WARRIORS ON HORSEBACK

THE INSIDE STORY OF THE PROFESSIONAL JOCKEY

WARRIORS ON HORSEBACK

THE INSIDE STORY OF THE PROFESSIONAL JOCKEY

JOHN CARTER

BLOOMSBURY
LONDON • NEW DELHI • NEW YORK • SYDNEY

NOTE
While every effort has been made to ensure that the content of this book is as technically accurate and as sound as possible, neither the author nor the publishers can accept responsibility for any injury or loss sustained as a result of the use of this material.

Bloomsbury Sport
An imprint of Bloomsbury Publishing Plc
50 Bedford Square
London
WC1B 3DP
UK

1385 Broadway
New York
NY 10018
USA

www.bloomsbury.com

BLOOMSBURY and the Diana logo are trademarks of Bloomsbury Publishing Plc

First published 2015

British Library Cataloguing-in-Publication Data
A catalogue record for this book is available from the British Library.

ISBN: HB: 9781472909688
ISBN PB: 9781472909695
ePDF: 9781472911520
ePub: 9781472911513

FSC www.fsc.org MIX Paper from responsible sources FSC® C020471

2 4 6 8 10 9 7 5 3 1

Acknowledgements
Cover photograph © Getty Images
Inside photographs © Getty Images with the exception of the following: pp. 112, 204 and plate section p. 7 © Press Association; pp. 78 and 80 © Wikicommons; p. 11 © National Horseracing Museum and p. 57 image supplied by Hollie Doyle
Horse illustration © Shutterstock
Typeset by Margaret Brain, Wisbech, Cambs
Printed and bound in Great Britain by CPI Group (UK) Ltd, Croydon, CR0 4YY

ACKNOWLEDGEMENTS

So much help, so many people to thank. The horse-racing community has been particularly supportive throughout my research. There are too many people and organisations to mention them all here, but in particular, and in alphabetical order, can I pick out Ron Atkins, Michael Caulfield, Bob Champion, Hollie Doyle, Martin Dwyer, Dale Gibson, Lisa Hancock, Martin Lane, Daloni Lucas, Richard Perham, Stan Singleton, Steve Smith-Eccles, John Snaith, Willie Snaith, Paul Struthers and Phil Taylor. Thanks also to Frankie Dettori and Hayley Turner, whom I had interviewed previously, as well as the team at Bloomsbury.

Meeting and talking to such fascinating subjects remains the best part of creating a manuscript. I learned so much.

Finally, thanks, as ever, to my long-suffering wife Paula and children Elisha and Joshua for their tolerance during the many hours when I was absent; either writing in my office or with them in body but not in mind as I shaped a paragraph in my head, eyes glazed over. Writing a book is deceptively time consuming. Thankfully they had the arrival of Bentley, the sausage dog, to keep them entertained. At times it was as if they didn't miss me at all ...

CONTENTS

Foreword **xiii**
Preface **xv**

PART ONE: PERSPECTIVES

1 Heart and soul **3**
2 The inner sanctum **16**
3 Location, location, location **30**
4 Have saddle, will travel **34**
5 Trailblazers **56**

PART TWO: ON THE FLAT: HISTORY, HEROES AND HEYDAYS

6 Black caps and spurs **65**
7 Tragic heroes **74**
8 From toads to princes **80**
9 Master craftsmen **87**
10 New age warriors **95**

PART THREE: OVER THE STICKS: HISTORY, HEROES AND HEYDAYS

11 Front runner **107**
12 Endless winter **114**
13 Raising the bar **119**
14 AP **126**

PART FOUR: OCCUPATIONAL HAZARDS

15 One piece **137**
16 Wasted **157**

PART FIVE: ANATOMY OF A JOCKEY

17 Horse-sense **181**
18 Look, listen, learn **191**
19 Pillars of professionalism **196**
20 Labour of love **204**
21 Just champion **210**
22 Bravery, bottle and goodbyes **214**

PART SIX: LAST HURRAH

23 National treasure **223**

Interviews **232**
Bibliography and further reading **233**
Index 236

MAP OF RACETRACKS AROUND GREAT BRITAIN

MAP OF RACETRACKS AROUND THE WORLD

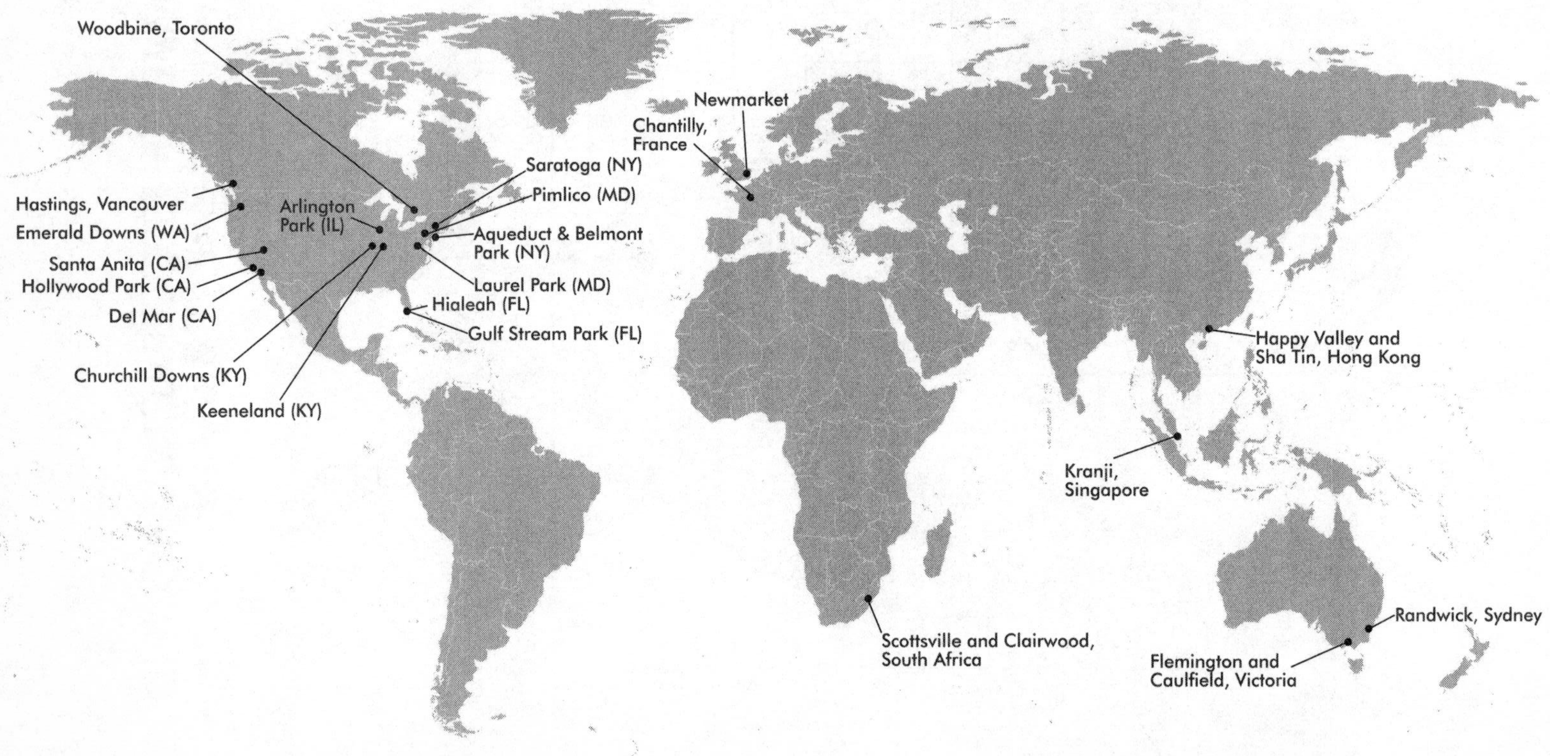

Woodbine, Toronto
Hastings, Vancouver
Emerald Downs (WA)
Santa Anita (CA)
Hollywood Park (CA)
Del Mar (CA)
Churchill Downs (KY)
Keeneland (KY)
Arlington Park (IL)
Saratoga (NY)
Pimlico (MD)
Aqueduct & Belmont Park (NY)
Laurel Park (MD)
Hialeah (FL)
Gulf Stream Park (FL)
Newmarket
Chantilly, France
Happy Valley and Sha Tin, Hong Kong
Kranji, Singapore
Scottsville and Clairwood, South Africa
Randwick, Sydney
Flemington and Caulfield, Victoria

WEIGHTS CONVERSION TABLE

Jockeys' body weights have been given in stone as is common in Great Britain and Ireland. For those less used to measuring body weight in stone, the following conversion table may be useful.

st and lb	lb	kg
4st 7lb	63	28.6
5st 0lb	70	31.8
5st 7lb	77	34.9
6st 0lb	84	38.1
6st 1lb	85	38.6
6st 2lb	86	39
6st 3lb	87	39.5
6st 4lb	88	39.9
6st 5lb	89	40.4
6st 6lb	90	40.8
6st 7lb	91	41.3
6st 8lb	92	41.7
6st 9lb	93	42.2
6st 10lb	94	42.6
6st 11lb	95	43.1
6st 12lb	96	43.5
6st 13lb	97	44
7st 0lb	98	44.5
7st 1lb	99	44.9
7st 2lb	100	45.4
7st 3lb	101	45.8
7st 4lb	102	46.3
7st 5lb	103	46.7
7st 6lb	104	47.2

st and lb	lb	kg
7st 7lb	105	47.6
7st 8lb	106	48.1
7st 9lb	107	48.5
7st 10lb	108	49
7st 11lb	109	49.4
7st 12lb	110	49.9
7st 13lb	111	50.3
8st 0lb	112	50.8
8st 1lb	113	51.3
8st 2lb	114	51.7
8st 3lb	115	52.2
8st 4lb	116	52.6
8st 5lb	117	53.1
8st 6lb	118	53.5
8st 7lb	119	54
8st 8lb	120	54.4
8st 9lb	121	54.9
8st 10lb	122	55.3
8st 11lb	123	55.8
8st 12lb	124	56.2
8st 13lb	125	56.7
9st 0lb	126	57.2
9st 7lb	133	60.3
10st 0lb	140	63.5

FOREWORD

BOB CHAMPION, MBE

Most people remember me for my Grand National win at Liverpool in 1981 on *Aldaniti*. Because of that, I suppose it's easy to overlook the fact that I spent 11 seasons as a professional jockey on the circuit in Britain. We certainly relished the big race days at Aintree, Cheltenham, Sandown and the like, but for much of the time we were riding in front of much smaller crowds at events in diverse locations, from Hexham to Hereford, Wetherby to Worcester.

Looking back it was certainly a great way to make a living and I loved my time as a professional jump jockey. Just working with racehorses every day was so gratifying. There can be few better feelings than to ride one in competition. And when you win, particularly a big race, the adrenalin buzz is addictive and makes you want more. I was fortunate to experience that buzz nearly 500 times. The jockey's lifestyle is dangerous and requires discipline and sacrifices, but the rewards make it all worthwhile and are what kept driving me forwards when times were tough.

Yet it wasn't just the racing and the wins that gave me such pleasure. It was the atmosphere and camaraderie within the weighing room that I missed most when I retired. Amid the laughter and pranks I made lifelong friends. Of course, we took it all seriously when we needed to – and I shared the weighing room with some of the truly great jockeys, such as John Francome – but we also had so much fun. And remember that in my time jockeys weren't breathalysed at the racecourse each day, so it was possible to have the odd night out and a few drinks.

That's just one aspect that has changed since my era. It's difficult to compare jockeys from different periods but I have no doubt that we are currently in a golden age. The riders are so professional and dedicated nowadays, none more so than AP McCoy, who would have been hugely successfully whenever he rode. He really is brilliant, so aggressive. I have never seen another jockey get a horse more quickly from one side of a fence to another.

I think John Carter's book accurately conveys life as a professional jockey, going back to the 18th century, through my era, right up to 2014. It is a world within a world and I hope the insights will be illuminating for readers. Jockeys are undoubtedly a rare breed and a special community that, to my mind, deserves to be recognised and celebrated.

Bob Champion
August 2014

BOB CHAMPION CANCER TRUST

If you would like to know more about the work of the Bob Champion Cancer Trust either:

email info@bobchampion.org.uk
call 020 7924 3553
or visit www.bobchampion.org.uk

PREFACE

In my pre-school years I was horse-racing mad, avidly watching it on television. My mum loved to relate the true story that I learned to read and tell the time at an early age because I needed to be able to check in the newspaper to see what time the racing was on. I cringe as I write these words, but I used to 'ride' a wooden rocking horse as each contest developed, as though I were a jockey involved in the race. I wore a cap and goggles, and used one of my mum's knitting needles as a whip. I tended to be Josh Gifford or Terry Biddlecombe.

Once at primary school I remember asking my teacher if I could be released early one afternoon so that I could make sure I was home in time to watch the Epson Derby. He said no, so I ran all the way home once school finished and just made it, breathless, before the stalls opened.

Somewhat thankfully, in time I grew out of my rocking-horse habit. Indeed I moved away from the sport, transferring my interests to football and cricket, activities for which my height – I developed into a sturdy 6-footer by my teenage years – was an asset rather than the hindrance it would have been had I carried on hoping to one day become a jockey.

Nevertheless, my awe for those who earn their living on horseback never left me. When I wrote two books on horse racing I came into close contact with many jockeys and the experience fuelled my desire to learn more, while reinforcing my opinion that they are a quite remarkable, not to mention abnormal, band of brothers and sisters.

Seriously, what possesses someone to earn a living by placing himself or herself in mortal danger every day? Who would want to starve their body of food and hydration 24/7 while attempting to maintain an elite athlete's level of fitness? Why would anybody want to get up at the crack of dawn seven days a week to rack up yet more miles on motorways for an annual income that Premiership footballers can earn in a week?

Those questions have nagged away at the back of my mind and, during the course of researching this book, I have tried to discover and document the answers. While doing so, I think that my previously limited involvement in the tight-knit horse-racing community has been an advantage: I don't view jockeys through the filter of personal experience or long-held opinions. I also know just enough to have been able to ask the right questions of the right people at the right time; just enough to have been capable of reflecting and capturing the views of experts who are truly in the know; just enough to tell it the way it is, unaffected by matey friendships.

Three moments during the researching and interviewing process gave me goosebumps and will stick in my mind long after the publication of this book.

First, I met a former National Hunt jockey who, at the age of 28, suffered a fall that left him in an induced coma for six weeks. Doctors demanded that he never rode again and for the past 30 years he has battled with both the injury and the mental torture of being unable to do the thing that made him happiest.

I asked him whether, if he could turn back the clock, he would have chosen a different, safer profession. To me – a pretty rational, logical, sensible member of society – the answer seemed obvious. But he dismissed the notion: he had no regrets and would choose the same path again.

Along with the words themselves, the tone and animation in his voice left no room for doubt. When he talked of life as a jockey his eyes were alive. Race-riding may have jilted him, but he has never fallen out of love with it.

Something clicked into place for me at that moment; I realised that once the race-riding bug has bitten you (the first win tends to be the point of no return), you've been infected and it's in your blood forever. There's more about the jockey in question in the first chapter of the book.

The second moment of enlightenment took place when I toured the weighing room at Aintree. At the back is a bleak, austere, beige room containing four beds surrounded by cutting-edge medical equipment that is, to all intents and purposes, a hospital ward. On race days medics wait there to treat the wounded. Intellectually, I knew this space existed before I visited it, but to see it for real disturbed me. It seemed too stark and sterilised to be located at the heart of such a celebrated sporting venue. Ideally, horse racing should be about entertainment, fun and glory; this was a sobering reminder that there is also a darker side.

The third goose-bump episode occurred while I was walking the course, alone with my thoughts, on Epsom Downs on Derby Day, 2014. Early rain on a steamy morning made for a warm, moist tour of this extraordinary stretch of racing turf: quirky is the word that comes to mind, so quirky that jockeys need their wits about them. From the starting stalls they follow an anticlockwise horseshoe shape, mainly easing left and downhill until they hit the long home straight and contest the most prestigious prize in the sport.

I'd done my research and I'd spoken to jockeys who had been there and won. I knew about the slopes, the cambers and the sharp turn at Tattenham Corner. And, for a blissful hour or so, as Epsom began to fill up, I was absorbed, lost in nostalgia. It was just me, the turf and the ghosts of races past, going back more than two centuries. Later that afternoon Joseph O'Brien eased Australia to victory in the 2014 renewal, and more names were writ large in the sport's annals. Dreaming of contesting, even winning, events such as this is why so many want to become jockeys – and long may it continue.

For me, these three different perspectives threw new light on this fascinating profession – and I hope this book as a whole does the same for you. Above all, I hope it celebrates a group of men and women who deserve our admiration.

PART ONE
PERSPECTIVES

1

HEART AND SOUL

When Willie Snaith, MBE, opens the door of his first-floor flat it is instantly apparent that a career in NBA basketball was never a serious option. Standing at a mere 4 feet 11 inches tall and taking a size 4½ shoe, he's a little 'un.

But the second and overriding impression is that even at the age of 85 the vitality and vigour of his active youth have not entirely left him. Yes, the craftsman's fingers that cajoled thoroughbreds around racetracks in his heyday as a top jockey have grown fleshy with arthritis over the years. Yes, he is rounder and plumper than he was in his youth. And yes, last year he spent some time in intensive care due to illness. But the grip of the handshake remains firm and the upbeat welcome is delivered in a booming voice. His speech, reflecting both his birthplace in the north east of England and the time he spent in Yorkshire, can have lost little of its power and projection. Moreover, there's still a twinkle in his eye and a sharp brain that can deliver a witty one-liner.

Certainly, his memory is undimmed by age. He struggled, for a moment and to his irritation, to recall the name of a trainer that he worked for (it was Matt Peacock) but that was the only blemish, blip or deviation during an hour-long trip down memory lane. He effortlessly recalled names and dates from a lengthy catalogue of anecdotes garnered over his long and successful career. Perhaps this reflects the post-jockey years he spent sharing stories as a tour guide for the National Horseracing Museum, but it's still a remarkable tour de force for an octogenarian.

During that hour it became apparent that if you want to meet someone who could restore your faith in humanity, let alone horse racing, then

Willie Snaith is the man. Yet it's not all been winning enclosures and MBEs. He had a challenging childhood that began in Gateshead between the First and Second World Wars. He lost his father, a shoemaker, at the age of five and his mother – who was even smaller than Willie and wore a size 2½ shoe – grafted hard, cleaning trams between 10pm and 6am each day. She was keen that her son wouldn't have to go down the mines and, fulfilling her ambition, when he left school at 14 Willie worked briefly in a wool shop before moving to Middleham in Yorkshire to train to become a jockey with Sam Armstrong.

Prior to this, the boy's only contact with horses had been pit ponies when he was evacuated to Hexham during the Second World War, but it soon became apparent to Armstrong's eagle eye that he was a natural. He just had a way with horses. Better still, he loved being a jockey, and this was a profession where wee Willie's lack of height was an asset. A sepia photo taken on a Brownie camera when he first started riding shows him on the scales weighing 3st 8lb which seems implausibly low. His own recollections confirmed this passion, with him asserting: 'I just loved it to bits. I loved the feel of the horse; that you were working together and the horse was with you. I'll never forget my first winner – it was in 1948 and I beat Gordon Richards by a short head. I was nicknamed the "pocket Hercules" because I was a strong little fella who used to get 'em past the post.'

Snaith stayed with Armstrong for nine years, becoming champion apprentice in 1949. Willie said of his mentor, 'Sam Armstrong was a tough man but he made me a jockey and he made a man of me.'

This period marked the start of a long career that spanned 27 years and the memories of those halcyon days are never far away, constantly being re-evoked by the location of his flat and the possessions contained within it. The brown-and-beige furnishings may be unremarkable, but the ex-jockey's neighbours certainly are not: 'Colin Casey lives in the flat upstairs. Jimmy Uttley, who won three champion hurdles on *Persian War*, is another neighbour. And Roy Baker. We're all ex-jockeys who have a flat here, provided by the Injured Jockeys Fund.'

All the flats overlook the Warren Hill and Side Hill gallops on Newmarket Heath, where hundreds of loose-limbed thoroughbreds exercise during dawn gallops. Willie can stand at his French doors and survey the territory where he once went about his riding-work duties decades ago. Even on a dank, drizzly, grey January morning it is a thrill to watch the class of 2014 canter up the hill. When they return, dragon-smoke puffs out from their flared nostrils.

The other outstanding feature in the living room is the quantity of memory-jogging mementoes and memorabilia. The space is a shrine to Willie's life, past and present. Even a cursory glance provides immediate evidence that he cherishes three aspects above all else: horse racing, his family and his association with the Royal Family.

The mantelpiece alone must trigger a thousand memories in his head. Towards the left-hand side is a black-and-white photo of Willie in his younger, early days. In it he has the look of the famous American actor Mickey Rooney about him and he is wearing the racing silks of the owner Jack Gurder, a 'gambling man and big friend of the trainer Sam Armstrong'.

In the centre of the mantelpiece is a black-and-white photograph of Snaith meeting Queen Elizabeth II for the first time in the paddock at Goodwood in 1954, just before he rode *Landau* to victory in the Sussex Stakes. The Queen's coronation had taken place the year before, but Willie was already in full flow and established in his profession by then. In total he rode five winners for the Queen and one for the Queen Mother in 1959, 'beating Scobie Breasley by a short-head at Sandown'.

The next time he met the Queen was some 50 years later when he was awarded with an MBE, an experience he recollects fondly: 'It was a great thrill and the greatest day. You get separated from your family as you wait to meet the Queen and I'm not ashamed to say that I cried my bloody eyes out. I couldn't help it. It was sheer joy. I was going to meet the Queen and really shake her hand.'

Further tokens of recognition can be found on either end of the mantelpiece. To the left: a foot-high dark iron statue labelled a 'lifetime in racing', which was presented to him by Princess Anne at Fakenham Races in 2008. To the right: another statue, this time awarded by his friends and family in Newmarket. He is one of a select group of jockeys to have a road in the town named after him, a distinction justified by his popularity, cheery demeanour, and long and illustrious career in the saddle.

Throughout the 1950s Willie was a leading lightweight jockey, riding for Noel Murless and Cecil Boyd-Rochfort. He rode in the Derby on Epsom Downs seven times, including an outing on *Landau* for the Queen, and achieved a third, a fourth and a seventh position. He also managed to win the Derbys in both Sweden and Norway, and spent nine successful winters in India.

Like almost all jockeys, Snaith has suffered his share of broken bones. In the past, he required the assistance of the Injured Jockeys Fund during a long layoff while he recovered from a punctured lung and damaged spleen resulting from an accident when his mount crashed through the wooden rails in the closing stages of a race at Lingfield in 1961. Despite the severity of the injuries, he recovered sufficiently to get back in the saddle and went on to ride until 1973, finishing with more than 900 winners to his name. Having retired as a jockey, he worked in Newmarket for Murless and his Warren Place successor Sir Henry Cecil.

Willie kept in contact with Sir Henry right up until his death and believes the joy of training the wonder-horse *Frankel* motivated Sir Henry to continue to fight cancer even when it became apparent it was a battle he couldn't win.

In truth, Willie knows everyone who's anyone in Newmarket and in the racing world. Sir Henry, Sir Gordon, Charlie, Lester – he knows them all and hasn't a bad word about any of them. That's not simply because he's trying to say the right things and be politically correct, but because that's the way he sees the world. He's a glass-half-full sort of 85-year-old.

When asked about Sir Gordon Richards, Willie replies: 'A marvellous man! I used to love riding work with him when we were riding for Sir

Noel Murless. He helped me, he helped everybody. On a horse he had great hands, beautiful hands. I looked up to him. Like me he was so small that he never struggled to make the weight.'

He is similarly complimentary about other colleagues, including Charlie Smirke: 'A great fellow and a great friend. He used to stop and lodge with me. When I had my accident at Lingfield he was the first to come and help.' Willie's admiration for his friend Lester Piggott knows no bounds:

> 'Oh Lester! My favourite man! A lovely fella who loved families and kids and was a wonderful horseman. He just knew the pace that they were going; he was a brilliant judge of pace. In the weighing room he was quiet and businesslike but during a race if you were creeping up on his inside and going to challenge him he'd soon squeeze you and get you into the rails. He was greedy to win winners. Even though he might have won thousands of races he still kept that same greed as though he had never ridden one before. He has a lovely, dry sense of humour. We're still great pals and he sends me two cards a year from his home in Switzerland, one on my birthday and one at Christmas.'

Twice a year Willie gets on his scooter – 'the little legs have seized up' he explains – and visits the stables of Sir Mark Prescott. However, although he clearly values those sporting relationships, it's Willie's family that keeps him going. Dotted around the flat are images of his two sons John and Derek, daughter Helen, eight grandchildren and two great-grandchildren. For the first time his voice cracks as he is asked about the highlight of his career and instead talks of his beloved and much-missed wife, Silvia: 'She was the highlight, God bless her. She was wonderful, a great person. We were pals and really loved each other. We were married for 61 years.' The subject is too sensitive to raise, but you know Snaith deeply regrets that he was too ill – in intensive care – to be able to attend her funeral after she passed away in July 2012.

His son John also became a jockey and there is clearly a great affinity between the two. 'I know he's my son, but he's a lovely man. We love each other to death. I know it sounds silly but the other day I went shopping into Newmarket on my scooter and we bumped into each other in Marks and Sparks, and we kissed each other on the cheek. I do that to all my children.'

The bond with John appears particularly strong. Perhaps because he chose the same profession, perhaps because of what he went through as a result. In this story of family fortunes Willie Snaith, MBE, is just part one. Part two is about John Snaith, and that episode of the story is altogether darker.

To do the story justice we need to rewind to 3.41pm on Thursday 7 April 1983. The venue is Aintree racecourse in Liverpool and the event is the 1983 Topham Trophy, one of the few races to be contested over the same fences used in the Grand National. It is run over 2 miles 6 furlongs and the day's spectacle will unfold under grey skies and on soft going. There's no sign of an early spring so far in northern England.

As we seat ourselves in the same saddle as John Snaith, a 28-year-old professional National Hunt jockey, we can hear the distinctive tones of Peter O'Sullevan, who is commentating for BBC television: 'They are coming down to The Chair, the third fence today and the 15th in Saturday's Grand National, one of the most daunting fences on the course. With *Nicky Tam* in the lead, from *St Taffy* and *Ballyhampshire* and *Oaklawn* ... and *Ballyhampshire*'s gone and so has *Durham Lad*.'

It's little wonder that 'The Chair' has just claimed another couple of victims. It is one of the most taxing and iconic fences in horse racing and the public revels in the history and war stories that surround it. Yet jockeys like you who are responsible for getting your mounts over it are more pragmatic. You are only interested in the mechanics of clearing the jump – and without doubt it poses a unique challenge: it is the tallest and narrowest fence on the racecourse, preceded by a 6-foot open ditch. The landing side is a disorienting 6 inches higher than the take-off side, the reverse of the arrangement at the even more treacherous Becher's Brook, a dubious delight to be encountered a minute or so later.

Back on the course, O'Sullevan looks down from his commentary gantry at the 17 remaining runners and riders. Among them you are a prominent front-runner, in racing colours of yellow and black, aboard a horse called *Oaklawn*.

After jumping the Water Jump you are in third place as the field moves out into the country, across the Melling Road. You are focused, wide-eyed and absorbed in the race, intent on preparing *Oaklawn* to negotiate each new test.

The journalist Simon Barnes once said that 'National Hunt jockeys have a hard and brutal life, but they also have free entry to the world's greatest brothel of the senses.' Today, the challenge of Aintree is bombarding these same senses: the feeling of riding a horse in a top-class competition; the sound of hooves rattling on the guard rail and the fir boughs cracking like gunfire as each fence is negotiated; the almost unconscious race awareness of the other horses and riders as, second by second, the picture evolves around you. Exhilarated, on the edge and so, so alive – this is what you live for. You love what you do, always have. Horse racing is your passion and the prospect of race-riding never fails to get you out of bed at an unearthly hour each morning.

In some ways this fervour is not surprising. Horse racing is, after all, in your blood; you are the son of the much-heralded and much-loved 'pocket Hercules', Willie Snaith. You had started going to the races with him when you were 11. The first time you had sat in the weighing room between your father and Tony Murray was at Newmarket's July Course where your senses – the same ones now being bombarded at Aintree – had first been brought alive by the sport. You can still remember, as though it were yesterday, the smell of leather and feeling in glorious awe of the jockeys as they had changed out of their suits into their vivid racing silks. You fell in love with horse racing that day.

You can also recollect how one morning in 1974, when you were 15 years old and weighed 5st, your Dad had announced without warning 'Right, say goodbye to your mum, pack yourself a bag and tomorrow morning I'm going to take you down to Epsom.' And the next day he had driven you there to become an apprentice with the trainer, Brian Swift. It had been tough love. He had sent you away from home, in the same way that he had been sent away from home, to become a jockey and to become a man. You had signed, without question or complaint, the indenture forms that had committed you for seven years, though you had actually stayed for nine. Since your parents had felt it was the right decision, no further discussion had been required.

Swift had paid for your board and lodging, a pair of boots, working shoes, a nice pair of slacks, a smart pair of shoes and a pair of jodhpurs, and, for the next four years, you had worked for a weekly wage of 60p. In the 1970s, work riders had worn a tie and a shirt and a flat cap, which they had turned around as they galloped off. There had been no safety helmets. Back in the present, however, as *Oaklawn* continues to negotiate the obstacles at Aintree, you have taken the precaution of wearing a primitive cork helmet under your racing cap.

As Peter O'Sullevan passes over the commentary to his colleague John Hanmer, *Oaklawn*'s jumping loses some of its zip. Twice the horse's leap is as much upwards as forwards. The landing is safe, momentum is lost and you fall back down the field, into the pack. Nevertheless the horse negotiates the ditch, which is to be the third fence when the Grand National takes place on the same turf, without alarm and then makes light work of the most feared fence in National Hunt, Becher's Brook. That's no mean feat: Becher's Brook is a 4½-feet-high nightmare of tightly packed spruce, with a blind drop of 5½ feet into a leg-buckling 45-degree upslope. Even after Becher's the iconic fences keep on coming: the Canal Turn, then Valentine's Brook.

Of course, the way racing normally works means you should be riding on the flat, like Willie did. You had initially followed this same path, riding 60-odd winners, but had found it a bit tame. The lure of National Hunt had proved irresistible. You had known it was the route you wanted to follow and, when the guv'nor had let you school with one of the top jockeys of the era, David Mould, the experience had reinforced your view.

John Snaith, after his career as a jockey had finished, but still very much in love with the sport

You had moved to a new trainer, Nick Gaseley, for three seasons, but it had felt claustrophobic in Lambourn and you had wanted to ride freelance and devote all your energies to National Hunt. The change had brought freedom but different frustrations. When you had been a stable jockey and had ridden the same horses out all the time you had got to know their quirks and foibles, strengths and weaknesses. As a freelance, though, you had ridden strangers. Trainers had rung up and said, 'can you come to Plumpton for two rides?' Of course you had needed the work and had taken up the offers, hopeful that the horses had been properly schooled. Yet some had been raw and dangerously incompetent jumpers.

You had begun to accumulate injuries: three broken legs, four broken collarbones, both your arms. You had lost your spleen and been knocked unconscious numerous times. A horse had jumped on the side of your face in France. Yet, dazed and concussed, you had always ridden the next day, never thinking of the dangers even though the scars, the breaks and the damage had been mounting up. One day at Towcester you had had a particularly bad tumble. You had come round in the ambulance room, walked back into the weighing room and said to your valet John Buckingham, 'John, remind me who drove me to the races?' He had replied, 'Sit down, John, you drove yourself.'

Back in the present at Aintree in the Topham Trophy, four fences from home, approaching the last ditch, you are now towards the back of the field, with *Oaklawn* increasingly fatigued by the challenge of the course's fences and the yielding ground. Snatches of commentary reach your ears: 'Over the next. *Man Alive* from *Private Jack*, *Tiepolino* then *St Taffy*, *Moonlight Rock* ... and *Oaklawn* has refused!'

At the moment of take-off *Oaklawn* makes a split-second choice that will change your life forever. He decides that he has run his race and aborts the jump. *Oaklawn* stops dead but you can't do likewise. Your body is propelled forwards and sideways at an unnatural angle, over the horse's neck. As you hit the turf, *Oaklawn* lands on top of you. Your skull hits the ditch with sickening force and you are knocked unconscious. Medical support rushes to your aid as the remaining runners move into the middle distance to contest the business end of the race. And as they do so, your life as a happy and fulfilled 28-year-old changes forever.

Back in the present day, 30 years later, John Snaith is sitting in the National Horseracing Museum, where he now works, and his booming voice – a trait he shares with Willie – frequently cracks with emotion as he casts his mind back to the dark days that followed as he shares the story of what happened next:

> 'I fractured my skull and spent six weeks in a coma. When I came out of it, the specialist said to me "John, you'll never ride again. We've monitored you now for three weeks, you can't walk straight, you can't hold a conversation, and your concentration is minimal. You've got the start of what we call 'Muhammad Ali' syndrome. You're punch drunk, and if you don't stop now the repercussions later on in your life will be horrific." So that was it really.'

The years since then have been beyond challenging: John has had to deal with the medical consequences of a serious brain injury and, above all, the reality that for the majority of his life he hasn't been able to do the thing he wants to do the most. He recalls how he reacted to this new, earth-shattering reality:

> 'I pined a lot. After that I knew I wasn't the same person. I suffered from depression, had two major breakdowns. The worst was 17 years ago when I ended up in hospital for four

> months. Not being a jockey and the medical condition drove me mad. I took myself off for four years with a rucksack and worked my way around the world trying to get it all out of my system, thinking the depression would only be part-time. But because it was medical – the injuries, the blows to the head – it was a difficult one. I retrained as a gardener – I was head gardener for Lord and Lady Phillips at Dalham Hall for a while – I laid roads in New Zealand, built houses in Australia, and then came back to England. I was just trying to find something. It's a big void to fill, not just for me but for many jockeys who have to retire early. Some fall by the wayside, some take to drink. I certainly dipped my toe in that one but fortunately I came out of the other side.'

When asked what he misses most, John replies:

> 'There's so much I miss. The best part was riding winners, riding into the winner's enclosure. But there was so much more than that. I loved going racing, the camaraderie of sharing a car, the craic, coming home. I loved being in the weighing room, with the banter and the camaraderie. Riders are the most loyal friends. We all look after each other and you can talk about anything to them. It was a wonderful environment. You felt safe in there and, having been a flat-race jockey, I found there was an even warmer feel to the atmosphere and the relationships in National Hunt.'

Fortunately, John has found a way of dealing with his life, post-riding, and for that he acknowledges the debt he owes to the Injured Jockeys Fund, which has supported him in numerous ways. He also thanks the National Horseracing Museum, which has provided him with meaningful employment: 'Working at the museum has helped enormously', John says. 'It's a job that I always look forward to. Nice people, surrounded by what I love. But I can honestly say that if the telephone went tonight and someone said "there are two rides at Plumpton, do you think you can get there tomorrow?" I'd be packing my bags.'

The National Horseracing Museum, Newmarket, England

Back in the present, John can be found deep in the bowels of the museum, bringing the exhibits to life with anecdotes and insight, whether he is aboard the horse simulator, encouraging visitors to give it a go, or at one of Newmarket's racecourses, where he can interpret the action for those who are new to the sport. Of the latter he says: 'I still get a buzz from being at the racecourse. I take visitors to about a furlong out, where the race is just beginning to unfold and you can hear the thunder of the hooves, the cracks of the whip and the jockeys shouting encouragement – it changes people's perspectives of racing.'

It must be a bitter-sweet experience to be close to the sights, sounds and smells that he misses so much, but even if John suffers moments of melancholy and what-might-have-beens, he still projects a boyish, naïve enthusiasm that the museum has been astute enough to take advantage of. In addition, when he says that his 'dad is looking down on me', the statement is factually accurate, because in the museum he spends most of his time about 10 feet away from a large sepia image of his father in action, watched by the Queen. You get the sense upon meeting John that he has, thankfully, come as close as he can to filling the void left by his abrupt departure from the thrilling world of race-riding. And those that visit the museum and chat to him receive an authentic insight into why the sport is so addictive for so many.

If further evidence is required, it's to be found in his answer to the awkward question that begged to be asked: 'So, if you knew then what you know now, would you ever have begun a career as a jockey?' The logical answer is: 'Of course not, why would I have wanted to put myself through all of this physical and mental suffering?' But being a professional jockey is not a logical, rational profession. So Snaith's response is immediate, unequivocal and from the heart: 'Oh yes, I would have still have been a jockey. I had such wonderful experiences.'

And that sums up the emotion felt so strongly by both father and son, and many other riders besides. Nowadays, Willie's thoughts gravitate towards the past, and those keepsakes on his mantelpiece are memory-prompters – of races, trainers, owners, royalty and family – that happily jostle for the attention of this cheerful and satisfied man as he enjoys his dotage. John's memory banks contain more challenging images, but his life story should be viewed with just as much admiration. He has demonstrated immense resilience and fortitude in the face of sustained adversity – and his tale supports the old adage that it is better to have loved and lost than to have never loved at all. For those of us trying to get our heads around why jockeys do what they do, John's story is the perfect starting point.

2

THE INNER SANCTUM

10.30AM WEDNESDAY 2 APRIL, 2014, AINTREE RACECOURSE

Aintree racecourse prepares for the eyes of the world once more. Tomorrow is the first of a three-day meeting that will culminate in the 167th running of the most famous horse race in the world, the Grand National. It's expected that a global audience of around 600 million will follow the action on television, with an additional 70,000 people watching at the racecourse.

Today, Aintree is comparatively deserted, though filled with the pre-event buzz of last-minute preparations. Cars and lorries edge along pedestrian walkways at the back of the stands; vendors, stewards and officials move purposefully around in high-visibility jackets; pathways are power-washed, with the spray chilled by a bracing northern breeze on a grey day.

Inside the jockeys' changing room, the sponsor's lime-green banners are erected above the saddle racks and electricians test the circuits. This is the calm before the storm.

To understand any species, you need to observe them in their natural habitat, where they are in private and at ease. For professional jockeys that place is the changing room, their inner sanctum. There is only one horse-racing professional here this morning but, having spent the last 28 years in changing rooms on the National Hunt circuit, there's no one better able to provide the inside track on this private world and the remarkable community that will bring this virtually empty room to vibrant life over the next few days.

Phil Taylor's official job title is Master Jockey's Valet (pronounced 'val-let' in horse-racing circles). For a percentage of the riding fees earned by jockeys in his care, Taylor and his team ensure that on race days all the jockeys need to focus on is the racing itself.

The 44-year-old from Birmingham is the current incumbent of a family business that has been passed down the generations. His father, Pat, was a valet for no less than 54 years, having followed in the footsteps of his own father. Whether the next generation of Taylors – Phil has a seven-year-old son – will continue the tradition remains to be seen, but if he does, he will be a busy man. Last week Taylor left home at 6.15am on Monday for Wincanton and came back at 8.30pm on Thursday after several days in the West Country. This week he will be in Liverpool from early on Wednesday until late on Saturday. His two vehicles cover 80,000 miles between them a year, and with the National Hunt circuit touring for 330 days a season, there's precious little respite.

Today, Phil Taylor's here early to prepare his area of the weighing room for what's to come. It's best to get organised because at Aintree you need to be ready for the unexpected. In 1997, for instance, a bomb scare caused the Grand National to be postponed and the course evacuated. Taylor was almost the last man out, accompanying the police's chief commander. 'That was the year we had the National on the Monday. It was a hell of a weekend', Taylor recalls fondly. 'None of us knew what was happening; none of us collected any belongings. I ended up sleeping on the floor of the Adelphi Hotel in Liverpool, along with some other lads. It was an almighty craic and the locals showed us amazing hospitality, people taking you in off the street. It was only late on the Sunday that they announced the race was going ahead the next day.'

The year after this scare, Taylor left his briefcase in the weighing room on the Friday only to later discover that bomb-disposal officers had blown up his 'suspicious device'. The Grand National meeting always brings human and equine drama, and Taylor is usually at the heart of it.

This morning, Taylor's notepad lies on the brown changing-room bench, suitably flanked by a ballpoint pen on one side and a packet of his favourite Marlboro Gold cigarettes on the other. The open page lists the jockeys in Taylor's 'stable' who will make use of his services over the next couple of days. Today at Wincanton there are 14 different jockeys with a total of 19 rides in eight races. Tomorrow 13 jockeys will ride at Taunton with 17 rides over seven races, while another 15 jockeys will be here at Aintree with 23 rides in seven races. Among Taylor's high-profile Aintree jockeys in his corner of the changing room will be Barry Geraghty, Robert 'Choc' Thornton, Leighton Aspell and Paul Carberry.

Part of Taylor's role is to make sure that these jockeys carry the right weights so that they meet handicapping requirements, and he will use the two old-fashioned sets of scales in the changing room to make sure they are pound-perfect when they are weighed by the clerk of the scales.

Over the next three days, however, Taylor and his team (two others join him on Thursday, three on Friday and Saturday) will be mostly making extensive use of the washing machines, tumble driers and the drying room in the small valets' area that adjoins the changing room. If one of their jockeys has worn it – socks, T-shirts, jockstraps, tights, britches, waterproof britches, gloves, mufflers, towels – they'll wash and dry it. They will also polish the riders' boots.

This is not an easy logistical feat. For a start, how can they tell who owns what? Taylor explains: 'Most of the racing gear is branded or sponsored or we'll stick a name on it, so it's not too difficult. Besides, when you launder their clothes 300 times a year, you get to know what they wear. I could pick up 20 different pairs of boots and have a damn good guess at which belong to whom.'

Taylor says that the room is most frenetic in the aftermath of the Grand National: 'There'll be 40 lads coming in, dumping 40 saddles on the table, plus all their clothing and boots, britches, tights. It takes some sorting out. Ironically, if you get fallers in the National it slows the amount of lads coming in so there're not so many saddles at one time, but we just want everyone to get round.'

On National day, as the jockeys begin to unwind away from the eyes of the watching world, it's rush hour for Taylor's team and around ten other valets that operate in the changing room: 'All the jockeys will be grateful they got back in one piece, a handful will be delighted with how their horses have run', Taylor says. 'I just want them to strip off so I can get their gear washed and boots polished and in their bags for Sunday, but they'll stand round the TV watching the replays, reliving it. Some will have been at the front and some at the back so they won't have all seen what went on. The National is not like any other race.'

Some will have a good, maybe even a life-changing race, but for every winner there are many more losers and, in National Hunt, adversity is never far away. That's where Taylor is of great value to his 'lads' because he's much more than just a logistics and kit man. He's also nursemaid, sounding board and personal assistant. 'If anyone's got a problem, they know my phone's on 24/7. I've been a marriage counsellor, I've been there when they've been seriously injured and I've been there when they've suffered bereavement.'

When Taylor says these words, the unblinking sincerity in his eyes leaves no room for doubt. He's a no-nonsense burly Brummie and his is not a superficial, put-on loyalty to the lads in his corner, it's straightforward and genuine – camouflaged by banter and swearing, but all the more real for that. Instinctively you know that he trusts them, they trust him and these deep-rooted allegiances are what keep Taylor on the day-to-day treadmill of life as a valet. Taylor's certainly 'been there' for Robert 'Choc' Thornton, who was an usher at Taylor's wedding (with some best-man duties thrown in). Of his friend, Taylor says:

> 'I love Choc to bits. 'We've been through a lot together, good and bad. He's had some horrific injuries. At Newton Abbott a few years ago he totally did his knee, there was basically nothing left of his ligament and cartilage. His knee looked like your elbow, facing out the wrong way. We spent a few hours together at the hospital that night and on the journey home I think I ended up stopping with him for about 24 hours.'

Taylor's admiration extends to all the members of his team, and not just for their ability to cope in adversity. Take Leighton Aspell, for example. Aspell is now 37 years old and a veteran in the weighing room. Seven years ago, dispirited, he retired from the sport, only to be drawn back 18 months later. He found he loved his job too much to stop before his time and, like many of the modern breed of jump jockeys, extended his career towards his 40s. Aspell is a straightforward guy who loves the sport and is brave as a lion, a fact that Taylor applauds:

> 'These jockeys have got more balls than me! You've got to admire them going out there, travelling at 35mph, jumping 6-foot fences – in the National 8-foot, 10-foot fences. They're incredible sportsmen; they can turn their hand to anything. A batch of my lads came with me to Scotland skiing for a few days. Jason Maguire had never skied before in his life, he was Bambi on ice and hilarious to begin with, but 24 hours later you could have pushed him off the worst slope and he'd have got it.'

Above all Taylor loves being part of the craic and joining in with the banter that flies back and forth across the changing room:

> 'They [the jockeys] talk about anything and everything in the changing room, but mainly about women! There's just a huge amount of craic between the lads. Because every ride could be your last ride, it's usually light-hearted. Cheltenham is very serious. The lads just stay in. But here at Aintree, we're all away from home for three or four days. Although we're not out until stupid o'clock – we might all be in bed by 10.30pm – between 7pm and 10pm we'll all sit round a table, have some dinner, maybe a bottle of wine, maybe a couple of beers and the craic between us all is brilliant. I can remember last year, the wife was up here with me, along with Davy Russell, Barry Geraghty, Jason Maguire, Robert Thornton, and we all went for a quiet Italian – it was probably the best night of the three days. We laughed and joked from start to finish. That's what it's all about. We do 17- or 18-hour days – particularly when travelling to the

> likes of Ffos Las and Fakenham – but the craic makes up for it. There's always a story.'

This camaraderie has always been present, with some jockeys acquiring kudos and legendary status not just for their skills in the saddle but for their sharp one-liners, pranks, teasing and practical jokes. Certainly Taylor's enthusiasm for the craic brought to mind an earlier chat with a jockey whose stories from the weighing room suggested that little has changed over the past 40 years.

In the 1970s and 1980s Derbyshire's Steve Smith-Eccles ('Ecc') was chief jester, usually to be found right in the hub of any unruliness in the weighing room, normally flanked by his great friend and ally, John Francome. Smith-Eccles was a high-class operator on the racetrack, riding in ten Grand Nationals and partnering over 900 winners, including eight Cheltenham Festival winners. Yet most stories about Smith-Eccles relate to his antics and exuberance away from the track. By general consensus it was something of an understatement when Smith-Eccles himself declared 'I worked hard, I played hard'.

Ecc is never short of a story, such as the one about a 'rubbish ride' at Uttoxeter: 'I got beaten on an odds-on favourite in the first and obviously one punter had lost a packet on it,' he said, 'because when I was going past the stands in a later race this dustbin came flying over the rails at me, accompanied by the words "Smith-Eccles, you cheating bastard." The bin was full ... [and] it only just fell short.'

Smith-Eccles also loves to talk about the practical joke he and Francome devised to play on northern jockeys:

> 'I'd say to them "Francome's mum – she's only gone and won one of these piano competitions, she's going to star on TV. He's a bit embarrassed about it; don't mock him." So, of course, the northern jockey goes up to Frankie and says "I hear your mum's a bit of a pianist." Francome was deadpan and says, "My f'ing mum got no f'ing hands." We played that one on Bob Champion and he said, "Well, how does she play the piano?" There are a million of stories like that. When you went to the races, it was

> like going to school. You did your business but you had half an hour between races and we just used to have fun.'

Phil Taylor was just starting his career as Ecc came to the end of his, and says that these days Matthew Batchelor has taken over the mantle as chief jester: 'Batch is a legend. Maybe AP [McCoy] gets beaten by a woman – it doesn't happen very often – and nobody will say anything until Batchy comes through and says "in all fairness champ, I think she'd have won on either one of them!" He always breaks up a silent moment.'

The light-hearted laughter, solidarity and kinship found within the weighing room is often commented upon by observers. Yet, strictly, they can only be labelled a team in the sense that they undertake the same jobs in the same location. In another way, these men and women are self-employed rivals and competitors – for winners and for business. They compete on the racetracks for prize money, glory and championships; and off it for rides, retainers and sponsorship. It is a cut-throat industry and the prosperity of their 'business' depends on success. Only the strong survive. Many will fall by the wayside. And, as in all professions, there is a range of different personalities: the loud, the quiet, the laid-back, the highly strung, the thinkers, the jokers, the leaders, the followers.

Yet, in their company, it is easy to overlook these discrepancies because they appear such a particularly close-knit band of brothers (and sisters). It helps that they spend more time together, either travelling or at racecourses, than they do with their friends and family, but the primary unifying factor, particularly on the National Hunt circuit, is the constant exposure to life-threatening danger. The effect of experiencing an ongoing and collective risk to life and limb has been well documented in relation to other walks of life and certainly brings the jockeys together. On the flat-racing circuit the constant wasting performs a similar role, although the general view is that there is a warmer, stronger bond in National Hunt. Taylor confirms this when he says:

> 'Yes, in no other sport would you eat together, change together, travel together, have nights out together, and compete against each other. The camaraderie exists because they go out there and

they might not be coming back. It's the only sport, apart from maybe motor racing, that requires two or three ambulances to follow you around while you do your daily job. I don't get ambulances following me around doing my job.

When something bad happens you can't fault them. Everyone pulls together, like when poor old John Thomas McNamara had a horrific fall at Cheltenham last year. The hairs stand up on the back of my neck when I think about it now. I'd looked after John Thomas for many years. He is a strange old character but one of the nicest guys you'd ever meet. It was probably going to be JT's last Cheltenham; and it would have been nice for him. They call him God in Ireland, God of the point-to-point circuit for amateurs. God bless him, he's still battling for some quality of life. That was horrible.

You always hope and pray they'll come back and safety gear has come on leaps and bounds in the past few year, but Jason Maguire, the day before the Cheltenham festival, was riding at Stratford, just looking to get the day out of the way, and broke his sternum, three of four ribs and had half his liver taken away. Ruby Walsh dislocated his arm and broke his shoulder at Cheltenham; Brian Cooper broke his leg there, apparently one of the worst fractures the surgeon had ever seen; Josh Hamer broke his collarbone; and Daryl Jacob broke his elbow, knee and his leg.

You've just seen Robin van Persie (the Manchester United footballer) out for six weeks with a tweaked knee. These lads would be riding the next day with that. They're a tough lot. If one of the lads lies down with an injury, you know he's hurt. AP's pain threshold is probably off the scale. A few years ago he broke his cheekbone at Plumpton and was back for Cheltenham. Everyone wants to ride there because it's our Olympics. They've got to be on crutches, in plaster or having an operation to miss out.

> So it's a dangerous game. But the lads will put themselves out. We'll help as much as we can, getting cars to wherever to pick them up from hospital. Whether it's stable staff, conditional jockeys, amateurs, everyone is in the game to help each other. It's a fantastic family to be part of.'

This view was echoed by Steve Smith-Eccles when he confirmed that it's the danger that bonds. 'It just brings everybody a little bit closer together,' he says. 'That is definitely a factor. I sat next to John Francome for ten years of my career – Francome one side, Scudamore the other – and you imagine the bond that we built. I'm sure it's just the same now with the jocks of today and that's because of the danger. There are times when you will need help, and if you aren't given help you could be in serious danger. So everybody tends to look after themselves and each other.'

This approach has always extended to jockeys talking through and sharing their plans for the first few fences of a race. This often happens in the weighing room and/or as the runners and riders mill around the starting gate. It's not fixing the race in any way; they are just getting organised, to minimise the risks. Taylor explains:

> 'Choc [Robert Thornton] will always say "the norm", which for him is third or fourth down the paint [on the rails]. That's his normal. Some lads will say "I'm going to bounce out [lead from the front]; I wouldn't mind a bit of company." Some trainers, like Donald McCain, love their horses being bounced out and making the running, possibly because he's got them so fit. But other lads will drop in stone last. Ruby Walsh and Timmy Murphy – they are geniuses at doing this. They'll drop a horse stone last and they'll just creep, creep, creep, creep throughout the race and then come the end of the race they always seem to be in the right place at the right time. You just look at them on the first circuit, maybe 3 lengths last, and then they make up a couple of places and then two out they're 2 lengths down, and then on the line they're there. They must get a huge buzz from

doing that. It's all down to judgement of pace and skill, and knowing what sort of horse you've got underneath you.'

In a close race, with the finishing post looming and glory to be won, there's no *team spirit*, no *kinship*: it's all about winning. These are, after all, athletes in the heat of competition – and they would not have reached the higher echelons of their chosen profession if they weren't warriors on horseback.

Conceding this, Taylor admits that there are times when tempers get frayed: 'Ninety-nine per cent of the lads that go out of the weighing room think they're going to win that race,' he says, 'even though the formbook says they're not. But I suppose that once you lose that belief then it's time to hang your boots up. It's hugely competitive. At the end of the day your adrenalin is pumping around and you're making split-second decisions and, yeah, occasionally there's a heated word.'

Of course most flare-ups between jockeys go unreported because they occur behind closed doors, and the unwritten code of the weighing room means that what goes on there stays there. That said, on the flat-racing circuit, stewards banned Kieren Fallon in 1994 for six months after he famously dragged another rider, Stuart Webster, from his mount shortly after they passed the winning line at Beverley, and it is common knowledge that Lester Piggott was once laid out by a punch from Geoff Baxter in the weighing room following an altercation.

Perhaps the conflict that reveals most about weighing-room ethics and attitudes was the one that took place between Richard Dunwoody and Adrian Maguire at Nottingham, when they were both competing to become British jump-racing champion jockey for that season. Tied almost neck and neck in this particular race, Dunwoody was just leading as they entered the home straight. Maguire, riding the odds-on favourite, attempted to pass Dunwoody on the inside as they approached the penultimate flight of hurdles. Dunwoody's mount appeared to veer left and Maguire's mount crashed into the plastic safety rail at the wing of the hurdle as he swerved away from the jump. Maguire lost his irons and nearly fell. Dunwoody's mount went on to win easily, but Dunwoody was disqualified and placed last following a lengthy stewards' inquiry. Dunwoody was banned for 14 days.

When this incident was raised with the normally outspoken Smith-Eccles – who was at Nottingham that day – he was clearly uncomfortable, shifting in his chair, and choosing his words with unusual precision:

> 'They were neck and neck throughout the latter half of the season, only a couple of winners between them. And Maguire came up Dunwoody's inside and Dunwoody put him through the rail. Now, that is a very, very dangerous thing to do. Okay, there is an unwritten law in race-riding that you shouldn't go poking up people's inner, but if you do you need to make sure you've got plenty in the tank to get there quick. Because if you pop up someone's inner and he or she shuts the door on you, then you've got nowhere to go apart from through the wing. And he brought Maguire down. Maguire shouldn't have done it, but not many people would have gone the whole way like Dunwoody did.'

Certainly it was a skirmish that caused quite a stir and some felt it violated the jump jockey's self-created code of conduct. It also allows an insight into various ways in which jockeys think and act. There will be times when the winning mentality that many elite sportsmen and sportswomen possess come into conflict with a team ethic. Dunwoody's autobiography was called *Obsessed: The Autobiography*, and the rider quite openly accepts that this title reflects one aspect of his personality.

It is also noticeable that even now, 20 years on, Smith-Eccles and Phil Taylor fall short of outright condemnation. Their body language, words and tone all suggest that they feel uneasy (or worse) about what happened, but even if they think in private that Dunwoody (or Maguire) breached the code they won't come out publicly and say so. That's one of the rules within the changing room, and you never hear quotes in the media from jockeys criticising a colleague.

So, while Taylor is happy to talk about how unlucky Maguire (one of the jockeys he worked with) was with injuries and what a remarkable buzz the photo-finish for the title created within the sport, when asked about the incident, he responds with the non-committal question, 'Is that how you become champion jockey? I don't know.'

Finally, it should be written for the record that despite the no-holds-barred battle to become British jump-racing champion jockey – flying from meeting to meeting, sometimes three in a day – Dunwoody and Maguire still stopped for a meal (albeit a rather uncomfortable one) together that night on the journey back from Nottingham.

Perhaps those kinds of altercations happen less frequently in the more politically correct world of the modern era. Certainly Smith-Eccles, for all his sense of fun, was a no-nonsense enforcer in the weighing room and saw it as part of his role as a senior to sort out those who crossed the line:

> 'If anybody started getting monkey, they got slapped down. If someone started taking the piss, sneaking up on your inside, they got slapped down. I did quite a bit of that myself. I'd take them into the loo and give them a f***ing good hiding. Sometimes I didn't have time to take them to the loo; it'd happen in the changing rooms. It's a tough old game out there and you don't need unnecessary hassle. I did it maybe six times during my career. I never really had to sort out any high-profile jockeys. These were young kids, learning the ropes and getting a bit cocky. Maybe they thought they were good, but they weren't. They just needed putting in their place. You worked hard, you played hard – and if anybody stepped out of line you'd soon sort them out.'

Smith-Eccles agrees that the modern changing room that Taylor inhabits is a more professional environment than the one he experienced when he was riding:

> 'In my day we could drink and, OK, you had to abide by racing rules but apart from that ... If I went to a race meeting and I rode in the first and didn't have a ride until the last race I would be expected by my owners and trainers to drink with them in the

> bar. I don't drink orange juice so I'd have a couple of whiskeys and other people did too. It was only after I retired that things became much more professional, quite rightly so, I must admit. I had the best of it, it was wonderful.'

Phil Taylor concurs with this view and describes how the culture is changing:

> 'Twenty years ago they would have been out on the lash. Nowadays the lads are going to the gym and a lot of the lads will run the track before racing. Jockeys will have ridden out in the morning – three or four lots maybe – driven to the racing, gone for a 3-mile run, and then they'll come back and sit in the sauna, and go out and have five or six rides. It's quite scary, the amount of physical exertion they do and then they've got to drive home for another 2–3 hours. The distance that Jason Maguire, for instance, must drive in a year is phenomenal, at least 60,000 miles. Jason lives in Gloucester and travels to Ayr, Hexham, all those northern meetings three or four times a week. It's madness. Nine times out of ten he'll drive himself. It's not a well-enough paid sport for you to be able to afford someone to drive you the whole time.'

Maguire's example highlights not only the relentless professionalism of the jockeys but also the pecuniary scraps they compete for, at least in comparison with more high-profile sports. In the last 20 years footballer's wages have increased beyond all recognition, but jockeys' incomes have been left at the gate. 'Wayne Rooney has just signed a contract for £300,000 a week – even a top jockey would be lucky to earn that in four years', Taylor explains. 'We're so far behind the times with jockey's wages, but if a jockey got £500 a ride there's not going to be many owners who can afford to pay that. By the time they've shelled out for the petrol for a 300-mile round trip, given a cut to their agent and paid me, jockeys are not earning a huge amount. If they have two rides per meeting, the first pays their expenses, only the second is profit.'

If jockeys viewed the profession purely in financial terms, they would simply choose another, more lucrative (and less dangerous) option, but such is the thrill of the competition and the lure of the camaraderie within the weighing room that the sport continues to draw in fresh, eager hopefuls and stars-in-the-making.

Those twin attractions of competition and camaraderie were reinforced three days later, on Grand National Day, which proved to be a happy one for team Taylor. There were no serious injuries and one of the jockeys who uses his valet services, Leighton Aspell, rode to victory on *Pineau de Re*.

Aspell's story of premature retirement, from which he returned within 18 months, was one that attracted media attention in the aftermath of his victory. Leighton said of this: 'I took a job with John Dunlop, but I decided there was still some unfinished business and life in the old dog yet. It's just a dream come true. The feeling is of pure elation when you cross the line. At my age, I won't have many more chances to win it. It's a wonderful day. This is what we do it for. I remember watching the National as a very young boy and as much as you enjoy sharing in everybody's success, you seek and crave it a bit too.'

3

LOCATION, LOCATION, LOCATION

A VALET'S GUIDE TO THE JOCKEYS' INNER SANCTUM

Strictly, the term *weighing room* covers the area in which the jockeys are weighed in and weighed out by the clerk of the scales. However, in general parlance it covers a wider area that includes several linked rooms that form the inner sanctum of the racecourse, with restricted access.

Jockeys' changing room

This is the largest room of the group, to which admittance is strictly monitored by a security officer. Inside the room is full of gear and banter.

There is a hierarchy to where the jockeys sit. AP McCoy, the acknowledged number one, has pride of place in National Hunt. Moving outwards from McCoy's position the seats go down the scale in terms of importance, with the more senior jockeys sitting closer to AP and the youngsters sitting further away. Jockeys have to work their way up, just as AP did, progressing from sitting round near the toilets to (hopefully) the number-one spot. In addition, jockeys who have the same valet tend to sit together.

Most changing rooms look similar, but they have their own subtleties. At Aintree, for instance, there are small bronze plaques on the wall underneath pegs bearing the names of previous winners.

The room has two sets of scales so jockeys and their valets can make sure they are the right weight before they are officially weighed by the clerk of the scales. There are also several television screens. There's a smaller women's changing room adjoining the men's one, which is identical, if a bit smaller.

Tea room

Jockeys tend to come into the changing room, hang their coat up, grab a paper and then go into the tea room unless they've got a light-weight race coming up, in which case they head for the sauna to sweat out a pound or two. They also come here between races to have a cup of tea or food. On the National Hunt circuit, Matt the tea boy travels around with the jockeys and provides refreshment.

Some jockeys won't get home until 9 or 10pm, so their only chance of eating a square meal is at the racecourse. There'll always be chicken, salad, fresh fruit and a fridge full of isotonic drinks, such as Lucozade, Red Bull or other brands. The lads tend to like full-sugar Coke rather than Diet Coke for the sugar buzz after they've been sweating weight off – it puts a bit of energy back into their bodies. A few drink only water, but a lot of riders will have a glass of ice with just a splash of Coke so they feel like they are taking in something. There's a television in there so they will have the racing on from various locations.

Valets' room

There are tumble driers and washing machines in this room. The valets transport the jockeys' clothing and equipment from meeting to meeting, lay it out in readiness for their arrival and wash it after their departure, ready to be transported to the next meeting.

They also have responsibility for the riders' saddles. These range in weight from 1lb upwards. It's easier to carry weight in a saddle than to wear weight cloths, so a jockey will normally use the heaviest saddle allowable if necessary.

The valets don't bring the racing silks. The colours of the silks are unique to each owner and are brought by the trainer.

Physiotherapist's room

The jockeys come in here to have niggling injuries treated and strapped up. Ten or twelve physios take it in turns to follow the racing circuit, and at the bigger race meetings there will be at least two in attendance.

Urinals, communal showers, saunas

The jockeys spend a lot of time in the sauna. By 9am in the morning the temperature in there is pumped up to 35°C (90°F) so it is ready for the first riders to come in. They may go straight in for 2 hours or so if they've got a light weight to make. If a jockey is particularly struggling, he or she will also have worn a sweat suit in the car in order to lose an additional 2–3lb on the journey.

Weighing room

This is positioned in the centre of the building. The jockeys are officially weighed here by the clerk of the scales before they go into the paddock. They carry their saddle, their weight cloths (which carry lead weights starting from ½lb) and their number cloth. The helmet is not weighed.

A jockey's weight must match the one printed on the racecard. Once the rider has been weighed, the trainer will take away the saddle and number cloth and saddle up the mount.

At the bigger meetings there may be two officials in attendance overseeing this operation and, in addition, clerks monitor the declarations. Once the horse is at the racecourse and is confirmed as going to run then it is *declared*. This must take place 45 minutes before the start of the race.

At the back of the room there may be a broadcasting office, from where PA announcements are made.

Clerk of the course's room

This is the small room that the clerk of the course uses as a base.

Steward's room

These differ from course to course, but at Aintree, for example, the steward's room is windowless and features a mahogany table surrounded by eight chairs. On the walls there are eight TV screens that show different angles of the course for replays of the race. If there is a stewards' enquiry, the jockeys come in here to explain their versions of events and provide evidence that will help the stewards to adjudicate.

Doctors'/ambulance room

This back room is the jockey's hospital ward and contains beds and medical equipment. Depending on the extent of the injury, a rider may come here for a medical examination before they are sent on to hospital. If, for instance, it appears likely that they've broken a collarbone, then they'll usually be examined at the course. If they need to go to hospital, then they often prefer to ask someone to drive them home to their 'local'; jockeys don't want to be stuck in hospital miles away from their homes if they can avoid it. However, if riders are extremely badly hurt, they'll be airlifted straight to the nearest hospital.

At a meeting such as the Grand National four or five doctors will be present. Some are A&E specialists, some are practising GPs. They will have seen everything from a broken fingernail to compound fractures and worse. Everyone is expertly trained and the medical care on racecourses is second to none; if you have to have a medical emergency, a racecourse is not a bad place at which to have it!

4

HAVE SADDLE, WILL TRAVEL

Riding work

Less than a fortnight after the longest day, dawn has long since broken when Martin Dwyer's alarm rings at 6.15am. Wiltshire's rolling countryside is already losing its night-time moisture under the warmth of unbroken sunshine so, despite a late return from Kempton Park yesterday, it is no hardship for him to get out of bed and start what will be another long working day.

Rising early – regardless of the elements – has been part and parcel of his job for more than 20 years, and he's used to leaving the family house before his wife, Claire, and his children, Joseph and Daisy, have stirred. He's been known to get up in the dead-of-night darkness of 4am to make the 2½-hour journey from Marlborough to Newmarket to ride horses to prepare them for a race. Sometimes he goes to Brian Meehan's nearby stables where he might ride out up to ten horses. But this July morning he travels the 25 minutes to Lambourn and works four horses at the stables of trainer Willie Muir.

He's back home 3½ hours later and, having showered, snatches some tea, a slice of toast (there're no light rides today; if there were, he might skip the toast) and his first glance at the day's *Racing Post*.

Dwyer turned 39 a week ago and is now a proven, seasoned professional. He first rode on the circuit in 1992 and since then has experienced all the rollercoaster highs and lows that go with being a jockey. On the one hand he's competed in prestigious races all over the globe and enjoyed more than a thousand of the adrenalin rushes that go with riding a winner. On the other he's suffered serious injury, a controversial suspension and dips in fortune when the rides and the winners have dried up.

He sips his tea and explains why jockeys ride work for trainers for free:

> 'It's to school the horses, get a feel for them and help the trainer make a plan: where he's going to run them, over what distance, on what ground, on which track, in which race. You try to assist them to build a profile of the horse and make the right decisions. It's a part of the job that a lot of people don't appreciate – and we don't get paid for it.
>
> The public wouldn't appreciate how much work we put in. A sprint race is run in under a minute, and people think we just fly in a helicopter, get on for 1 minute, get the glory and the prize and go home again. But we can be up at all hours working these horses towards these races. There wouldn't be many sportsmen or women who have a schedule like we do. We compete every morning, every day and often at night-time as well.'

Martin Dwyer at work, riding Code Red to victory in The Scott Dobson Memorial Doncaster Stakes at Doncaster Racecourse, October 2014

There are around 450 working jockeys in Great Britain and Ireland across both codes (flat-racing and jump-racing), and today, for example, a total of 146 (of which 55 are apprentices or conditional riders) will be riding at the meetings at Haydock, Great Yarmouth, Epsom, Newbury, Leopardstown on the flat or at Perth over jumps. In addition, 43 are suspended and 42 injured.

Dwyer won't always rise early to ride work but it's a common occurrence, and the first part of a daily cycle that he, and most professional jockeys, will follow. After riding work comes some preparation time, and then it's a routine of travelling, race-riding, travelling and sleeping. That cycle is punctuated by numerous phone calls, moments when he studies the form, and weighing-room banter with colleagues. Sometimes he walks the course, sweats in the sauna or goes to the gym. And, very occasionally, he eats and drinks. But essentially the cycle is the same and has been the same for the 22 years that he has been riding. All that changes is the backcloth. For Dwyer yesterday it was Kempton, today it's Great Yarmouth and at the weekend he flies to Frankfurt in Germany. He welcomes these changes in location because he values variety and new challenges more highly than stability and a comfort zone. Dwyer positively likes not knowing where he will be all the time, and is fully aware that if he wore a suit and worked in the same office each day, nine to five, it would drive him to distraction.

Indeed, Dwyer had craved an active, outdoors life ever since his childhood, brought up on the deprived outskirts of Merseyside. He was a restless, adventurous, thrill-seeking boy; always on the go, usually playing football with his mates, often involved in scrapes. It shaped a personality that has stood Dwyer in good stead over the years: fearless, gutsy, streetwise, sociable, always ready with a sharp one-liner.

From the age of three he followed his dad's lead and became a devoted fan of Everton (he remains an ardent supporter and explains you are either *born* a blue or *become* a red). Like all the other lads in the area in the 1980s, football was his first love until his head was turned in an unexpected direction, as he explains:

'Where we lived, the sister of a friend of mine owned a pony next to a football pitch. When she wasn't there we'd climb over the wall and drag the pony out of the stable. We couldn't ride it very well at all but we'd gallop up and down the grass verges by the side of the road and in the field. We did it for a laugh, and I got into horses that way. Where we grew up in Merseyside it wasn't the done thing for lads to ride ponies. Everything was football. I remember falling off the horse with my football boots on but no helmet.

I started taking a more general interest in horses and did a work-experience placement when I was 14 with a local family who owned a farm. They taught kids how to do showjumping. I was good at handling horses and they told me how to ride. I wanted to work with horses because I enjoyed it and I was good at it.

I always loved the thrill of riding horses. I remember we were on holiday in Wales and there was a stone wall with a load of horses in a field, and the lads bet me I wouldn't jump on one particular horse's back. So I stood on this great big stone wall, next to which the horse was eating grass and I just dived on it. I landed on its arse. I fell down and it kicked me back over the wall. I was lucky: it could have killed me.

As the other kids grew and got bigger I never got picked for the school football team so I went in a different direction and did something I was good at.

At the end of my school days my dad, a big racing fan, wrote a letter to the trainer Ian Balding, who is based in Kingsclere, a small village in Berkshire, just the other side of Newbury. They had a reputation for taking youngsters under their wing and he decided it was good for me not to be at Newmarket with all the distractions.'

Balding responded positively to the letter and, in January 1992, the 15-year old Dwyer was dropped off by his dad at Balding's Park House

Stables. He was told to 'work hard, keep out of trouble and you'll be fine'. Taking the advice to heart, Dwyer undertook all the apprentice jobs, competing against the others, trying to impress the guv'nor and get rides. He had only one that year but progressed well enough to finish as the runner-up in the apprentice jockeys' championship in 1996. It was clear that he'd got ability and that he'd found a job that he adored: 'That enjoyment of riding and love of horses is so important. You need to have that', Dwyer explains. 'The first big thing for me was the thrill of the speed. It's an unusual feeling because you're travelling at nearly 50mph on the back of a live animal and you can't explain what it feels like to anybody. You have to do it. You do get used to it but when you first start it's an unbelievable experience.'

Working the phones

It's 10am. The period between riding work and travelling to the races is the prime time for Dwyer to communicate with his agent and other connections within racing. This is an often-overlooked but critical part of a jockey's life. In fact it might be *the* most important task because without his network Dwyer would be lost. As a self-employed businessman his whole survival depends on the strength of these relationships. Dwyer explains:

> 'I'll spend half an hour of the phone with my agent, Simon Dodds, making a plan of which meetings I'm going to go to, informing him about the horses I've just ridden. I'll say "I've ridden a horse this morning, I've discussed it with the trainer and we're going to ride him in a mile race at Newbury and not the mile-and-a-half race somewhere else." So Simon knows not to accept another ride in that race if he is offered one. Nowadays you have to have an agent. He's vital when it comes to getting the rides for you, and the schedules are so tight you can't do it for yourself. He manages where you go and what you ride each week. We keep in touch each day but you also have to leave them to it a bit. I'll also make other phone calls to trainers.'

It's pretty clear that the subject of trainer–jockey loyalty pushes Dwyer's buttons. He thinks attitudes have changed over the years, and not for the better:

> 'It seems to me that there's been a shift. A lot of the older trainers have retired and now there are younger trainers and jockeys coming through with completely different ideas. That's a natural thing in any business or sport, but the attitudes have changed. There's no loyalty in racing any more, between trainers and jockeys. The old-school trainers that have slowly dwindled away had different values.
>
> The blame game is more prevalent in racing now than it ever was before. If you look back, the big stables had their jockeys and stuck with them. Nowadays, trainers use different jockeys every day of the week. The younger trainers run handicap horses in group races and, when they don't win, they blame the jockey. They over-egg the horses, then sack the jockey. And it's happening every day of the season. A trainer will run a horse six times, with six different jockeys. If the horse doesn't win, it must be the jockey's fault so they get a new jockey. But if they look back over their season they must see they aren't better off for having done that.
>
> I rode a horse last season. The trainer was running it over the wrong distance and I told him so. He disagreed, he ran it over the same distance again and it was beaten. Then he started riding it over the right distance. I rode it, and we won three big handicaps with it, going up 30lb in the ratings and it was third in a group race. This year he decided he needed a change. The horse since has run twice, with two different jockeys on it, and been stuffed well out of sight. I'm not saying I would have won on it, but what was that decision-making based upon?
>
> In my opinion, the most successful outfits are the ones that build a team and stick with it. Richard Hannon and Richard Hughes have had the same trainer, jockey, head lad and vet for

> years. They're one team and they all work together. They make mistakes some days but that happens.'

These days, Dwyer is a freelance jockey. He rides most of the horses at the stables of Willie Muir, his father-in-law, but in the past fortnight he has also ridden for George Baker, Jo Hughes, Andrew Hollingshead, Sylvester Kirk, Bill Hughes, Pat Eddery, Marcus Tregoning, David Griffiths, William Knight, Mick Channon and Ismail Mohammed.

It hasn't always been this way. Eight years ago he made a well-meaning business decision at the height of his career that had serious consequences. At a time when he was a top-ten jockey riding frequent Group One winners he secured a move to become second jockey to trainer Sheikh Hamdan bin Rashid Al Maktoum, being paid a retainer to be available to ride for him as and when required.

Dwyer expected that he would inherit the number-one spot when Richard Hills retired. He waited and persevered for two seasons, but things didn't go to plan. Hills's worthy endurance meant he kept on riding and Dwyer was constantly waiting for him to make up his mind – as is a first jockey's prerogative – which of Sheikh Hamdan's horses he would ride. Pulled in different directions, it was impossible for Dwyer to juggle his options. He messed other trainers about with late switches and eventually they lost patience. Ties were broken, most notably those linking him to friends and allies such as Andrew Balding and Marcus Tregoning, with whom he had worked so successfully during the first half of his career.

In time, Dwyer decided that he had to terminate his connection with Sheikh Hamdan and go back to being freelance. He was pretty much back to square one, as he explains:

> 'At the time I thought going to Sheikh Hamdan would be a step sideways rather than forwards but that I'd still ride nice horses and, in the long run, when I got the first job it would all be worthwhile. But it didn't work out like that. Being second jockey and with so many horses with different trainers, by the time we'd figured out who was running and Richard had decided where he

> was going, it was too late to pick up other rides. It damaged my career massively and I have no one to blame but myself.
>
> When you are letting people down, they don't come back after a while. The job wasn't working out and I felt my career was suffering. It could have been different if I'd got the first jockey job but I couldn't wait any longer. I had to leave and start almost from scratch. It's racing, it's life, it was disappointing because I never stopped working hard and didn't do anything stupid but I really suffered for it.'

When asked how he spends the precious, small amount of time left between riding work and travelling to the races these days – other than working the phones and managing those all-important relationships – Dwyer replies:

> 'Riding is seven days a week now so there's no time for gym work. I only use the gym if I've had an injury and I'm coming back to fitness. There's a great rehabilitation centre in Lambourn, which is brilliant, but at the height of summer there's no time to go to the gym. Anyway, there's nothing you can do in the gym that simulates riding in a race.
>
> I don't do the books either. Most jockeys haven't got the time or are too thick to do any paperwork or keep accounts together, which is an absolute nightmare. I'm lucky that my wife Claire does all that for me.
>
> I do, however, spend time doing loads of research to prepare for upcoming rides. Nowadays, with the Internet, it's very easy to look up the form of horses so I put time into that, in the morning then throughout the day, reading the *Racing Post*, studying form. And the trainers will also tell you about the horses you're going to ride.'

If, like today, he has ridden work nearby then he might also get a few minutes with his young family. To his consternation his daughter, Daisy, broke her finger a couple of days ago, so he gets an update on her recovery. Dwyer is a devoted family man and the demands of the job mean that he sees less of them than he would like: 'It's difficult, but I spend as much time with them as I can and try to strike a balance', he says. 'I was suspended last weekend and we all went to Ross-On-Wye in Gloucester and stayed with friends. I turned off my phone and we went mountain biking through the forest one day, then on the Sunday canoed down the river and had a pub lunch. It was not until Sunday night that I turned my phone back on. I feel I've got to make the time when I can. I'm not a golfer so I spend all my spare time with the kids.'

On the road

With calls made and form studied, the way is clear to start a round trip of 436 miles to Great Yarmouth. The venue is not one of his favourites, simply because of its location. It's out on a limb and all jockeys hang their heads in the manner of travelling salesmen when they talk of the constant challenges they face negotiating the congested roads on this little island:

> 'The travelling is crazy', Dwyer confirms. 'Being away from your family, it's hard to lead a normal home life. I do 40,000–50,000 miles a year, easily. I have a new sponsored Audi and the best things about it are that it's got comfy seats, good sat nav and it doesn't break down. They're the most important things for a jockey.
>
> I've missed races loads of times because of the traffic. There's nothing you can do about it. The roads in Britain are unpredictable. There are accidents, the motorway gets closed.
>
> But it's better than being stuck in an office. You end up doing a lot of driving yourself but you need to share when you can, because you can't do it all and you need to relax a bit. Some of the jockeys that are doing well have a driver and in years gone by I've also used drivers, but you need to be doing well and earning enough money to pay someone else. It's physically and mentally tiring. You can drive 400 miles in a day and it can be

a nightmare, but if you have a winner or two you don't worry about it. However, when you've had a bad day and then you've got a long drive home, it's tough.'

There is often both afternoon and evening racing, and Dwyer rushes from one to the other. He could be required at any of flat-racing's 30-odd racecourses, from Musselburgh in the far north to Brighton on the south coast, or from Ffos Las in the west to today's destination in the east. These can be long days. Up early, home as late as midnight.

Winter brings some respite; he will either be working abroad or travelling shorter distances to the all-weather tracks at Kempton, Wolverhampton or Lingfield. But that's no consolation today. Moreover, the trek is being made just for one ride. To an accountant's mind there is no logic to this unless the horse, *Beakers N Num Nums*, features in the

HITTING THE ROAD

With the season in full flow, the racing schedule is remorseless and the amount of time spent on motorways is astonishing. Here is Dwyer's travel over the previous fortnight, this is fairly typical:

Kempton Park	(132-mile round trip)
Bath (twice)	(66-mile round trip)
Great Yarmouth	(436-mile round trip)
Leicester	(208-mile round trip)
Salisbury	(70-mile round trip)
Brighton	(234-mile round trip)
Windsor	(112-mile round trip)
Chepstow	(112-mile round trip)
Ayr	(760-mile round trip)*
Royal Ascot	(106-mile round trip)

* Travelled by aeroplane

prize money. Dwyer knows, however, that if he were to reject a ride simply because it's too much trouble and not worth his while it would be tantamount to professional suicide. He just can't do it. So he views today as an investment for the future.

Dwyer will be paid £115.32 for the ride (the same amount is paid to every jockey, regardless of the trainer or the stature of the race) and this amount will barely cover his bills. If the horse wins, then Dwyer will get 6.9 per cent of the prize money (the first prize for this race is £4,400).

As a member of the Professional Jockeys Association, Dwyer receives the benefit of welfare support and services. These include various schemes that help with legal insurance for disciplinary matters and motoring offences (the latter being especially handy bearing in mind the number of miles travelled and the potential for speeding points); medical expenses, both at home and abroad; and professional and public insurance, as well as career ending insurance. In addition, the Professional Riders Insurance Scheme (paid for by racehorse owners) makes disbursements for a certain period when a jockey is injured.

However, balanced against the positives are heavy expenses. Dwyer has to cover agents' fees of 10 per cent, valet fees and Professional Jockeys Association membership fees (3 per cent of the riding fee), as well as having to pay for group insurances and physiotherapy services. On top of these, there is the cost of the petrol required for travelling to the races and to trainers' yards to ride out. On average, one-third of his earnings is eaten up by these expenses.

Because Dwyer has enjoyed an unusual amount of success in his career he earns more than most, but the average annual wage of a flat-racing jockey – including apprentices just starting out with 25 rides a year – is around £30,000, the same as the average *weekly* wage of a Premier League footballer.

Some, like Dwyer, are able to supplement their British earnings overseas, predominantly during the winter, where the prize money and other associated benefits are better. That's why he will ride in Frankfurt on Sunday and that's why he has ridden so frequently in India.

His time in the subcontinent has provided both happy memories and big-money wins in the past – such as when he rode *In The Spotlight* to success in the Indian Derby in 2012 – but the good experiences have been irrevocably soured by what he describes as the lowest low of his career. This occurred when Dwyer finished a narrow third on the heavily backed favourite *Ice Age* at Mahalaxmi racecourse in February 2013, a ride that left a number of race-goers unhappy.

He originally had a 55-day suspension imposed for allegedly preventing his mount from running on its merits. An appalled Dwyer strongly denied the allegation, citing that the horse had been bleeding heavily from the nose during the race, but the ban was extended to eight months after an appeal board sent the case back to Royal Western India Turf Club (RWITC) stewards. Normally the ban would have applied worldwide but, to Dwyer's immense relief, the British Horseracing Authority took the unprecedented step of not recognising the foreign jurisdiction, enabling him to continue to ride in Britain.

Dwyer is keen to draw a line under the controversy: 'I first went to India years ago when I was 23 and have been back, on and off, for 18 years', he says. 'I used to go over for a couple of weeks, but in 2012 I spent three months there during the winter, riding *In the Spotlight*. We won everything. It's a fantastic place, so it's a shame about the controversy. I guess you're not going to go through life without bumps along the way.'

In the saddle

The M25 and Norfolk's single carriageways negotiated, Dwyer arrives at the Yarmouth coast with time to spare before his race, the sixth on the card. By then the race meeting has begun, attended by a small, shirt-sleeved crowd of holidaymakers and locals basking in 25°C (77°F) sunshine, cooled by a breeze off the sea. It's one of those bread-and-butter meetings that keep the bookies ticking over.

Dwyer aims to get to each meeting at least an hour before the start of the first race in which he is riding. If he needs to walk the course, spend some time in the sauna to sweat out a couple of pounds or see a physio he gets there earlier, but none of those things are required today. Dwyer explains:

> 'I only walk the course if there are extremes in weather or I haven't ridden the track for a while, just to familiarise myself with it. On Sunday I'm flying to Hamburg, and when I get there I'll walk the track, as I haven't ridden there since last year.
>
> I'll also walk the course if they've moved in the rails to see if there is any advantage to be had in the ground. I remember at Deauville once they moved in the rail by just a couple of metres, so I decided to stick to the rail the whole way on the fresh ground. And I did, mostly at the back, but in the straight I got room and got up and won. Knowing about the fresh ground won me the race.'

Dwyer's trusty valet Dave Mustoe is in the weighing room, busy as usual. Dwyer clearly appreciates his services: 'He's a good lad, Musty', Dwyer says. 'He keeps all my stuff together. If riders didn't have valets, all the races would be off late, the three o'clock would be run at quarter to four, because if we had to organise ourselves ...'

Today, there are small cards so the weighing room is sparsely populated with jockeys and is quieter than normal. Dwyer's arrival adds to the noise levels. He's one of the most vocal, winding people up, telling jokes, joining in with the banter, as he admits:

> 'There's a lot of mocking. You have to have a strong character. If you show any weakness, everyone will jump on it. We stick together, but there is a lot of teasing. The only way to describe the weighing room is like a school classroom when the teacher leaves for a minute. It's good fun. We're like a travelling circus. On Sunday we're going to Germany for the German Derby and I think there are seven of us. We're staying the night in Hamburg and God knows what's going to happen.
>
> You can be riding in Hong Kong and three or four of you will stay in the same hotel. There was a phase where people put bills

> on other people's hotel rooms. That got a bit out of hand for a while. It started in Japan, when [Jamie] Spencer put the drinks bill on [Kieren] Fallon's room and signed for it. That started a bit of a war for a while. I've been trapped in my room before too. They got all the furniture off the landing and barricaded me in.'

Other than the chat and gossip, Dwyer, as usual, relaxes, rests, plans for the race, goes through the form of the horses and builds up a picture in his mind of how he's going to ride.

As he changes out of a shirt and pair of jeans into orange-and-yellow striped racing silks, the scars on his trim, pencil-slim frame are reminders that this is a perilous profession. The small blemish on his chest can be disregarded – that came from a hamster bite in his youth – but there's a more prominent one on his left elbow from a particularly bad fall at Leicester, which required three operations. He also broke his right hand that day. The injury drove him crazy. He couldn't shave or take the lid off a jar, and it had serious professional consequences, not least because he was sidelined for four months and he missed out on a Breeders' Cup Turf winner on *Dangerous Midge*.

The scar on his ankle is the result of a fracture in 2010 that also cost him four months, but there's less visible damage from a more recent fall that threatened his career for a few days. He had looked set to make his first mount of 2014 a winning one at Southwell when the horse, *Columbian Roulette,* jinked unexpectedly in the final furlong and ejected him. His legs hit the ground first before he flipped over and struck the right side of his head. The blow left him unconscious for six minutes and the force of the impact split his helmet. He regained consciousness before being taken to the Queen's Medical Centre in Nottingham where he was later discharged after undergoing a battery of tests. He recalls:

> 'I don't remember anything of the day. I woke up in the hospital and I didn't know what had happened. It was a weird experience. My wife and father-in-law came later on in the evening and I was in a ward, and that was when I got my bearings back. They

told me that my brain had taken a bashing and it obviously controls everything. I had bruising on the brain. There was a time that evening when I couldn't feel the left side of my body and I thought "this is serious". But because I'd damaged the right side of my brain the left-hand side of my body had just stopped working, like a dead leg. That was frightening – everything goes through your mind. But within an hour or so the feeling came back.'

When asked if he ever watched a video of the fall, he replies: 'Yes, when I came round my father-in-law told me that people had been emailing *At the Races* saying I'd jumped off the horse', he says. 'I had no memory of it and I'm thinking "shit, does it look like that?" But when I watched it I realised it wouldn't even physically be possible to jump off a horse like that. The horse swerved underneath me. It's done it so many times since. It's broken somebody's shoulder, somebody's leg. It goes at 40mph or more and then it just swerves from underneath you – and it's just not possible to stay on a horse when it does that.'

There is no suggestion that the fall has altered Dwyer's mindset towards danger. Indeed, the risk remains something he positively welcomes. Maybe it goes with the territory for thrill-seekers, a fact that Dwyer acknowledges: 'There is an element of danger in racing every day. We're the sportsmen who go to work every day and get followed by an ambulance. I like that in a way because not everybody can do it. In the middle of a race you feel alive, when you're inches away from the horse in front of you, travelling at 40mph, making split-second decisions. It's a unique occupation.'

With several injuries, the move to Sheikh Hamdan and the controversy in India, the second half of Dwyer's career has posed more challenges than the first, which featured a steady ascent to the summit of a Derby win. Winners and rides are slightly less frequent these days but there are still plenty of them – and the result this particular Thursday in the 4.40pm at Great Yarmouth on *Beakers N Num Nums* is to add to the list.

Dwyer rides a stealthy race in a field of four, easing ahead in the final couple of furlongs to secure a comfortable 22nd win of the season from his 194th ride on the 7–4 shot. This is a low-key triumph on a low-key race day, yet Dwyer is still pleased. It makes the journey worthwhile, financially and psychologically. He says the day when any kind of win fails to improve his mood will be the day he takes the decision to stop racing.

But Dwyer has had many better days than this, winning Blue Riband races all over the globe. He teamed up with Andrew Balding, son of his first trainer Ian, to land his first Group One victory aboard *Casual Look* in the 2003 Epsom Oaks. That year he also won the flat 'Ride of the Year' at the Professional Jockeys Association Awards for winning the Jockey Club Cup on *Persian Punch*, Dwyer's favourite horse, whom he recollects fondly: 'He had his own personality', he says. 'You had to push him the whole way, and he'd always fight back. I remember winning the Goodwood Cup on him and the noise from the crowd in the stands was unbelievable. After the race I took him back down to the crowd, a spontaneous thing, and they rushed to the front rail to see him and it was just an amazing feeling to be part of something like that. He had his own fan club.'

The Dwyer–Balding combination proved potent in the ten months that followed the Goodwood Cup, particularly with *Phoenix Reach*, who won them big international races in Canada, Hong Kong and Dubai. Dwyer describes the feeling: 'You can't beat winning a big race. It's just the thrill, like scoring a goal, serving an ace. The buzz, there's no feeling like it – and if that ever goes, you've got to pack up, because if you can't enjoy that then there's no point in doing it.'

Dwyer's biggest buzz came at the sun-drenched 2006 Derby on Epsom Downs. A few jockeys are awarded letters after their names, honoured by royalty, but this was the day when Dwyer put some important initials before his name: DWJ, Derby Winning Jockey. What a race it was. Not only did he win on the biggest stage in racing, but he also won with élan and flair, showcasing his talent to the watching world. Dwyer's lilac racing silks onboard the 6–1 shot, *Sir Percy*, could just about be spotted in the pack towards the rear of the field as they approached Tattenham Corner and swung into the home straight. But he crept through the pack down the long run-in – ever closer, still with petrol in the tank, easing through the gears – then in the final few yards executed an award-winning riding manoeuvre up the inside to snatch a dramatic, short-head victory on the line.

Even now, eight years on, the seasoned, seen-it-all pro becomes boyish and proud as he relives the moment:

> 'It was a rough race. I just had to go where there was room, and take chances by going up the inside and hope the gaps would come. I remember making my move, and I went for a gap on the rail, and I made a split-second decision to go left instead of right, and just put my head down and hoped. And the horse dug deep.
>
> My gut instincts told me I'd up just got up on the line and won, but it was a photo finish, and then, while I was pulling up, somebody said Daryll Holland had won. I was deflated. I thought "shit, they must have seen the result", but when we turned round and came back and I saw that I had won it and I just felt elation.
>
> I couldn't begin to describe the feeling. You just think you've arrived and you've achieved the ultimate, the pinnacle, like scoring in the FA Cup Final. All the memories came back from when I started riding. I thought back to when I was 16 and my Dad had driven me down to Ian Balding's stable with my sandwiches, wrapped in silver foil. He had said "Behave yourself, I don't want to be coming back to pick you up next week". To have got from that point to winning the Derby was just unbelievable.'

Dwyer received a 7 per cent share of the first prize of £740,695, but what impact did such a headline-making success have on his life? He explains:

'Financially, it makes a difference but it doesn't make you a millionaire. What matters more is the fact that you've won the best race in the world. It establishes you. They can never take that away from you. Like today, I was going down to the start and Derek Thomson bellowed out "Derby-winning jockey, Martin Dwyer" and that still makes the hairs stand up on the back of my neck. That's where it changes things. There's only one Derby a year. There are more than 200 current jockeys and not many have won it. Ask anybody around the world about horse racing and they'll know three things: the Grand National, the Epsom Derby and Lester Piggott.

And I did it before Frankie [Dettori] as well, that was quite nice! I gave him plenty of stick but he won it the next year.

You remember little things. I always remember the morning after Colin Mackenzie from the *Daily Mail* called our house. My wife and I had gone out and my dad was watching the children. I'm named Martin after him.

[Colin] says "Morning, Martin, it's Colin Mackenzie here." And my dad says, "Morning, Colin, how are you?" although he doesn't know him. So Colin Mackenzie thinks he's talking to me and starts conducting an interview with my Dad, who still doesn't know who he's talking to.

The conversation goes on: "How do you feel about yesterday?" My Dad says, "Best day of my life." and Colin says, "Oh brilliant, I'm so pleased for you. Were you nervous before the race?" And my Dad says, "Oh yeah, I don't mind telling you, I was shitting meself. I had to have a few drinks just before the race to calm me nerves." Colin says, "No, really?" and Dad says, "Yeah, I had a couple of beers and a whisky." Colin said, "Are you joking?" and Dad said, "No, no." That nearly got in the paper. God, it was funny.'

Back home

The journey home always feels quicker after a winner. Dwyer returns home to Marlborough after the children have gone to bed to tuck into a small plate of pasta, the largest meal of his day. He doesn't get to eat often, and that can be hard, as he reveals:

> 'Sometimes you think, "when did I last have a meal?" You just pick at things. Eating sporadically, your stomach shrinks anyway. I never eat puddings or chocolate. Some of the lads who are naturally above 9st really struggle. I'm always between 1st and 10lb underweight. I'm 8lb 4oz now but I need to be just over 9st. I drop a few pounds to ride light weights by losing fluids. Everyone's the same. George Baker and Richard Hughes are tall, big lads and if they filled out, they'd be 10st. But we've got more support now, though every jockey manages their weight in their own way. And the minimum weights have been raised, sensibly, over the past few years, which is better. It's a lot more professional nowadays.'

What of the future? The average jockey retires at 33½ (although this statistic is increasing each year) and Dwyer is now 39. He has recently set up an events company with jockey Steve Drowne, and they successfully run parties and music festivals. Yet he has set his sights on riding, barring injuries, until at least 45. 'Why not?' he suggests; Kieren Fallon is 49. Moreover, Dwyer knows his skills in the saddle are undiminished:

> 'I think I'm a better jockey now than I've ever been. You need to be fit and strong, but a large part of being a winning jockey is your decision-making skills and you make better decisions with maturity and experience.
>
> Besides, you're only as good as the horse you're riding. When Frankie Dettori lost his job with *Godolphin* he only rode about six winners in two months, but he hadn't suddenly forgotten how to ride. You can't do it without the horse underneath you. It's a vicious circle. You don't get the winners and people don't put you up and you end up riding a lesser class of horse. James

Doyle was always a great jockey but he was going to give up – he was going to become a plumber and did a course – and then he got on one decent horse and won on it and the rest is history.

Jockeys definitely go in and out of fashion. Confidence is important but if the most confident jockey in the world rides a donkey they've got no chance. It's 95 per cent the horse. And there are a lot of good jockeys who are not getting the chance. A lot of it is down to luck.'

Finally, he gives his advice for aspiring jockeys: 'Enjoy the good times and be aware that it doesn't last forever. Someone said to me the other day that age is like a petrol tank: when you're young it goes on forever, but when you get to the second half of the tank it just drops away.'

MARTIN DWYER – CAREER RECORD IN GREAT BRITAIN (as at 3 July 2014)

YEAR	WINNERS	RIDES
Total	1,216	**12,168**
2014	22	194
2013	47	536
2012	42	535
2011	53	497
2010	68	478
2009	86	789
2008	64	675
2007	70	657
2006	90	862
2005	82	718
2004	82	848
2003	90	789
2002	106	964
2001	65	810
2000	61	554
1999	36	525

1998	46	535
1997	57	603
1996	36	379
1995	6	150
1994	6	60
1993	1	9
1992	0	1

MARTIN DWYER – COURSE-BY-COURSE RECORD, LAST FIVE YEARS (as at 3 July 2014)

COURSE	RIDES	WINNERS
Total	2,240	232
Kempton (All-weather)	332	34
Woverhampton (AW)	239	26
Lingfield (AW)	225	28
Newmarket (July)	120	7
Windsor	117	10
Newbury	109	4
Newmarket	102	4
Goodwood	95	9
Leicester	94	11
Ascot	83	6
Bath	76	15
Sandown	71	6
Nottingham	61	5
Brighton	60	5
Salisbury	57	11
Southwell (AW)	47	3
Doncaster	40	8
Haydock	40	3
Ffos Las	37	10
Epsom	33	2

Lingfield	32	4
York	28	3
Yarmouth	26	3
Warwick	22	2
Chepstow	20	2
Folkestone	18	2
Pontefract	13	2
Chester	12	1
Redcar	11	2
Ayr	4	0
Beverley	4	1
Thirsk	4	0
Ripon	3	1
Catterick	2	1
Hamilton	2	0
Newcastle	1	1

5

TRAILBLAZERS

Recent years have seen waves of talented young female riders trying to break into the ranks of professional jockeys – and 17-year-old Hollie Doyle from Hereford is one of them.

Currently an amateur, this week she is undertaking a five-day course at the British Racing School in a bid to prove her competence and be awarded an apprentice jockey's licence. The licence allows riders aged between 16 and 26, in full-time paid employment with a trainer, to ride against professional jockeys, with a weight allowance to compensate for their inexperience.

During the week, Hollie is being lectured and assessed on diet and nutrition, sports science, rules and regulations, and integrity – and she will also need to impress in the practical elements of the course: riding work and on the simulator, entering the stalls and demonstrating her fitness.

As Doyle takes a brief lunchtime break to talk about her fledgling career she fiddles with a folder that contains all the notes and handouts from the course. Hollie admits she's found the sessions more of a challenge than anticipated and has at least one eye on the clock as she chats, a diligent pupil acutely aware that she soon needs to be back in the classroom.

What becomes immediately evident is that Doyle has the pedigree to succeed. Her upbringing is steeped in all things horse: her grandparents used to breed Arabs, her mother rode in Arab races before becoming an apprentice and her dad was an apprentice to trainer Richard Hannon before weight got the better of him and he went as a conditional jockey to John Edwards. Later he trained point-to-pointers before obtaining a full trainer's licence.

Consequently she's ridden and felt at home around thoroughbreds since before she could walk. As Doyle has developed, she's excelled in pony riding, showjumping and as an amateur race-rider, and now she's hell-bent on graduating to the next level.

So far Doyle has ridden as an amateur in 15 races – at racecourses such as Salisbury, Wolverhampton and Lingfield – and has already notched up three winners. Those races, those wins, have whetted her appetite for life on the pro circuit. At first she says she felt 'overwhelmed at being in the same weighing room as George Baker and Richard Hughes', worried that they would be questioning why she was there. But Doyle soon settled and became addicted to the 'adrenalin buzz of jumping out of the stalls, riding in races and the feeling you get when you do well.'

Doyle works at trainer David Evans's yard in Abergavenny in south Wales and initially says, simply, that her ambition is to 'have as many winners as possible.' In truth, modesty aside, she's aiming higher. Like most teenagers she has lofty dreams and ambitions that are not as yet quite matched by her confidence and self-belief. So when she adds, timidly, that she'd like to be champion apprentice, she soon clarifies that she accepts that this is very unlikely.

Young hopeful, Hollie Doyle, one of an increasing number of female jockeys

Part of Doyle's uncertainty is caused by the sheer number of teenagers who share her dream of wanting to turn pro. She explains that this was a surprise: 'It's a shock to find it's not just you. There's a lot of competition. You realise how many people you are up against. You're not the only one who wants it. It makes you think "oh God, am I going to do any good here? I don't know what I'll do if I don't ..."'

If Doyle does fall short, it won't be for want of determination or willingness to work hard, two traits that she knows are essential and thinks she's got. She also knows that standing just 4 feet 9 inches tall and currently weighing 7st 2lb will help. She says she hasn't grown for a year or two now and, while she may muscle up, she's unlikely to struggle with the weight-management issues that some taller, heavier jockeys – particularly males – battle with 24/7.

And Doyle is tough. She hasn't been fazed by a broken arm (in 2012) and a broken leg (in 2013); she has already adopted that stereotypical matter-of-fact, put-it-at-the-back-of-your-mind approach to the dangers of the sport that is so prevalent with jockeys. 'You can get injured walking across the street', she states with finality.

Nor does she think being female puts her at a disadvantage. It is noticeable that the majority of the attendees on the apprentice course are female, and more and more are breaking through into the sport. Doyle agrees: 'There are more opportunities for girls now', she says. 'I don't think it's as hard for us now as it was ten years ago. It's still harder for us than for boys, because we're not as strong, but you wouldn't think "there's a girl riding in that race" any more. There're a lot of female riders. It's pretty even.'

So, when Doyle chooses Cathy Gannon and Hayley Turner as her role models, she has selected them from an increasingly large list. How things have changed. It wasn't until 1966, 212 years after the formation of the Jockey Club, that women were even granted licences to train, and their success was only achieved following a verdict handed down by the court of appeal after a long-running battle with the Jockey Club.

It took another six years before women were allowed to ride in races on the flat under Jockey Club rules, with Meriel Tufnell becoming the first female winner in 1972. Four years later, ladies were given clearance to ride under National Hunt rules, leading to Charlotte Brew becoming the first to compete in the Grand National in 1977. It was another 19 years until Alex Greaves became the first woman to ride in the Derby in 1996, finishing last on a 500–1 shot trained by her husband, and another 16 years before Hayley Turner became the second female participant.

That Turner should be the latest to fly the female flag in Britain's most prestigious horse race was no surprise. Her career, which began in 2000, has long lit up a career pathway that Hollie Doyle would love to follow. If Doyle does manage to do so, she could look forward to becoming champion apprentice jockey; riding Group One winners both in the UK and internationally; riding in Blue Riband races in Dubai and the USA; riding in the Epsom Derby; and above all, enjoying season after season of racking up the winners. The years since 2005 (the season in which Turner shared the apprentice title with Saleem Golam) have yielded Turner 34, 53, 36, 56, 100, 73, 88 and 92 winners respectively. This is quite a tour de force, the product of a long-lasting career that has demonstrated that not only can Turner compete with male jockeys, she can rank among the best of them.

So far, although her career is in its infancy, Hollie Doyle can claim at least parity with Hayley Turner in terms of background. They both grew up with horses, had some success in eventing and showjumping and felt the thrill-seeker's urge to go faster and live on the edge.

However, Doyle's first, never-to-be-forgotten victory in her first race – 5 May 2013, Salisbury Racecourse, onboard the 8–1 shot *The Mongoose* – compares favourably with Turner's torturous equivalent at Southwell. But it is actually Turner's bitter-sweet debut that highlights the kind of qualities that will be needed if Doyle is to keep pace and sustain a career as a pro, and withstand the banter. 'On the day of my first ride I needed to ride light and the trainer said "get in the sauna", Turner recalls. 'Of course the lads were all there with nothing on and I'm 16, with a towel wrapped round me. And they were the worst lads you could have in there, y'know, with all the banter. And I was so embarrassed and they were just teasing me. That was the start of a really bad day.'

With her proud mum and dad waiting down by the finishing post, the race began but then, in the heart of the action, inexplicably, her mount broke its leg. 'The horse looked after me and it didn't fall and I jumped straight off', Turner says. 'They had to shoot it and I had to hold the horse. The adrenalin was rushing through me; it was such a shock. I didn't cry even though I wanted to. I just thought "there's no way I'm going to cry". I had to untack the horse when it was dead and then I was trundling back down the course with my saddle and my mum and dad are asking "Where is she? What's happened?" It didn't put me off, and if that didn't put me off, then nothing was going to.'

Turner's whole career, starting on that day at Southwell and for the following years, highlights the need for a no-nonsense, bloody-minded, keep-calm-and-carry-on determination to not be put off. One of the other big challenges for Turner in a male-dominated community was to be able to build trust and credibility with owners and trainers. In horse-racing's hierarchy, the owners and trainers hold sway and are the ones to impress. So they need to rate and trust the custodians of their highly strung, highly valuable thoroughbred Olympians.

Turner states that the owners questioned her suitability to ride their horses, a fact that she puts down to them 'paying so much money that they always want the best jockeys'. As such, she found it difficult to get owners to allow a female on their horse. Looking back, she believes that she wasn't ready to be a jockey when she was 17: 'I think that was about strength really and I do think that male jockeys are stronger earlier on.'

That challenge became all the greater when Turner couldn't benefit from the weight allowances gifted to an apprentice. Initially she was able to claim a weight advantage compared to a pro – 7lb until she had won 20 races, 5lb until she had won 50 races and 3lb until her 95th win – and that made her a more appealing option for a while. But, thereafter, she was exposed, vulnerable and fending for herself in a harsh marketplace, touting for work and being judged at parity against proven performers.

This stage is undoubtedly the pivotal moment in any race-riding career and many riders vanish without trace along with their weight advantage.

For most females this has proven to be an insurmountable challenge. Before Hayley Turner, the only women to have ridden out their claim in Britain were Alex Greaves, Emma O'Gorman and Lisa Jones – and of those only Greaves stayed the course, partnering 300 winners in a 15-year career. Yet Turner both survived and flourished.

The final aspect in which Turner has needed her mindset to 'not be put off' is that of coping with the inevitable injuries. She's had some bad ones. In March 2009 she sustained serious head injuries that required a prolonged period of recuperation after an accident putting a horse through the starting stalls on the Newmarket gallops. In 2013, she ended the year early to have surgery on an ankle; then, having returned, a fractured pelvis and three broken bones in her back once again forced her out. Undaunted, she's back, still riding winners, still an example to the new wave of women hopefuls.

It would be optimistic to expect Hollie Doyle or any of the aspiring young female jockeys in Britain to emulate the achievements of Hayley Turner, but there is no doubt that they are lining up to have a go. It's a trend that Paul Struthers, Chief Executive of the Professional Jockeys Association, believes will continue:

> 'It has helped that we've had trailblazers like Hayley and, to a slightly lesser extent, Kirsty Milczarek and Cathy Gannon. If you speak to the racing schools, they are getting a greater number of females going through their licensed courses, and that is going to happen because of weight.
>
> The minimum weight has risen to 8st but there are fewer and fewer people who can do that weight, even as a youngster. When they go on to their first licensed course on the flat their target has to be 8st 3lb. This factor makes one think that there is going to be a greater number of female jockeys coming through, and statistics suggest women are getting more rides as a collective group than they used to.'

But are women now competing on a level playing field against the men? Struthers considers:

'Do I still think there is a problem with female jockeys being given a chance? Yes. But that's not unique to racing. That's true in any walk of life. Hayley's first Group One winner came by chance. Someone was injured and she got the ride and won. Prior to that, although she was getting plenty of winners, she wasn't given the opportunity in Group One races. As soon as she got one she won. It is frankly the same for most jockeys. As for many professions, most people are much of a muchness in terms of their ability – and it's the same with jockeys. Some will rise to the top through professionalism and dedication and application; others are naturally more talented. But racing is not a solitary sport, you're sitting on a half-tonne animal and if you're not on a good enough horse you're not going to win races. It becomes self-fulfilling. You start coming up, getting better mounts, getting more winners and it takes off.'

Postscript

Hollie Doyle passed her apprenticeship course at the British Racing School and is now beginning to live her dream; competing with the likes of Hayley Turner on Britain's racecourses, and aiming to turn pro.

PART 2
ON THE FLAT: HISTORY, HEROES AND HEYDAYS

This section highlights the most iconic and influential jockeys down the years and their daring exploits rather than attempting to construct a comprehensive history, which would require infinitely more space than is available. While a lot of the focus is on riders from Great Britain and Ireland, some key figures from around the world are also featured.

Whether the most appropriate riders have been selected is up for debate (indeed, that's partly the point), but what is without doubt is that all those who are included were outstanding in their day and have played a part in the development of professional jockeys over the past 250 years.

6

BLACK CAPS AND SPURS

Originally the term *jockey* meant *horse dealer* or *owner*, and it only gradually acquired its current meaning of *rider*. This was because owners, who were usually rich and held an established position in society, tended to ride their own horses in competitions. At the start of the 18th century, for instance, most events took the form of match races, usually contested by just two horses, of which records were kept in private books and diaries.

This form of racing remained popular throughout the 18th century until, as racing became more organised and attracted more and higher gambling stakes, owners began to delegate riding responsibilities to minions. In keeping with their lowly status, these early jockeys were dressed like servants and grooms – right down to the crested buttons on their masters' frock-coated livery – and treated as such. They needed to be able to ride and they needed to be small; the smaller the better, so that they didn't burden the horses with excessive weight.

In those days, horse racing was very different from its 21st-century equivalent. Black caps were the norm, making it hard to distinguish between riders as the sport grew in popularity and the numbers of entries in each race increased. In 1762, to address this problem, the newly formed Jockey Club announced a 'resolution and agreement of having the colours annexed to the following names worn by their respective jockeys for the greater convenience of distinguishing the horses in running and also for the prevention of disputes arising from not knowing the colours of each rider'.

Those silks or racing colours consisted of a patterned or coloured jacket and a cap worn with cream breeches. The combined weight of the fully clothed jockey and their saddle could be no more than 8st. In those days, there were no number boards giving details of the runners, no organised parades or appearances in the paddock, and little punctuality when it came to the race starts. The match races had no preliminary heats and the newly instituted idea of having only one race to decide the winner was unacceptable to many. The power of the Jockey Club had yet to grow, and the races were contested with limited and vague codes of conduct, so roughhouse tactics were actively encouraged. Crossing and jostling were allowed, often leading to disagreements and fights. Certainly, the jockeys could be brutal with their whips and their spurs on both the horses and each other.

The status of professional jockeys was low and most had a bad reputation that reeked of corruption and lack of class. In *Great Jockeys of the Flat*, Michael Tanner and Gerry Cranham cite reports that jockeys, particularly in the north of the country, were 'remarkable for their slovenly, dirty and unworkmanlike appearance … it is no uncommon occurrence to see these wretched apologies for jockeys ride in dirty jackets, dark greasy corduroys and gaiters of similar complexion'.

Northern jockeys also were renowned for a particularly aggressive approach to races that often caused danger to others. They won at all costs. In comparison, the same book revealed that southern jockeys appeared 'on horseback with a neatness and cleanliness bordering upon elegance; their performance is, for the most part, of a superior order to their rivals from the north; they are illiterate, ignorant men'.

Yet regardless of geographical location, there were inescapable truisms that encouraged jockeys to turn to the dark side. The growing preoccupation with gambling and popularity of the sport created a conflict of interest that remains to this day. It is a simple fact: horse racing attracts gambling, and no one is in a better position that the person who rides the animal to have an effect on its speed and performance and, in turn, the result of the race. That influence can be brought to bear in ways that the rule-makers would expect – riding the horse with skill and commitment – but there is also a shadier option: hindering the horse and interfering with its chance of success.

This potential for corruption has always been an unwelcome aspect of the sport and there‘s no reason to believe that it will change. And in the unregulated 18th century one who came under constant suspicion was Samuel Chifney Senior.

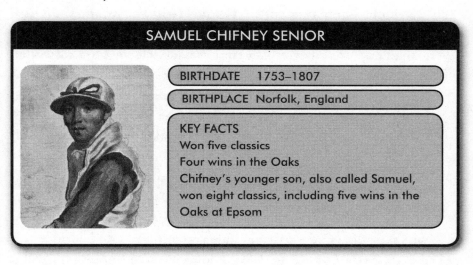

SAMUEL CHIFNEY SENIOR

BIRTHDATE 1753–1807

BIRTHPLACE Norfolk, England

KEY FACTS
Won five classics
Four wins in the Oaks
Chifney's younger son, also called Samuel, won eight classics, including five wins in the Oaks at Epsom

Born in 1753, Samuel Chifney Senior was the first jockey to attract the public's interest. Perhaps this was down to his idiosyncratic appearance – he would wear ruffles and frills on his racing silks, ribbons on his boots and lovelocks would hang down from beneath his cap – and his haughty mindset. No doubt, he was a dandy and a show-off, with an ego the size of his home county of Norfolk. It was entirely in keeping with his carefully cultivated image that he rode for aristocrats such as the Duke of Bedford, Lord Grosvenor and then George IV, the Prince of Wales.

Certainly, Chifney revelled in being dubbed a 'luminary of the first brilliancy', yet although this description might have been excessive he did possess substance as well as style. He could get a tune out of a horse and he knew how to win. In fact, Chifney was the first to introduce recognisable tactics into race-riding.

In the Georgian era, most jockeys went at a breakneck gallop from the moment the flag fell to the instant they charged past the finishing post. Chifney, though, played a waiting game; riding long in the saddle with a slack rein, sitting back, both on the horse and within the race. Having held up his mount he would make a late and often decisive swoop as the front-runners tired. This tactic became known as the 'Chifney Rush'. He was good, a fact he was only too aware of.

In his autobiography, entitled *Genius Genuine*, Chifney boasted that 'by 1773 I could ride horses in a better manner in a race to beat others, than any person ever knew in my time'. He went on to give an explanation of how he had reached such lofty heights, saying:

> 'the first point in riding a race is to command your horse to run light in his mouth ... it keeps him the better together, his legs are the more under him, his sinews less extended, less exertion, his wind less locked; the horse running thus to order, feeling light for his rider's wants; his parts more at ease and ready, and can run considerably faster when called upon, to what he can when that he has been running in the fretting, sprawling attitudes, with part of his rider's weight in his mouth.'

The main reason, however, for the longevity (and notoriety) of his reputation in the horse world is the part he played in a high-profile drama that led one of horse racing's celebrated benefactors, the Prince of Wales (who was to become George IV), to sell all his horses and abandon the sport for five years.

Chifney had been hired by the Prince of Wales as a 'rider for life' for 200 guineas a year in 1790. At that time, the Prince owned around 40 horses and enjoyed gambling, largely on match races in which his horses would run against those of his aristocratic counterparts.

On 20 October 1791, Chifney rode one of the Prince's horses, *Escape*, at Newmarket. The horse, despite being highly fancied, came last in the race. The next day, at much improved odds, Chifney won on the same horse. There was bedlam. Chifney, it was alleged, had deliberately pulled *Escape* in the first race to improve the odds and make a financial killing in the second event. Although nothing was ever proven, the circumstantial evidence was entirely in keeping with the general opinion of Chifney's ethics. He had a poor reputation: it was said that Tattenham Corner (the tight turn into the final few furlongs at Epsom Downs) was straighter than Chifney.

Following an inquest, Sir Charles Bunbury of the Jockey Club informed the Prince that no members of the Jockey Club would 'make matches' or run horses if Chifney were riding. The Prince was appalled at the outcome. He turned his back on the sport but remained loyal to the jockey, awarding Chifney his full annual retainer even though the Prince no longer owned any horses for him to ride.

Despite the financial benefit of the Prince's loyalty, Chifney's golden days were over. He lost his confidence and sold that retainer in 1806 for £1,260. Moreover, he became indebted to a saddler and ended up in Fleet Prison for a time, dying a year later at the age of 52 in a nearby hovel. Aside from his individual story, his legacy to the sport was two sons who both became famous in the horse-racing community: William, who also served time in prison; and Samuel Junior, who became a well-known jockey.

Chifney Senior would certainly not have been shy about proclaiming that he was 'the man' of his era, and this may be true to a certain extent. Whether Chifney's personal qualities made him a suitable role model for those who followed is open to debate. Fortunately for the sport's reputation, however, in Chifney's rather murky wake came a man who shared his predecessor's intuitive understanding of horses and tactical nous for race-riding, but whose personality and integrity could not have been more different.

Frank Buckle, the son of a Newmarket saddler, was born 13 years after Samuel Chifney Senior. He left home at the age of nine and found employment at the stables of Lord Grosvenor. He rode his first race at the age of 12 – weighing 3st 13lb – and became a diligent student of Chifney's style of riding and his tactical inclination to bide his time.

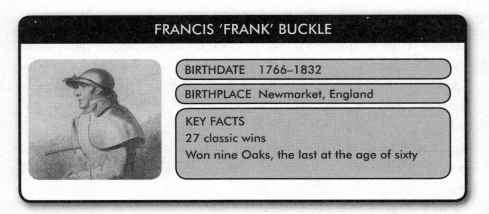

FRANCIS 'FRANK' BUCKLE

BIRTHDATE 1766–1832

BIRTHPLACE Newmarket, England

KEY FACTS
27 classic wins
Won nine Oaks, the last at the age of sixty

Buckle shared Chifney's nerve and intuitive sense of pace and timing so, regardless of the distance of the race, he preferred to save his horse for the 'Chifney Rush', a tactic particularly well suited to match races. Buckle astutely believed that winning by a couple of lengths wasn't any more effective than winning by the length of his arm.

That, however, is where the similarity between the two jockeys ends. If Chifney was as bent as Tattenham Corner, Buckle was as ramrod-straight as the Rowley Mile at his native Newmarket. Buckle became a respectable and enthusiastic member of the racing community. The extent of his honesty and fair play are evident from his actions at a race in Lewes. Being without a ride, Buckle bet heavily (at that stage jockeys were allowed to bet on races) on one of the runners and prepared to watch the event. At the last moment, he was offered a ride on another horse in the same race. He accepted and went on to win, thereby losing significant amounts of his own gambled money.

That integrity, allied to stamina and longevity, allowed this small, tough man to win 27 classics and sustain a career until he reached the age of 65. Buckle's style of riding was also ideally suited to match races and he took part in one of the most prominent of the era at Newmarket's Craven Meeting in 1799. Buckle rode the Yorkshire-stabled St Leger-winner *Hambletonian* against *Diamond* over 4 miles 1 furlong and 138 yards for a purse of 3,000 guineas. Newmarket was alive, with interest levels akin, in the modern era, to those surrounding a high-profile world championship boxing contest. The inns were full and the town was heaving with spectators buzzing with anticipation. Bookmakers took thousands of pounds amid unprecedented gambling.

At the end of an epic race of 7 minutes and 15 seconds, Buckle drove *Hambletonian* to a hard-fought victory by just half a neck. Although Buckle was renowned for his composed horsemanship it is a sign of Georgian times that *The Sporting Magazine* wrote: 'Both horses were much cut with the whip, and severely goaded with the spur, but particularly *Hambletonian*; he was shockingly goaded.'

This was an era when spurs were allowed, there were no punishments for excessive use of the whip and little concern for animal welfare. But that shouldn't dilute our admiration for this most professional of jockeys. When Buckle died of inflammation just three months after his last ride, his tomb in the parish churchyard where he was buried carried the following inscription, which highlighted that for almost half a century England's 'Pocket Hercules' distinguished himself and his profession, thereby going some way to rectifying the public's perception of jockeys:

> *'No better rider ever crossed a horse;*
> *Honour his guide; he died without remorse;*
> *Jockeys attend – from his example learn*
> *The meed the honest worth is sure to earn.'*

During Frank Buckle's heyday at the stables of trainer Robert Robson, for the Duke of Grafton, he went about his business under the doleful gaze of a young man called James (Jem) Robinson and, just as Buckle learned from Chifney Senior, Robinson learned from Buckle. Born into a family of Newmarket farm labourers in 1794, James Robinson spent 13 formative years with Robson, during which time he learned lessons in race-riding from Buckle until, as his idol's powers began to diminish, the two increasingly duelled in match races. Their greatest match, in October 1821, resulted in a dead heat.

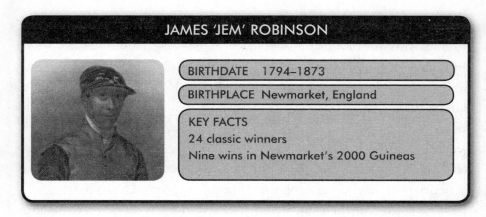

JAMES 'JEM' ROBINSON

BIRTHDATE 1794–1873

BIRTHPLACE Newmarket, England

KEY FACTS
24 classic winners
Nine wins in Newmarket's 2000 Guineas

Robinson certainly had something of Buckle about him: the honesty, the absence of mistakes, an even temper and great skills in the saddle. And his career figures are similarly impressive. He won the 2000 Guineas nine times – which remains a record – and the Epsom Derby six times. His haul of 24 classics was impressive, not least the two victories in 1824 that allowed him to win a bizarre wager that within seven days he would ride the winner of both the Derby and the Oaks, and get married.

However, compared with Buckle, Robinson could be excessive in his use of the whip, even when judged by what would seem to be the brutal standards of the time. According to John Day, of all the jockeys riding Robinson could 'punish his horse most in the least time'. And off the racetrack, whereas Buckle was always the diligent pro, Robinson's lugubrious, melancholy long face gave a misleading impression of his attitude towards partying: he lived the high life and after each flat-racing season was over, Robinson would head to London and make merry, indulging in food and drink, frittering away his earnings. During the winter off-season his weight ballooned but, come springtime, he knuckled down again and wasted, sweating out his indulgences.

Before moving on from this period in horse racing's history, we need to touch the peak of our cap towards the Suffolk-born Elnathan 'Nat' Flatman, who was the first British flat-racing champion jockey in Great Britain. Flatman began his 34-year racing career as an apprentice jockey aged 15, and by 1840 he was the dominant rider in British racing, winning the British flat-racing champion jockey title 13 years in a row. He also won ten classics riding for significant owners, including Lord George Bentinck (the Earl of Chesterfield), Admiral Rous, Lord Stradbroke and Lord Derby. With Flatman, the horse was in safe and competent hands, though there were more gifted and talented jockeys around.

However, by the time of Buckle and Robinson, thoroughbreds were no longer owned exclusively by the aristocracy and the new wave of owners were comparatively uncouth, unsavoury characters who took the sport into disrepute. For a period horse racing became particularly anarchic, shady and corrupt, jockeys included. This was reflected in the press of the time, with Charles Greville, owner of the 1835 1000 Guineas winner *Preserve*, saying: 'The sport of horse racing has a peculiar and irresistible charm for persons of unblemished probity. What a pity that it makes just as strong appeal to the riff-raff of every town.'

7

TRAGIC HEROES

For a spell, horse racing became even more corrupt than it had been during Chifney's time, but gradually villainy and underhand dealings were replaced by new standards of honesty and efficiency in Victorian England. During this same period in the second half of the 19th century, two quite outstanding jockeys emerged on the equine scene: George Fordham and Fred Archer.

The two men were born 20 years apart, with Fordham being the elder. They died within a couple of months of each other, though in very different circumstances. Fordham and Archer were the class acts during a golden period for race-riders, despite the age difference. Fortunately, Fordham's long career meant that the two were often able to pit their wits against each other, giving the watching public the chance to judge for itself which of the riders was the greater. Certainly the black-and-

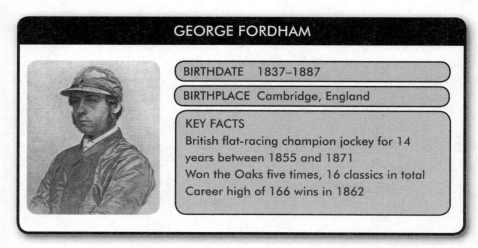

GEORGE FORDHAM

BIRTHDATE 1837–1887

BIRTHPLACE Cambridge, England

KEY FACTS
British flat-racing champion jockey for 14 years between 1855 and 1871
Won the Oaks five times, 16 classics in total
Career high of 166 wins in 1862

FREDERICK JAMES ARCHER

BIRTHDATE 1857–1886

BIRTHPLACE Cheltenham, England

KEY FACTS
British flat-racing champion jockey for 13 consecutive years
21 classic wins
Archer left £66,662 (worth around £6 million/ US$9.6 million today) to his daughter

white statistics support Archer. In a tragically curtailed career – of which more later – he rode 2,748 winners on the flat compared with Fordham's 2,369; and, while both were British flat-racing champion jockey 13 times, Archer won 21 classics to Fordham's 16.

Archer's father was a jump jockey, winning the 1858 Grand National, and, as a boy, Fred started to ride ponies almost as soon as he could walk. That childhood experience helped to build horse-sense, and with time he

Winning Edge. Fred Archer wins the 1880 Epsom Derby

developed an uncanny judgement of pace and an obsessive will to win. Though he was conservative in his dress and demeanour, he was not shy in the saddle. There was a deeply ingrained inner drive. He was a winner, and the phrase 'Archer's up' gave comfort to gamblers everywhere. Yes, there were more elegant jockeys on the circuit, but he invariably forced a strong enough finish to take him to the winner's enclosure. Certainly he could be merciless and harsh, both with other jockeys and with the horses that he rode. There is a story, surely exaggerated over the years, that on one occasion he was found in tears, miserable that he couldn't have ridden both winners in a dead heat.

Yet, in terms of pure horsemanship, most well-informed observers of the age felt that Fordham was the greater of the two rivals. Born in Cambridgeshire, the son of a bricklayer, Fordham rode his first winner at Brighton in 1851, and in 1853 weighed just 3st 12lb when he won the Cambridgeshire on *Little Dravid*. He led from start to finish (such was his lack of strength that he was unable to stop the horse until it had reached Newmarket's town centre) and among the prizes he received was a gold-headed whip that proclaimed 'honesty is the best policy'. That became his mantra. He was kindly and good looking, described as the 'most unassuming and modest of men' by many, and by Archer as the 'old gentleman'.

Fordham was no stylist, though. He rode with fairly short leathers, got well down on the mount's back and slewed his head and body sideways in ungainly fashion during a race, with his shoulders hunched up high. Though it may not have pleased the eye, his horsemanship became increasingly admired, most notably his ability to 'get a tune' out of almost every horse. Even animals that stronger men could do nothing with became putty in his soft hands.

So, those in the game rated him and were eloquent when singing his praises, sometimes at the expense of his peer. Trainer George Morton said: 'I think I would rate him as a greater jockey than Archer. Not only was he more skilful but he possessed the greater finishing power and one could count on the fingers of one hand the races he threw away.'

Another trainer, Richard Marsh, agreed: 'For Fred Archer I had the greatest admiration as well as respect. He had some uncanny means, I thought, of imparting extra vitality to his horses ... Yet, on the whole, I am inclined to name George Fordham as the greatest all-round jockey I have ever known. He was a master in judging pace in a tight fit, and no one knew better where the winning post was better than he did.'

Jockey Tommy Heartfield was of a similar opinion:

> 'Archer was a fine horseman, without a doubt, but I should certainly not say in the same class as Fordham. Everybody, when speaking of great jockeys, always tried to put Fordham in a corner by himself and then talked about the others. I never knew how he could make horses win races that nobody else could ... Archer would win races with 10lb in hand and make it appear that he had got 21lb in hand, Fordham would win a race with 10lb in hand and make it appear he had got home by the skin of his teeth. Old Fordham was a man to sit and nurse 'em; yet he was a powerful jockey at the same time.'

Archer in action. A chromolithograph featuring Fred Archer's last Epsom Derby victory, riding Ormonde, *circa 1886*

Yet within a year both were gone. Fordham died in 1887 at the age of 50, but by then the younger Archer had already been buried, with the tragic nature of his death playing a part in creating his legend. It is thought the long-term impact of *wasting* on his health and his psychological well-being, allied to the sadness he felt after the heart-rending death of his wife in childbirth in 1884 – just a year after they were married – resulted in Archer becoming very ill. In a fog of confusion while suffering from a fever, he put a shotgun to his head and took his own life. He was just 29 years old. The news of his death released a great outpouring of sorrow from the British public. Clearly he was much loved. On that day, buses in London stopped every few yards so that the passengers could get off and buy a paper and, later, the Prince of Wales sent a wreath to the darkest of funerals as Archer was buried next to his wife and William, his son, who had also died prematurely.

Archer was not the only tragic hero of the time. Across the Atlantic, the African-American Isaac Murphy, dubbed the 'coloured Archer', experienced similar trials and, like Fred, was a shining star that lit up the sky all too briefly.

Isaac's father served in the Union Army in the American Civil War until his death as a prisoner of war. The family moved to Lexington to live with his grandfather, Green Murphy, and when he became a jockey

ISAAC BURNS MURPHY

BIRTHDATE 1861–1896

BIRTHPLACE Frankfort, Kentucky, USA

KEY FACTS
Won Kentucky Derby on three occasions
628 career wins
At its creation in 1955, he was the first jockey to be inducted into the National Museum of Racing and Hall of Fame

at the age of 14, he changed his last name from Burns to Murphy in his grandfather's honour.

A brilliant exponent in the saddle, Murphy was one of the first jockeys to hold up his mount for a charge down the home stretch, a Stars-and-Stripes equivalent of the 'Chifney Rush'. He rode upright and encouraged with words and a spur rather than the whip.

His win in the Travers Stakes at Saratoga Springs in 1879 catapulted him to national fame. This was followed by three Kentucky Derby wins and, in 1884, he won the first American Derby in Chicago, the most prestigious race of the era. Even though he rode before jockeys received a share of the winnings, for a time Murphy was the highest-paid athlete in the USA, earning close to $20,000 a year at his peak in the late 1880s. Though some of the figures are disputed, most records credit Murphy with 628 wins and an unprecedented 44 per cent success ratio.

By the mid-1890s, however, his ongoing battle against weight and alcohol had truncated his career and forced him into retirement. Sadly, ten years after Fred Archer's death, Murphy died of pneumonia at the tender age of 34 and is now buried next to the American wonder-horse *Man o' War* at the Kentucky Horse Park's entrance. The comparisons with Archer are evident: talent, success, acclaim, wealth – and a struggle with the day-to-day realities of life as a jockey that resulted in their tragic and premature demises.

The passing of Fordham, Archer and Murphy signalled the end of an era. The dawn of the 20th century saw many social and economic changes in Britain, and in horse racing the wind of change saw an increasing amount of American jockeys travelling across the Atlantic to try their luck, something that Murphy never pursued. One rider in particular adopted a groundbreaking riding style that bore no comparison to the Murphy template. Yet he succeeded so brilliantly that he could lay claim to becoming the most influential jockey to have travelled to these shores.

8

FROM TOADS TO PRINCES

For 200 years, British jockeys – and many American ones as well, including Isaac Murphy – had ridden in a similar way: erect, with long leathers and long reins. Then along came James Sloan, who was so abnormally tiny (he never weighed more than 6st) with stumps for legs that his father rather unkindly nicknamed him 'Toad'. In time the nickname evolved into 'Tod'.

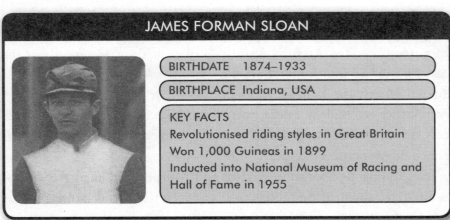

JAMES FORMAN SLOAN

BIRTHDATE 1874–1933

BIRTHPLACE Indiana, USA

KEY FACTS
Revolutionised riding styles in Great Britain
Won 1,000 Guineas in 1899
Inducted into National Museum of Racing and Hall of Fame in 1955

Sloan's eureka moment came when his horse bolted and he regained control by climbing out of the saddle and on to the horse's neck. It dawned on him that this shift in his riding position had enabled the horse to run more freely, so he changed his approach. He shortened the stirrups, crouched forwards in the saddle with his head bent over the horse's withers and rested his body on its neck and shoulders. By leaning into his run and buffeting the wind with his collarbone there was less wind resistance.

At first Sloan was ridiculed for his 'monkey on a stick' style, but his success encouraged others to follow suit. Hand in hand with his riding style, Sloan mastered the new tactics of leading from the front. This was not an unthinking, headlong, top-gear blitz from the start – he would not have won many races with that approach – but a strong, steady sprint that still kept something back for the latter stages. For a while the local jockeys continued to adopt the traditional 'pull' from the gate (gates had been introduced in 1897) in the hope that Sloan would burn his horse out through his 'impetuosity'. Often, though, they were disappointed. Sloan won many a race and built his reputation with his innovative tactics.

Going out on your own soon became known as going out 'on your tod', a phrase that remains in common parlance in the UK to this day. It worked to the extent that he rode 254 winners from 801 rides in England between 1897 and 1900, and earned an unusually lofty retainer of £5,000 from Lord William Beresford. Race times at tracks around Britain improved as a result of his new approach.

Steve Donoghue, the next riding icon in line, modelled himself on Sloan and was lavish in his praise. In *Great Jockeys of the Flat* he is quoted to have said: 'He was one of the finest jockeys and one of the most accomplished horsemen I have ever met. He could do anything with a horse; he was fond of them and he understood them. He had wonderful balance, beautiful hands and was a marvellous judge of pace. He used to crouch right up on a horse's neck, balanced like a bird and he could get the last ounce out of his mount.'

Sloan's horsemanship and influence on future generations of English jockeys were certainly well worthy of the compliments from Donoghue and others. Less so, his behaviour out of the saddle. English trainer Richard Marsh wrote in his book *A Trainer to Two Kings*: 'he was full of brains and a vitality which he shared with the horses he rode. His brains made him a wonderful judge of pace, while he had extraordinary hands. He inspired his horses and it was a thousand pities that off a horse he was devoid of those brains.'

That lack of 'brains' brought a swift end to his heyday. He liked fat cigars, flash clothes and expensive champagne. He was conceited and corrupt. And he was an insatiable gambler who mixed with loose women and steely-eyed gangsters. In 1901, he was convicted by the Jockey Club for illegal betting and his licence to ride was not renewed. In 1915, after barely four seasons, he was deported from England for running an illegal gaming house in London, and in 1933 he died in the charity ward of a Los Angeles hospital. Donoghue reflected that 'I really do think that the life of Tod Sloan, the awful failure and waste of it, should be a lesson to any jockey.'

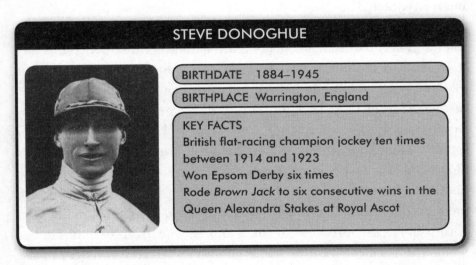

STEVE DONOGHUE

BIRTHDATE 1884–1945

BIRTHPLACE Warrington, England

KEY FACTS
British flat-racing champion jockey ten times between 1914 and 1923
Won Epsom Derby six times
Rode *Brown Jack* to six consecutive wins in the Queen Alexandra Stakes at Royal Ascot

In Britain, the short-lived nature of Sloan's career as a jockey meant that the baton was passed to a man who had much admiration for his predecessor's riding skills. Steve Donoghue became British flat-racing champion jockey ten consecutive times between 1914 and 1923, and rode the acclaimed *Brown Jack* to six consecutive wins in the Queen Alexandra Stakes at Royal Ascot. These achievements were fuelled by an outstanding talent on horseback that was most apparent on the rollercoaster contours of Epsom Downs, where he became an acknowledged specialist, winning six Derbys.

One newspaper article of his era stated: 'the reason why Donoghue always distinguishes himself at Epsom is that he is so clever at getting off and gets going so well that he is rarely if ever bunched in going downhill ... Donoghue knows every inch of the track at Epsom and his presence on a horse is the equivalent of lightening the animal's weight by at least 7lb.'

Jockey George Duller saw other reasons for Donoghue's success: 'There is not one secret of astonishing success, there are many. If the horse tries to fight for his head, Donoghue will lean over and give him a reassuring pat on the neck or, dropping his hands, will take his ear. The effect is magical. The mount becomes calm and tractable immediately.'

One facet of his character that they didn't pass comment on was his ruthless pursuit of the best horses. Donoghue had won the Derby on *Humorist* in 1921 and *Captain Cuttle* in 1922, and earmarked a horse called *Papyrus* to complete the hat-trick in 1923. However, *Papyrus* was owned by Mr Ben Irish rather than Lord Woolavington, who paid Donoghue's retainer. Donoghue made his desire to ride *Papyrus* so blatantly obvious that Woolavington became peeved at this treachery, cancelled his retainer and announced that Donoghue would never ride for him again. Perhaps Donoghue felt the end justified the means – *Papyrus* went on to win, cementing Donoghue's place in the record books – yet in time this trait cost him dearly with owners and trainers, some of whom lost trust in him.

Donoghue had a long affair with the actress Lady Torrington, who committed suicide when, in 1929, Donoghue opted to marry the dancer Ethel Finn. Donoghue himself died in 1945, from a heart attack.

By this time, the mantle of main man had passed to Gordon Richards, a rider of spotless reputation, who watched, learned and then put into practice much of Donoghue's craftsmanship in the saddle. Richards once said: 'I never took my eyes off him. I was watching everything that Steve did, trying to do the same ... and Steve began to take an interest in me. It was a marvellous bit of luck for a kid who didn't know the first thing about riding.'

SIR GORDON RICHARDS

BIRTHDATE 1904–1986

BIRTHPLACE Donnington Wood, Shropshire, England

KEY FACTS
British flat-racing champion jockey 26 times
Only jockey to have been knighted
Won Epsom Derby at his 28th attempt

Richards first rode ponies bareback as soon as he could walk and by the age of seven drove the pony-and-trap passenger service run by his family. He became a stable boy aged 15 and his riding skills were soon commented upon, resulting in him being given apprentice rides. He emulated the upright body position that Donoghue had increasingly been forced to adopt as a result of a shoulder injury, guiding his mount with the ideal combination for a jockey of tree-trunk strong legs and soft hands.

Richards became a fully fledged professional jockey in 1925, just after Donoghue's dominance had begun to wane, and immediately became a champion. Just as the 21-year-old's career took off, however, Richards contracted the debilitating disease tuberculosis, and was sent to the English countryside to convalesce in a sanatorium – as was the custom in those days. Recovery was painfully slow, but once he was well again there was no stopping him or the horses that he rode. In 1932 Richards became stable jockey to trainer Fred Darling and broke the long-standing record for the number of wins in one season. What followed was an accumulation of statistics that highlighted his dominance: British flat-racing champion jockey 26 times, 4,870 winners.

Ex-jockey and journalist Brough Scott has always been able to sniff out talent. Writing for the Injured Jockeys Calendar 2001, he recalled a trip to the races:

> 'One day, it must have been 1950, my father took me to Brighton to watch him [Richards]. A tiny, serious-looking man so big in the chest and short in the leg that if he had not been a legend you would almost have thought him a circus dwarf. In the saddle he should have been something of a pea on a drum but even by the time he left the paddock I could see he was part of the horse beneath him. But it was the finish that was fantastic ... When things got tough going to the furlong pole [Gordon] stood bolt upright and threw the reins forwards and waved his whip in tempo. With anyone else the horse would have rolled all over the South Downs. With Gordon, 8st of solid Shropshire muscle on top of legs of Hercules, it was the clamp of victory.'

By the time Scott watched Richards in action retirement loomed, but there was one notable gap on the jockey's CV: Richards had never won the Epsom Derby, despite 27 attempts. Then came 1953, the year of Queen Elizabeth II's coronation, when he rode the giant *Pinza*. He took the lead two furlongs from home and was carried down the home straight to the finishing post by the warmth of the crowd's cheers. Photo-finishes had been introduced in 1949, but thankfully Richards was spared the trauma of putting this innovation to the test. He won by a distance and the long-awaited victory was celebrated by the sporting nation, not least the new and grateful Queen who knighted him, so far the only jockey to be honoured in this way.

Richards's story – from the dark days of tuberculosis to royal recognition – is one of triumph against adversity. Around this time, the Canadian Red Pollard displayed many of the same qualities.

Pollard was fortunate enough to be the first-choice jockey for the American wonder-horse *Seabiscuit* in 26 consecutive starts. They embarked on a formidable run, initially on America's west coast, then the east. However, as with most epic stories, the hero had to endure adversity and suffering before he could re-emerge triumphant – and in 1938 Pollard suffered an awful fall that compressed his chest and fractured his arms and ribs. He only just survived the extensive surgery,

JOHN M. 'RED' POLLARD

BIRTHDATE 1909–1981

BIRTHPLACE Edmonton, Canada

KEY FACTS
Best known as regular rider of *Seabiscuit*
Founding member of the Jockeys' Guild in 1940
Inducted into the Canadian Horse Racing Hall of Fame in 1982.

bravely working again only a few months later, before he was hit by the double whammy of two broken legs – one caused by a runaway horse, the other by a fall.

These misadventures were thought to have ended the much-vaunted Pollard–*Seabiscuit* partnership, but the horse's owner, Charles S. Howard, remained loyal to the jockey, paying for his hospital stays and treating him like a son. Through Howard's charity, Pollard found a wife – he fell in love with the nurse who attended him – and then bounced back against the odds on the racecourse, celebrating a joyful reunion with the then 7-year-old *Seabiscuit* by winning the Santa Anita Handicap at Santa Anita Park in California in front of 80,000 spectators.

By then, Pollard's leg, which had never fully healed, was withered and he was blind in his right eye; yet his indomitable spirit had not been broken. The *Seabiscuit*–Pollard story was so inspirational that it was made into the movie *Seabiscuit* in 2003, featuring Tobey Maguire as Pollard.

9

MASTER CRAFTSMEN

LESTER KEITH PIGGOTT

BIRTHDATE 1935–

BIRTHPLACE Wantage, England

KEY FACTS
4,493 career wins
30 classic wins
British flat-racing champion jockey 11 times

1953 was the Derby that featured Richards's swansong to an adoring public. One year later, a new household name was announced as a precocious 18-year-old, Lester Piggott, won the same race on *Never Say Die*. A year later, Piggott took over from the retiring Richards as first jockey to Noel Murless – the top riding job in British racing.

Piggott's pedigree was strong. He came from a family steeped in horse racing: his father, Keith, was a jockey and trainer, and his grandfather rode the winners of two Grand Nationals. As the trainer Vincent O'Brien once said, 'God gave him a gift and he exploited it to the full.'

By common consent Piggott was a 'genius' with horses. Following Lester's ninth Derby win on *Teenoso*, journalist Tony Morris was happy to employ the word in relation to him, describing him as 'the supreme artist plying his craft from the saddle, his genius as sublime as that of a Rembrandt or a Beethoven, and his accomplishments on the same plane.'

And there were few better qualified than his predecessor, Sir Gordon Richards, to pass judgement and endorse the use of the 'G' word: 'the secret of his success is his confidence in his own genius. For me he is a genius, as Steve Donoghue was before him', Richards said. 'From the very beginning he has instinctively known what to do and when to do it ... We come back to the word genius – a man's ability to communicate something to a horse.'

Allied to the ability to communicate with his mount, Piggott possessed a fiery, Archer-like, win-at-all-costs mentality. Hugh McIlvanney, the award-winning Scottish sports writer, described him as 'a volcano trapped inside an iceberg' and, while he didn't say much (though this was in part due to a hearing disability and a related speech impediment) and appeared cool and calm on the surface, there was fire in his belly. In particular, he didn't care much for journalists and authority; while, generally, he paid lip service to owners and trainers – indeed other jockeys – he cared only about being first past the post. If that made him unpopular then so be it.

In 1954, aged just 18, Piggott fell foul of the Royal Ascot stewards for his riding on *Never Say Die* in the King Edward VII stakes. He had supposedly ridden dangerously when going for a gap just after the turn into the home straight and he was suspended from riding until further notice. The stewards of the Jockey Club advised him that they had 'taken notice of his dangerous and erratic riding both this season and in previous seasons and that in spite of continuous warnings, he continued to show complete disregard for the rules of racing and for the safety of other jockeys'.

The Australian jockey Edgar Britt, who won every English Classic except the Derby and was inducted into the Australian Racing Hall of Fame, confirmed that Piggott paid no respect to seniority or reputations, noting in his autobiography *Post Haste* that 'in his early apprenticeship days he was a menace to the older jockeys in a race. He would stay on the fence, sending his mount through when there was insufficient room.' Speaking of Piggott, Britt also said: 'Lester is smart at the barrier, uses

Another classic win for Lester, with victory in the 1957 Oaks, riding Her Majesty Queen Elizabeth II's horse, Carrozza

his brains throughout a race and can ride patiently … he relies a lot on his whip to get the best out of his mount and can really make a last horse move.'

Sir Gordon Richards agreed: 'Even in those first days you could tell Lester had a touch of the devil and a touch of genius. Of course he ran into trouble with stewards. It was inevitable I suppose. If he saw a gap, he would go through. If he didn't see a gap and he couldn't go inside, outside, over or under he would just go through. He didn't seem to understand the notion of being a loser.'

Piggott was also pushy when it came to making sure he rode the mount of his choice. One of his peers in the changing room, Pat Eddery, said: 'Lester rarely says anything to anyone unless he's asking you about horses. He never asks me because he knows I won't tell him. But the only way some jockeys can get anywhere to him is by telling him about what such-and-such horse is like to ride. They're mad. I won't tell him anything. No way. Because for sure he'll pinch it.'

Sure enough, in racing circles people still talk in disapproving tones of Piggott's Donoghue-like behaviour when he 'jocked off' (stole a ride from) W. Williamson from *Roberto* in the 1972 Derby at the 11th hour. Piggott lost no sleep, explaining 'it is part of a jockey's job to get on the best horses, and if that involves ruffling a few feathers so be it'.

Piggott's career record suggests he rode plenty of the best horses: 30 classic winners in Britain, nine Derbys, British flat-racing champion jockey 11 times. No doubt he feels that those stats justify the fact that he upset a few people and fell foul of the authorities. Certainly, the achievements are all the more remarkable for a 'long fellow', who by normal rules should have been too tall to make even a decent living as a jockey.

Part of Piggott's 'genius', though, was to adapt his approach. And he became instantly recognisable on the racecourse for his unusual riding style with pulled-up stirrup leathers. Piggott explained:

> '[One of the] disadvantages of being big is style. Style is the way you look. If you are small it doesn't matter so much how you look because there isn't much of you to be seen and your legs don't take up so much room. If you're big you can be seen better and there's less horse showing. I smile when people ask me why I ride with my bottom in the air. Well, I've got to put it somewhere.'

Piggott firmly believed that:

> 'A horse responds to a good weight on its back, live weight – not dead weight, lead, under the saddle. When a biggish jockey gets up, the chances are that the horse feels the authority ... If you've got a good length of leg you can communicate more with the horse, squeeze him with your knees, control him generally – show him you are there.'

Of course there was a sad postscript to Piggott's story after he announced his retirement in 1985. He was convicted for tax fraud and sentenced to three years in prison, though he actually served just one day over a year. His OBE, awarded in the 1975, was stripped from him. Two years after coming out of prison, at the age of 54, Piggott rode professionally again, adding his 30th classic to his list of achievements. He also went to Belmont Park in America and worked the old magic with a win in the Breeder's Cup Mile.

That the last hurrah happened so far from home highlighted how the nature of horse racing, and the role of the jockey, had changed in the course of his era, a period during which the sport progressed more than ever before. Equipment changed, notably with the introduction of starting stalls in 1965 and, a year later, the first woman trainer was licensed by the Jockey Club. Female jockeys would follow. And in Piggott's time it became trendy, and financially possible, for the best of British to travel around the world in pursuit of the Blue Riband prizes. Equally, high-class foreign jockeys came to ply their trade on these shores.

So it became apparent that Piggott, for all his genius, wasn't the only master-craftsman of his era. Arthur Edward Breasley – more commonly known as 'Scobie' after the famous Australian trainer James Scobie – from Wagga Wagga in New South Wales was another.

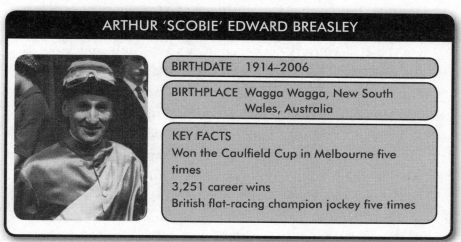

ARTHUR 'SCOBIE' EDWARD BREASLEY

BIRTHDATE 1914–2006

BIRTHPLACE Wagga Wagga, New South Wales, Australia

KEY FACTS
Won the Caulfield Cup in Melbourne five times
3,251 career wins
British flat-racing champion jockey five times

Breasley was one of the first Australian jockeys to try his luck on British racetracks, and his innate horse-sense allowed him to adapt to differing conditions. Towards the end of an illustrious career he came to post-war Britain in 1950 to compete with Piggott and his peers. This move enabled Breasley to construct an impressive international portfolio: more than 3,000 winners, of which more than 2,000 were in Britain, where he was British flat-racing champion jockey four times. Among these wins were Australia's Caulfield Cup, England's Epsom Derby (twice) and France's Prix de l'Arc de Triomphe.

Although he was Piggott's senior by 21 years – coincidentally he got married on the same day that Piggott was born – they shared some notable duels and held each other in mutual respect. Piggott recognised that Breasley was a textbook rider with an intuitive sense of what made a racehorse tick. He mainly used his hands and heels to ease his mount forwards, seldom resorting to the whip.

Sir Gordon Richards, who became a trainer at the end of his riding career, used Breasley extensively and was flattering in his praise of the rider:

> 'His horsemanship was equal to anyone's and when I began to train it never crossed my mind to want another man as my stable jockey. He's riding with his head the whole time and he's a natural horseman. Me, I was more of a trustful rider. Scobie is persuasive. Like all Australians he's got all the guts in the world. On those sharp tracks out there they've got to be quick out of the gate, get a good position, keep it and go the nearest way. Sometimes they get in trouble with these tactics but if they make a success out there then they are natural riders with cool heads and guts. I could trust him completely and never give him any instructions. He knew what he was doing, and in any case he wouldn't have taken any notice of them if I had.'

In fact Breasley wasn't the only classy Australian race-rider with a 'cool head and guts' who gave the Brits a run for their money. Queenslander George Moore was similarly skilled and subtle in the saddle. The majority of his success was found in his homeland but he also starred in France and on British shores, most notably during 1967 where he swept all before him with wins in the 1000 Guineas, the Derby Stakes and the

King George VI and Queen Elizabeth Stakes. Little wonder that he also won the BBC's Overseas Sports Personality of the Year award that year.

WILLIAM LEE SHOEMAKER

BIRTHDATE 1931–2003

BIRTHPLACE Fabens, Texas, USA

KEY FACTS
8,833 career wins
Flat-racing champion jockey in the USA five times
12 America classics/Breeders' Cup wins

Despite Moore's impressive CV, the third master-craftsman in this group is the American Bill Shoemaker. He won 11 Triple Crown races (America's equivalent of the classics) – four Kentucky Derbys, two Preakness Stakes and five Belmont Stakes – and at the 1986 Kentucky Derby became the oldest jockey (aged 54) to win the race. In all he rode between 1949 and 1990, and amassed 8,833 wins, but it was style as well as stats that made Shoemaker remarkable. Sports journalist Simon Barnes wrote that Shoemaker was a 'spring of pure natural talent; he finds it hard to imagine what it must be like without such talent. He is, simply, the most wonderful horseman. More than any Mexican groom he will tame your outlaw horse. Put him on some rogue animal that has been scattering work riders like confetti, and the horse will turn into a lamb at once. And he does nothing. You see him sitting there, not moving, not doing a thing, and the wickedest horse in the world is acting good as gold.'

Like all the great performers, Shoemaker possessed the knack of making something complex (and riding a racehorse *is* a complex craft) look so straightforward you might wonder why everyone can't do it. Simplicity is genius, and Shoemaker made it look ridiculously simple.

Other jockeys watched and admired him, including American jockey Steve Cauthen, who said: 'Bill doesn't do a lot but he keeps beautifully in the centre of balance, so that a horse can run for him more easily.' Lester Piggott confirmed this view: 'He's a phenomenon. Some of the things he does, with his whip and his reins in a tangle, you would think would slow the horses down, but they just go faster.'

Shoemaker himself was at a loss to know why horses went faster for him, and was not inclined to waste much time trying to work it out. It certainly wasn't in his DNA. There was no history of horse racing in his family and he took up the sport late. Yes, he possessed the kind of coordination and ball sense that helped him also to become an accomplished golfer, but if it hadn't been for his tiny stature he would surely have worked in another profession.

When Shoemaker was born he weighed just 2½lb. Medics were pessimistic about his chances of lasting the night, but nevertheless placed him in a shoebox in an oven set to a very low temperature to keep him warm and see if he would survive. This Shoemaker did, but his difficult start in life may have affected his later development, for once fully grown he stood a diminutive 4 feet 10 inches in height, and weighed 7st 9lb. So a jockey he became – and one of the finest horsemen in an era of master craftsmen.

10

NEW AGE WARRIORS

Who have been the icons of the modern era? There are plenty of contenders to consider; when the sport became more professional, the top jockeys did not stand out quite as much from the rank-and-file as they had done in the past. This was true in Great Britain, true the world over. The best of the best weren't as distinguished anymore – largely due to the higher collective standard of the competition.

In Australia, for instance, the modern era has showcased the talent of the rugged race-rider Mick Dittman, Darren Beadman and Perth's Damien Oliver – to name but three.

Plying their trade in the United States of America has been an ever deeper reservoir of talent, including Laffit Pincay Jnr, Angel Cordero Jnr from Puerto Rico, Pat Day of Colorado, Chris McCarron and Jerry Bailey of Dallas. Nor can the inspirational story of Gary Stevens be overlooked. He made a sensational return to the saddle after a 7-year gap, having conquered his personal demons.

Of those who have mainly ridden in Britain, some observers would make a case for the inclusion of another American, Steve Cauthen, who was a precociously talented teenager from Kentucky when he crossed the Atlantic to ride for owner Robert Sangster. Later he became first rider for the all-conquering Henry Cecil stable. Cauthen was a truly international jockey, equally at home on American and British shores.

Others will point to the riding and record of County Kildare's Pat Eddery. He had a drive to be first past the post that was Piggott- and Archer-like in its intensity. But that ambition was not apparent from his riding style. It was said that Eddery had the best hands in racing and, because of this, he became a role model for aspiring jockeys. Those hands were always quiet and his laid-back, Zen-like demeanour was transmitted to the horses that he rode.

Many spectators will support the claims of the lavishly talented Kieren Fallon, this time from Crusheen, County Clare in Ireland. Fallon and controversy have frequently ridden together – but there's no doubting the horsemanship, the six British flat-racing champion jockey titles or, at the time of writing, 16 English classic wins.

In addition to these greats, the English jockey Ryan Moore has gradually established himself over the past few years as the foremost race-rider of his generation. Serious, silent and deadpan, Moore's hands and heels do all his talking for him – and the major titles are mounting up.

All of the above would deserve selection as a modern icon, yet the two icons who most reflect the changing face of being a jockey in the modern era are an American and an Italian, one female, one male. Their importance lies both with their skills in the saddle *and* their wider influence: both have changed horse racing forever.

The first of these two trailblazers is a 4-foot-10-inch-, 7-stone pocket dynamo who smashed to smithereens the glass ceilings that once existed for females in American horse racing. Inspired by Steve Cauthen, Julie Krone became a hall-of-famer who rode 3,704 winners, amassed US$90 million in prize money and became the first female jockey to win a Triple Crown race when she won the Belmont Stakes in 1993. This was a brilliant display of race-riding, shepherding *Colonial Affair*, a 14–1 shot, around the rain-soaked track to win by 2¼ lengths. In doing so she stopped being a novelty act – a girl with long blond locks doing surprisingly well among the lads – and became a top-ten, top-notch jockey.

Krone was great with horses. She developed an unusual and intuitive warmth and empathy with thoroughbreds that can be traced back to solitary 5-mile rides – at the tender age of three – on her pony *Daisy* in Michigan, coupled with her experiences as an accomplished show horse rider. This sensitivity helped Krone on the racetracks of America, where

JULIEANN LOUISE 'JULIE' KRONE

BIRTHDATE 1963–

BIRTHPLACE Benton Harbor, Michigan, USA

KEY FACTS
3,704 career wins
First woman to secure a Triple Crown win
First woman inducted into the National Museum of Racing and Hall of Fame

the emphasis is less on physical brute strength and more on balance and cajoling the horse to go for you.

By contrast, towards the human species Krone was so strong-willed, feisty and up for a fight that she was named by *USA Today* as one of the ten toughest athletes in America. Krone did not suffer fools at all, let alone gladly. She knocked one jockey off the scales at Pimlico, had to be pulled off another at Keystone, and at Monmouth Park Krone was fined for smashing another over the head with a deck chair after he had pushed her into the swimming pool.

Maybe that rock-and-roll spirit helped Krone deal with the litany of broken bones and hospital visits. On one occasion two stricken horses pitched down on her, one after the other. It took 4½ hours of surgery to save her left arm and, three months down the line, the injury required a bone graft from her hip.

Having made her riding debut in 1981, Krone survived in the industry for 18 years, until the accumulation of severe injuries forced her into retirement. She focused on media work for four years before returning to the saddle and enjoying the ups and down of race-riding once again: there were more winners, including a Blue Riband victory in the Breeders Cup, but also more brutal injuries, including fractures to two bones in her lower back and several ribs as well as muscle tears. By 2004, her body could take no more and this time her retirement was for good. She left behind a legacy of accomplishments that no one in horse racing would have believed could be possible in the first half of the 20th century: a true warrior on horseback.

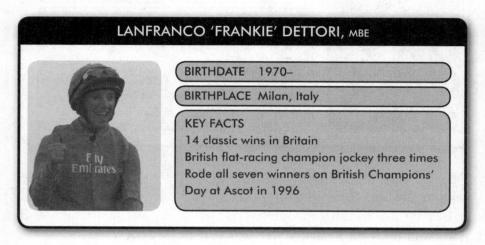

LANFRANCO 'FRANKIE' DETTORI, MBE

BIRTHDATE 1970–

BIRTHPLACE Milan, Italy

KEY FACTS
14 classic wins in Britain
British flat-racing champion jockey three times
Rode all seven winners on British Champions' Day at Ascot in 1996

The other modern groundbreaking icon is Lanfranco Dettori. This diminutive Italian, the son of a multiple-title champion jockey, rode his first winner at the age of 16 and became the first teenager since Piggott to ride 100 winners in one season.

Further success followed, and on 20 September 1996 he won all seven races on the card in a single day at Royal Ascot. This was unprecedented. As Dettori kept on being first past the post, race after race, it gradually dawned on the bookmakers that the 25,000–1 odds they had given on the seemingly impossible event of him winning all the races were becoming more and more likely to come through. For some bookies this day led to financial devastation. The crowd, however, were less worried, aware that they were witnessing history being made.

Dettori is at his best when his mood, confidence and form are high. When he's hot, he's hot – and that day he was unbeatable, carried along on a wave of momentum. He said, 'Horses have that ability to catch your mood and the horses really caught my mood that day. I wasn't even on the ground – I was flying and they were running just that little bit faster.'

SEVEN: THE MAGIC NUMBER

Race 1 – *Wall Street* –½ length win in a Group Three race
Race 2 – *Diffident* – Dettori told the head lad 'I'll bare my bum under the Newmarket tower if he wins' but the 12–1 shot won by a short-head
Race 3 – *Mark of Esteem* – A Group One triumph with the horse, a 2000 Guineas winner, showing a notable burst of acceleration
Race 4 – *Decorated Hero* – the most trouble-free win of the day, by 3½ lengths
Race 5 – *Fatefully* – the short-prized favourite survived a steward's enquiry to win – just
Race 6 – *Lochangel* – the penultimate win, by ¾ length
Race 7 – *Fujiyama Crest* – Dettori got a standing ovation all the way to the start before the horse won, by a neck

Dettori has won 14 English classics, including, belatedly and much to his relief, Epsom's Derby aboard *Authorized*. But he sees that early autumn afternoon at Royal Ascot as the pinnacle of his career. 'Well, the Derby was just one race, Ascot was seven in one day', he said. 'Of course the Derby was a huge notch on the bedpost of my CV but in 300 years of horse racing I'm the first one to have ever done it [seven winners in a day] and I'm probably the first living person to have a statue [Dettori's statue, commemorating the achievement stands at Ascot]. Normally, you only have a statue when you're dead!'

Yet for all this, Dettori's selection in this section may be a controversial one. Many within the horse-racing community might contest that Dettori has not been the outstanding jockey of his era; they will have other favourites. These are valid claims, but the choice of Dettori as a pivotal figure is not just down to the brilliance of his riding, it is also due to the significant role he played in changing the social status of jockeys, and the impact he had on the wider sport. Until Frankie, it appeared to be almost illegal for a jockey to smile while in public view. Riders generally undertook their duties with an undertaker's deadpan reverence and subservience. Some were more animated and chatty than others, but they rarely exhibited much emotion or excitement. The rituals of the sport seemed to demand no less and each new up-and-coming jockey, not surprisingly, imitated the style and demeanour of their role model.

Yet over recent times, society as a whole has loosened its top button, become less starchy and more willing to express emotion, particularly when a goal, a win, is achieved. Horse racing, with its deep-rooted culture and embedded class system, was slower than some sports to follow this trend, particularly on the flat. But, slowly, times changed. Willie Carson became known outside racing circles for his infectious laugh and cheeky-chappie manner, and when Dettori came along he single-handedly signposted a quantum leap forwards in terms of riders' behaviour and profile.

Although by no mean the first jockey to achieve household-name stardom, Dettori was one of the first to bask in the fame. He was one of the new breed, a world traveller in the pursuit of glory in Blue Riband events. He was also media-savvy, basking in the limelight, promoting himself and his sport with a ready smile and a quick wit. Frankie represents a new and entirely different type of role model, and younger jockeys have learned that displays of emotion and excitement at a big win are no longer deemed undignified or unprofessional. He has become a thoroughly modern tribal icon for the warriors on horseback.

BRITISH FLAT RACING CHAMPION JOCKEYS					
Season	Jockey	Winners	Season	Jockey	Winners
1840	Nat Flatman	50	1873	Harry Constable	110
1841	Nat Flatman	68	1874	Fred Archer	147
1842	Nat Flatman	42	1875	Fred Archer	172
1843	Nat Flatman	60	1876	Fred Archer	207
1844	Nat Flatman	64	1877	Fred Archer	218
1845	Nat Flatman	81	1878	Fred Archer	229
1846	Nat Flatman	81	1879	Fred Archer	197
1847	Nat Flatman	89	1880	Fred Archer	120
1848	Nat Flatman	104	1881	Fred Archer	220
1849	Nat Flatman	94	1882	Fred Archer	210
1850	Nat Flatman	88	1883	Fred Archer	232
1851	Nat Flatman	78	1884	Fred Archer	241
1852	Nat Flatman	92	1885	Fred Archer	246
1853	John Wells	86	1886	Fred Archer	170
1854	John Wells	82	1886	Charles Wood	151
1855	George Fordham	70	1888	Fred Barrett	108
1856	George Fordham	108	1889	Tommy Loates	167
1857	George Fordham	84	1890	Tommy Loates	147
1858	George Fordham	91	1891	Morny Cannon	137
1859	George Fordham	118	1892	Morny Cannon	182
1860	George Fordham	146	1893	Tommy Loates	222
1861	George Fordham	106	1894	Morny Cannon	167
1862	George Fordham	166	1895	Morny Cannon	184
1863	George Fordham	103	1896	Morny Cannon	164
1864	John Grimshaw	164	1897	Morny Cannon	145
1865	George Fordham	142	1898	Otto Madden	161
1866	Sam Kenyon	123	1899	Sam Loates	160
1867	George Fordham	143	1900	Lester Reiff	143
1868	George Fordham	110	1901	Otto Madden	130
1869	George Fordham	95	1902	Willie Lane	170
1870	William Gray/ Charlie Maidment	76	1903	Otto Madden	154
			1904	Otto Madden	161
1871	George Fordham/ Charlie Maidment	86	1905	Elijah Wheatley	124
			1906	William Higgs	149
1872	Tom Cannon, Sen.	87	1907	William Higgs	146

Season	Jockey	Winners	Season	Jockey	Winners
1908	Danny Maher	139	1943	Gordon Richards	65
1909	Frank Wootton	165	1944	Gordon Richards	88
1910	Frank Wootton	137	1945	Gordon Richards	104
1911	Frank Wootton	187	1946	Gordon Richards	212
1912	Frank Wootton	118	1947	Gordon Richards	269
1913	Danny Maher	115	1948	Gordon Richards	224
1914	Steve Donoghue	129	1949	Gordon Richards	261
1915	Steve Donoghue	62	1950	Gordon Richards	201
1916	Steve Donoghue	43	1951	Gordon Richards	227
1917	Steve Donoghue	42	1952	Gordon Richards	231
1918	Steve Donoghue	66	1953	Sir Gordon Richards	191
1919	Steve Donoghue	129	1954	Doug Smith	129
1920	Steve Donoghue	143	1955	Doug Smith	168
1921	Steve Donoghue	141	1956	Doug Smith	155
1922	Steve Donoghue	102	1957	Scobie Breasley	173
1923	Steve Donoghue/ Charlie Elliott	89	1958	Doug Smith	165
			1959	Doug Smith	157
1924	Charlie Elliott	106	1960	Lester Piggott	170
1925	Gordon Richards	118	1961	Scobie Breasley	171
1926	Tommy Weston	95	1962	Scobie Breasley	179
1927	Gordon Richards	164	1963	Scobie Breasley	176
1928	Gordon Richards	148	1964	Lester Piggott	140
1929	Gordon Richards	135	1965	Lester Piggott	160
1930	Freddie Fox	129	1966	Lester Piggott	191
1931	Gordon Richards	145	1967	Lester Piggott	117
1932	Gordon Richards	190	1968	Lester Piggott	139
1933	Gordon Richards	259	1969	Lester Piggott	163
1934	Gordon Richards	212	1970	Lester Piggott	162
1935	Gordon Richards	217	1971	Lester Piggott	162
1936	Gordon Richards	174	1972	Willie Carson	132
1937	Gordon Richards	216	1973	Willie Carson	164
1938	Gordon Richards	206	1974	Pat Eddery	148
1939	Gordon Richards	155	1975	Pat Eddery	164
1940	Gordon Richards	68	1976	Pat Eddery	162
1941	Harry Wragg	71	1977	Pat Eddery	176
1942	Gordon Richards	67	1978	Willie Carson	182

Season	Jockey	Winners	Season	Jockey	Winners
1979	Joe Mercer	164	1997	Kieren Fallon	202
1980	Willie Carson	166	1998	Kieren Fallon	204
1981	Lester Piggott	179	1999	Kieren Fallon	200
1982	Lester Piggott	188	2000	Kevin Darley	155
1983	Willie Carson	159	2001	Kieren Fallon	166
1984	Steve Cauthen	130	2002	Kieren Fallon	136
1985	Steve Cauthen	195	2003	Kieren Fallon	207
1986	Pat Eddery	176	2004	Frankie Dettori	192
1987	Steve Cauthen	197	2005	Jamie Spencer	163
1988	Pat Eddery	183	2006	Ryan Moore	180
1989	Pat Eddery	171	2007	Seb Sanders / Jamie Spencer	190
1990	Pat Eddery	209			
1991	Pat Eddery	165	2008	Ryan Moore	186
1992	Michael Roberts	206	2009	Ryan Moore	174
1993	Pat Eddery	169	2010	Paul Hanagan	191
1994	Frankie Dettori	233	2011	Paul Hanagan	165
1995	Frankie Dettori	211	2012	Richard Hughes	172
1996	Pat Eddery	186	2013	Richard Hughes	208

PART 3
OVER THE STICKS: HISTORY, HEROES AND HEYDAYS

11

FRONT RUNNER

Two fine Irishmen, one from the North and one from the South, bookend the history of National Hunt. In some ways they are similar – accomplished race-riders, fearlessly brave – yet in others they are poles apart. AP McCoy is the icy-cool professional, and there is much more on this obsessive, serial winner later in this section. Even seasoned observers within the horse-racing community speak in awe at the very mention of McCoy's name, struggling to find sufficient superlatives, acknowledging that we shall not see his like again. The other 'bookend', Captain Martin Becher, also broke the mould, but his cavalier, swashbuckling style, both on and off a horse, was not all AP-like.

Becher is believed to have been born in an area of County Cork, just outside Limerick, which had been the location of the first point-to-point 45 years previously. It was there that that Edmund O'Brien and

CAPTAIN MARTIN WILLIAM BECHER

BIRTHDATE 1797–1864

BIRTHPLACE County Cork, Limerick, Ireland

KEY FACTS
Rode in the first Grand National in 1839
Aintree's Becher's Brook is named after him
Served in the military during the Napoleonic Wars

Cornelius O'Callaghan, two keen fox-hunters (the sport's foundations lay in hunting) inadvertently became responsible for the birth of steeple-chasing. They agreed to race over 4½ miles point to point, steeple to steeple, for a cask of wine. As news spread of the wager, a curious group of spectators flocked to watch the event on the appointed time and date.

By the early 19th century, the term *steeplechase* began appearing on official racecards in Ireland. Although the 13-year-old Becher was now hunting on a pony, he was too young to be involved in what became recognised as the first steeplechase over fences (eight of them, standing at 4 feet 6 inches) at Bedford in 1810.

By then, Becher was maturing into a hale and hearty fellow, and he became a mimic, singer and raconteur, brimming with stories, bonhomie and much-heralded party pieces, such as leaping on to a mantelpiece from a standing jump. It is little wonder that he became popular with everyone – not least the ladies – and that wherever he went, laughter and carousing went with him.

Yet it wasn't all fun and games. Becher's ancestor, Colonel Thomas Becher, became aide-de-camp to King William of Orange at the Battle of the Boyne in 1809 and Martin also went into the military, serving during the Napoleonic Wars. He was stationed in Belgium at the time of the Battle of Waterloo, though it is unknown whether he actually took part in the battle. Upon being released from service, Becher took a commission as a captain in the Buckinghamshire Yeomanry, which left him with sufficient free time to pursue his passions of revelry and cross-country riding.

So Becher's ruddy features (later to be adorned with thick side whiskers) and rugby hooker's frame – squat and thickset – became an increasingly familiar sight on horseback in the formative years of National Hunt.

By 1823, Becher had donned racing colours for the first time and was present for – though not directly involved with – a pivotal date in the sport's progression at St Albans in 1830, when 16 runners raced for 4 miles from Arlington Church to the Obelisk in Wrest Park, near Silsoe.

Modern-day jockeys take on the challenge of the fence named after Captain Becher

Scaffolding poles tied with sheets were placed at the start and the finish and the jockeys' only instructions regarding the course were 'leave that church on your right, and the clump on your left, and get to the hill beyond'.

The race was a storming success and, word having got around, the first renewal in 1821 saw carriages and horsemen pouring into the town, blocking its outskirts. Becher rode in this one, on *Wild Boar*, and looked sure to win until the horse slipped and fell close to home.

By now, though, Becher was established as a prominent horseman – no stylist in the saddle, but blessed with fine hands and pluck – and was a central figure in what became a renowned 'match' run in 1833. Becher rode Colonel Carritic's grand jumper, *Napoleon*, against *Grimaldi*, trained, owned and ridden by 'Squire' Osbaldeston. The race covered 6 miles across rugged cross-country terrain comprising fields, hedges, brooks and the River Lem, with a prize of £1,000 on offer for the winner.

The contest was nip and tuck as the two reached the river. Becher and *Napoleon,* better on land than in the water, disappeared for so long that spectators feared for their safety, but they eventually emerged, albeit now 100 yards behind. Although they made up much of the lost ground in the run in, the 'Squire' and *Grimaldi* just prevailed, though they finished on the wrong side of the flag. As a result, the outcome was deemed indeterminate and the bet was amicably cancelled.

By now, National Hunt was growing at speed, with new races bubbling up: at Cheltenham in 1834; at the Vale of Aylesbury in 1835; and at Aintree in 1835. Becher competed at the latter venue in both its first hurdle meeting and its first-ever steeplechase when he rode *The Duke* to a 1-length victory. Then, in 1839, in what was to become regarded as the first Grand National, Becher rode the 20–1 shot *Conrad*. This event, founded by hotel owner William Lyn, immediately caught the public's imagination. People massed to Liverpool by railway, steamer, coach, gig, wagon, on horse and on foot. Hotels slept four to a bed. Seventeen runners contested the 4½-mile marathon with conditions stating that 'no rider was to open a gate or ride through a gateway, or more than 100 yards along any road, footpath or driftway'.

Although some of the 29 obstacles were small, others were more challenging, including a 5-foot-high stone wall in front of the grandstand. In addition there were two brooks. The first – a 'strong pailing, next a rough, high jagged hedge and lastly a brook about 6 feet wide' – presented a particularly formidable test of fortitude and bravery and it was here that Becher inadvertently put his name into history and his purply-pink weather-beaten features into the drink.

The 40-year-old led the cavalry charge up to the brook with typical bravado. He attacked it boldly, perhaps too boldly. *Conrad* hit the pailing at speed, catapulting the Captain head-first into its icy waters. Legend has it, he remarked later that 'water should never be taken without brandy'. Of course that brook became known as Becher's Brook and remains one of the biggest challenges at the 21st-century version of the Grand National. Becher remounted, but his race ended for good when

Warriors off to work. Jockeys leave the weighing room during a race meeting at Lingfield Park

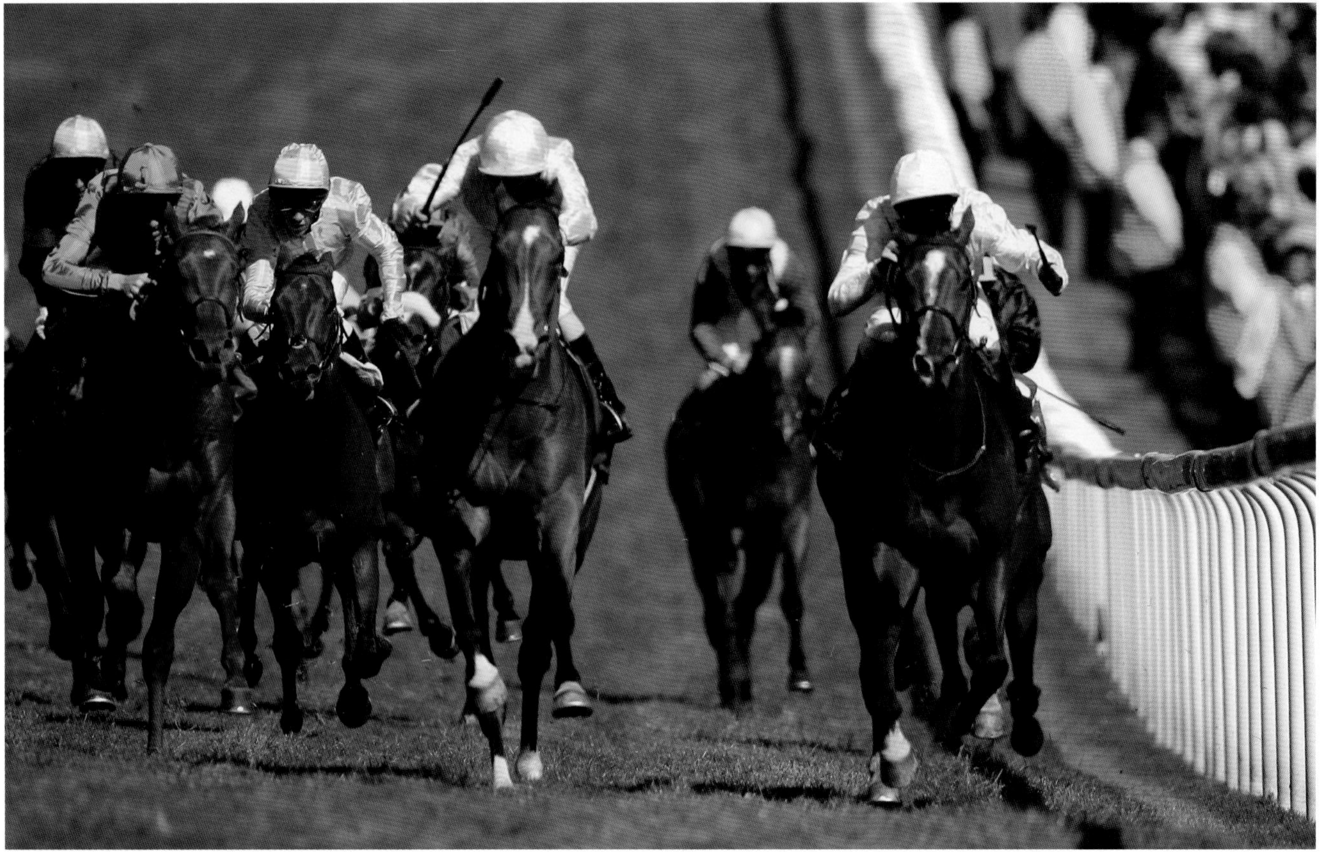

Martin Dwyer rides Sir Percy *(R) to victory during the Vodafone Derby at Epsom on 3 June 2006*

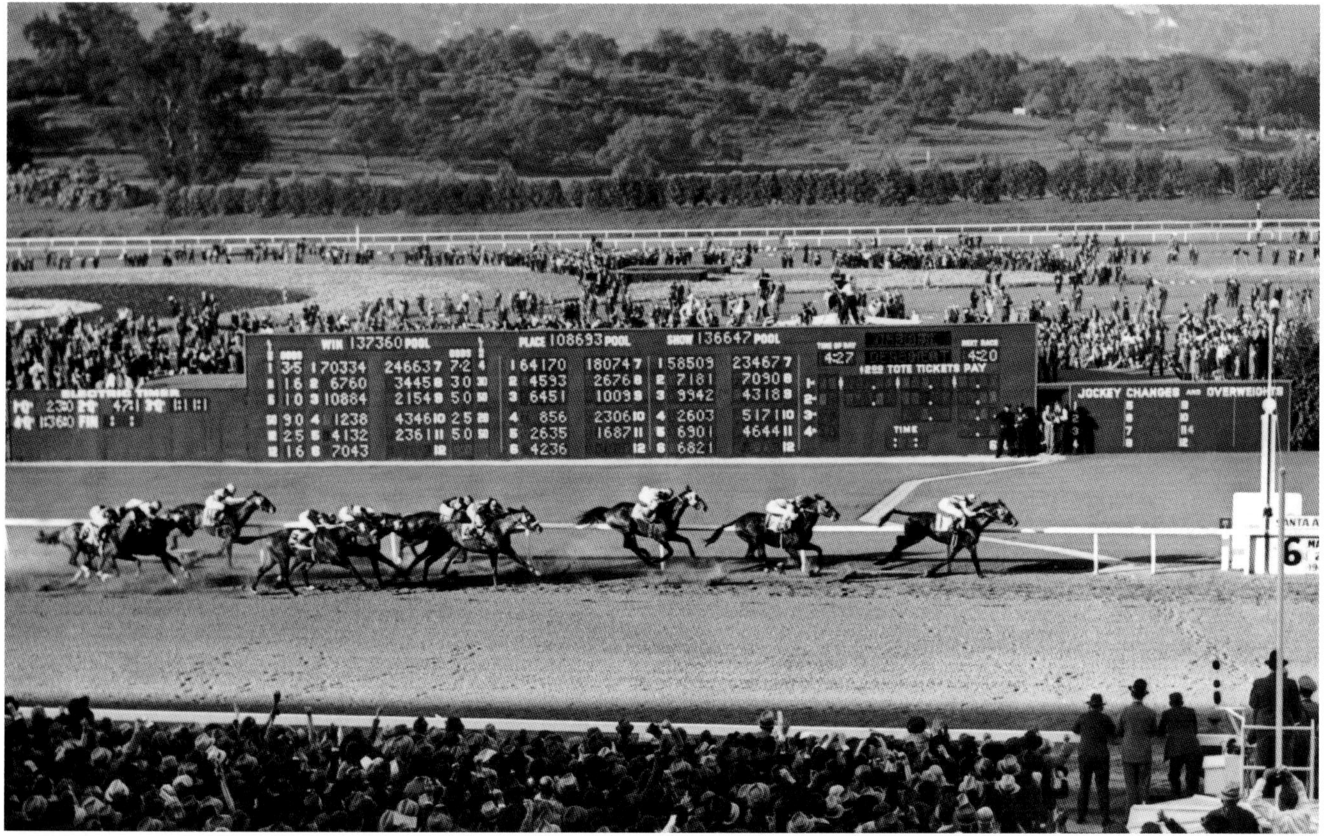

The legendary wonder-horse Seabiscuit *wins at Santa Anita, California*

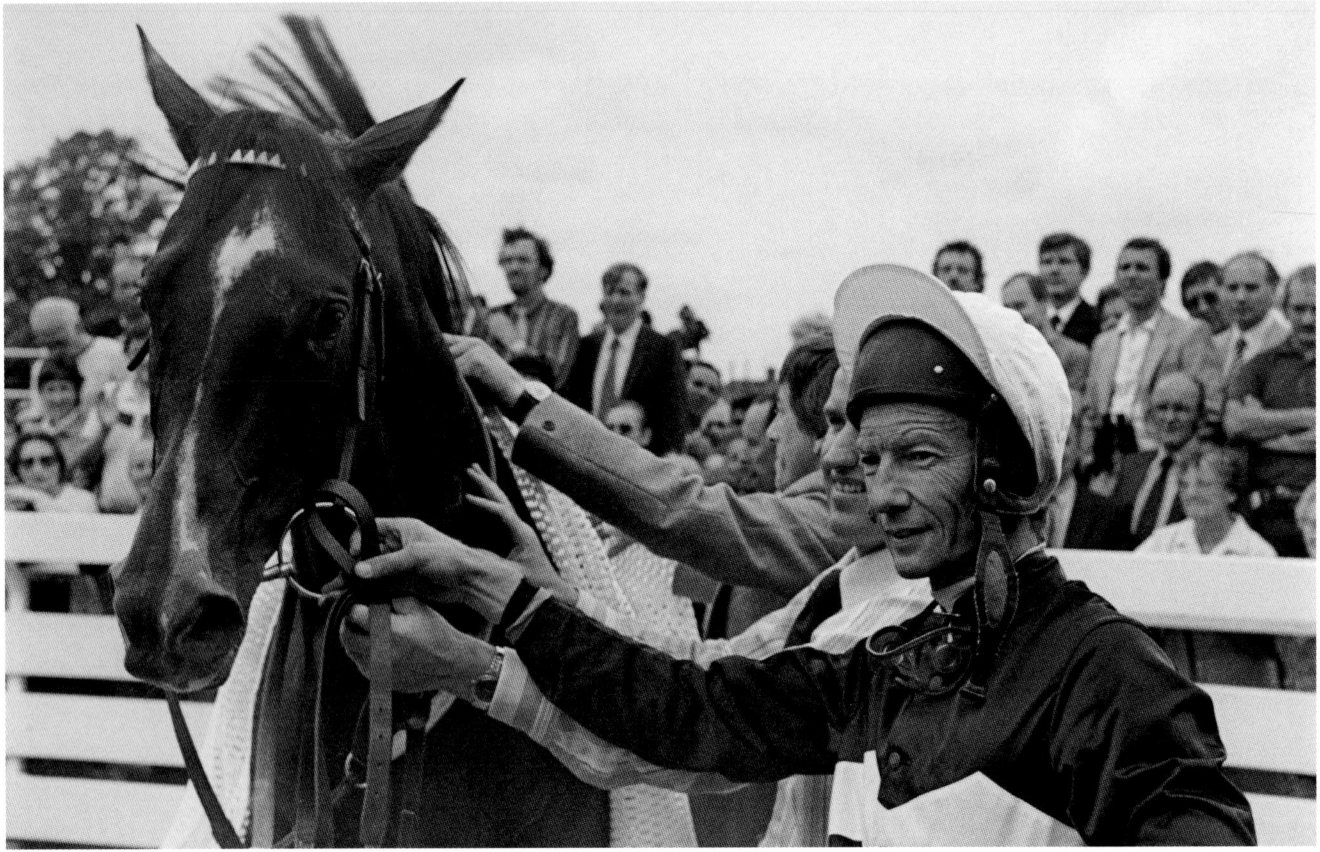

A thoroughbred Jockey and an icon within the sport. Lester Piggott, after riding his 4,000th winner

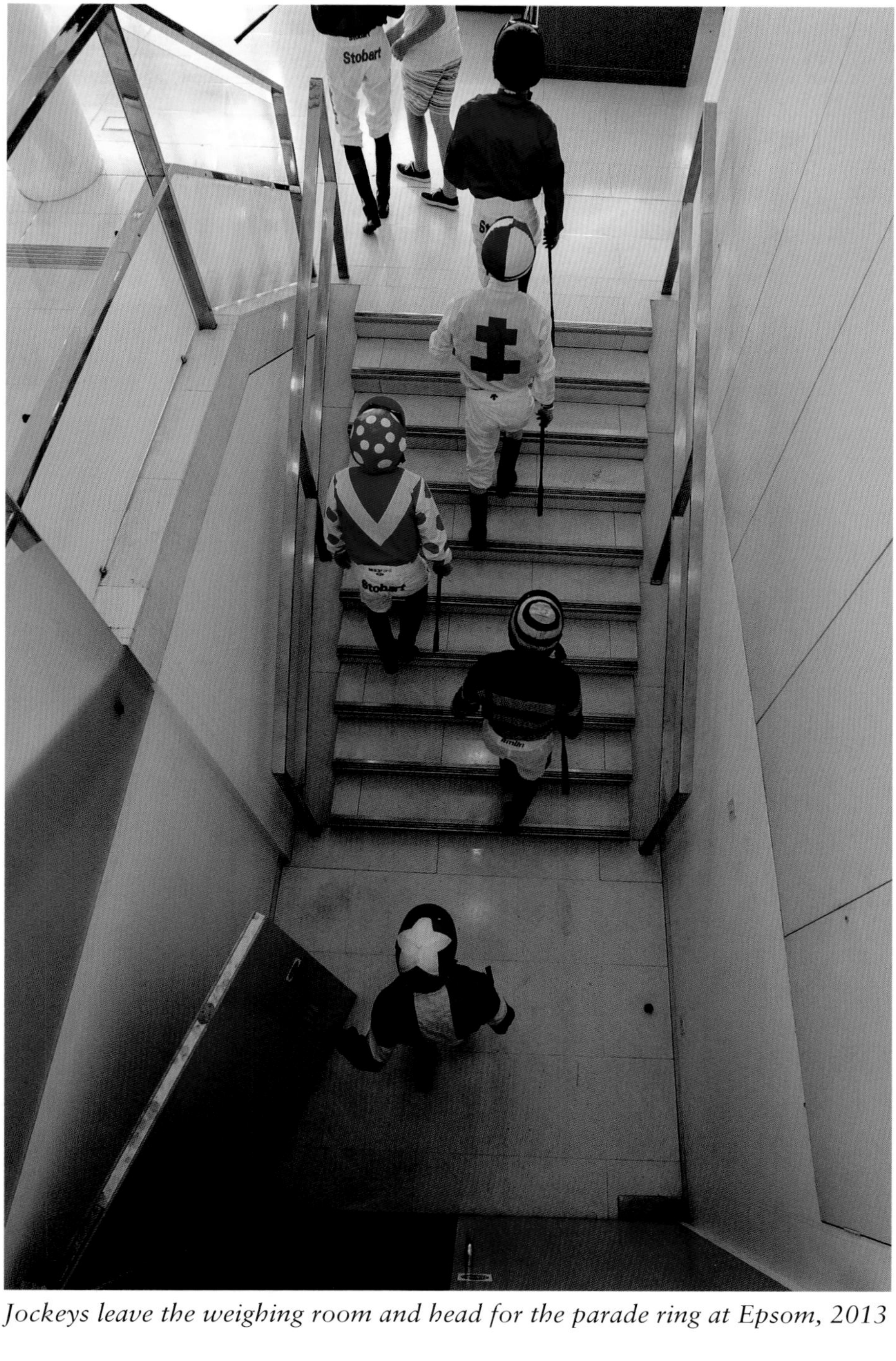

Jockeys leave the weighing room and head for the parade ring at Epsom, 2013

Champion's Story. One of the greatest moments in modern-day sport. Bob Champion recovers from cancer to win the 1981 Grand National

Frankie Dettori celebrates on Fujiyama Crest, *after winning the seventh and last race at Ascot, breaking the record*

Tony McCoy in typically dynamic action, driving his horse forward at Worcester in October 2014

he was also deposited into the water at what is now called Valentine's Brook.

That first Grand National race was won by professional jockey Jem Mason, appropriately on a horse called *Lottery,* but for a while the race was dominated by wealthy amateurs, like Becher, who frequently had military connections.

With his legacy unknowingly secured, Becher took his leave of the National Hunt scene, spending his autumnal years happily until, after a brief illness, he died in 1864 at the age of 67. By then the code of the horse-racing sport that he helped to pioneer was going from strength to strength and other jockeys were becoming known for their accomplishments. One, George Stevens, became the man to beat, particularly at Aintree. He won the Grand National five times (1856, 1863, 1864, 1869 and 1870) and instigated the tactical approach – still widely followed – of hunting conservatively around the first circuit in the pack, conserving energy. In addition to his wins at Aintree, Stevens notched up more than 100 winners in total, an impressive haul during an era in which there was much less racing in the sporting calendar.

Yet this paucity of race meets was changing and by the end of the 19th century National Hunt was mushrooming in popularity around the globe. In the USA, for instance, the first Maryland Hunt Cup was contested in 1894, posing a 4-mile, 22-obstacle challenge to horse and rider.

Britain, though, remained the hub of racing and from 1900 onwards a formal jockeys' championship title was awarded to the rider who notched up the most winners each season. The first to dominate was Frank Mason, who was British jump-racing champion jockey on six occasions, starting in 1901. Indeed, Mason was so outstanding that he was paid £300 *not* to ride for the fortnight before the 1905 Grand National by owner Frank Bilby, a Liverpool manufacturer. Bilby wanted Mason fully fit and available to ride his horse, *Kirkland*. It turned out that Bilby had invested wisely because *Kirkland* and Mason won the Grand National by 3 lengths.

Others to dominate were Fred Rees (five-times British jump-racing champion jockey between 1920 and 1927) and the diminutive and lively Billy Stott, who took on his mantle and also reeled off five championships, this time on the trot. Stott enjoyed the delight of riding one of the greatest horses of all time (perhaps only second to *Arkle)* when he won the Cheltenham Gold Cup on Ireland's *Golden Miller* before that honour was withdrawn. He was replaced in the Grand National that year in favour of Ted Leader before riding duties were awarded to Gerry Wilson.

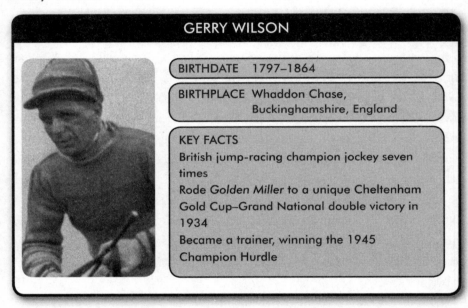

GERRY WILSON

BIRTHDATE 1797–1864

BIRTHPLACE Whaddon Chase, Buckinghamshire, England

KEY FACTS

British jump-racing champion jockey seven times

Rode *Golden Miller* to a unique Cheltenham Gold Cup–Grand National double victory in 1934

Became a trainer, winning the 1945 Champion Hurdle

Gerry Wilson, brother-in-law to the celebrated jockey–trainer Fred Rimell, was a supreme horseman, whose skills were acquired as a boy in the hunting field and then as a jockey during his apprenticeship on the flat. He was an upbeat character with a steely resolve, which was tested as it took him a decade to progress from his first winner (in 1921) to reach the higher echelons of jockeys, eventually becoming British jump-racing champion jockey in 1932/3.

Wilson went on to win the title on seven occasions but is best known for his alliance with the wonder-horse *Golden Miller*. In winning the title so many times, Wilson became part of one of those scarce jockey–horse partnerships – across both horse racing codes and around the globe – that earn a place in the history books through their shared accomplishments. Other pairings that come to mind include: *Arkle* and Pat Taaffe; *Seabiscuit* and Red Pollard; Ron Turcotte and *Secretariat*, who together in 1973 secured the America Triple Crown; Australian jockey Glen Boss, synonymous with *Makybe Diva*, with whom Boss won three consecutive Melbourne Cups in 2003, 2004 and 2005; and last but not least Tom Queally, whose name automatically evokes the brilliance of *Frankel*.

The reputation of the Wilson–*Golden Miller* partnership is due mainly to the unique double they achieved in 1934. By then, the rhythm of each jump season had become established, with a gathering of momentum through the winter that culminated in two celebrated festivals. The first took place at Cheltenham, National Hunt's equivalent of Royal Ascot because of its series of world-class races, including the Gold Cup. The second was the Grand National meeting at Aintree.

No horse has won both the Gold Cup and the Grand National in the same year apart from *Golden Miller*, who raced into the annals of history with Wilson on board in 1934. The Gold Cup was a comfortable win and, 17 days later, he also made light work of carrying 12st 2lb to win by 5 lengths at Aintree in a record time.

In 1935 the two went for the double double. *Golden Miller* narrowly beat *Thomond* in an epic duel for the Gold Cup and, at 2–1, started as the hottest favourite in Grand National history. Alas, it wasn't to be. *Golden Miller* fell and the double was not to be repeated.

12

ENDLESS WINTER

Danger? What danger? In the days of Gerry Wilson, jockeys wore little more protection than Captain Becher had done over a century earlier. They remained indecently exposed to the inevitability of injury and even the eminent jockeys of the day suffered: Fulke Walwyn (Grand National winner in 1936) fractured his skull in 1938 and was unconscious for a whole month; and the career of Fred Rimell (four-times British jump-racing champion jockey) ended when he broke his neck at the 1947 Cheltenham Gold Cup. These were not uncommon injuries. Fortunately, both men recovered sufficiently to go on to enjoy illustrious careers as trainers.

Back protectors and goggles had yet to be employed, and the cork crash-helmets of the day frequently came off when a jockey was unseated as they had no retaining strap under the chin, or split upon impact. On-course medical supervision was primitive. If a jockey felt he was able to ride after a bad fall, he was allowed to do so. On top of all that, there was no Injured Jockeys Fund, and insurance companies ignored what they saw as a foolhardy pursuit.

Viewed rationally, being a jump jockey was a mug's game, yet, despite the hazards, the period just after the Second World War saw a crop of strapping, gutsy, dogged men contest the major titles in National Hunt. They may not have been intuitive riders with the horse-sense of a John Francome or Ruby Walsh, but this was a lion-hearted group who had survived the wartime years and now took up the challenge of riding over fences professionally.

One of the finest of these was County Limerick's Tim Molony, who turned professional in 1940 and came to England after the war. Between 1948 and 1955 Molony was British jump-racing champion jockey five times, and had more than 900 winners to his name. He rode *Sir Ken* to three consecutive Champion Hurdle wins and *Hatton's Grace* to four consecutive Champion Hurdle victories.

Molony was noted for his strength in the saddle and his gritty resolve – and the same could be said of a man who contested the British Jump Jockeys Championship with Molony, and became entirely synonymous with jump racing and all that it stands for. He cleared 120,000 fences and galloped over 10,000 miles during more than 4,000 races – winning nearly a quarter and being placed in half of them. There were other jockeys around like Fred Winter – in a way his story is their story – but no one person epitomises the era better.

FREDERICK THOMAS WINTER

BIRTHDATE 1926–2004

BIRTHPLACE Andover, Hampshire, England

KEY FACTS

923 career winners, breaking the previous record

British jump-racing champion jockey four times and champion trainer eight times.

Only person to have won the Cheltenham Gold Cup, Champion Hurdle and Grand National as both jockey and trainer

Racing flowed through Winter's veins from birth. His father had been a flat-racing jockey, precocious enough to win the Oaks as a 16-year-old apprentice, and who subsequently set up as a trainer on Epsom Downs in 1929. By the time Fred was 4½ years old, he was riding out each morning with his father's string. He was educated at Ewell College and

Over the last. Fred Winter negotiates the final fence on his way to victory in the 1961 Cheltenham Gold Cup

was allowed the day off, aged 13, for his first ride in a race, on the flat at Newbury. The boy was cheered all the way back to the unsaddling enclosure.

After this early promise, Winter left college and started work as an apprentice in Newmarket. Within two years his weight forced an end to his aspirations to ride on the flat and, at the same time, Britain went to war, and horse racing became an irrelevance. Fred enlisted in the Army, and from 1944 to 1947 he was attached to the 6th (Royal Welch) Battalion Parachute Regiment, serving in Palestine for nine months.

Demobbed in 1948, the year after he met Captain Ryan Price, Winter became the captain's stable jockey and the two men formed a jockey–trainer partnership that spanned Winter's 16-year riding career. Winter, by his own admission, was not a natural, tending to 'fall off a lot' in his formative years. His first racecourse fall had shaken him to the core;

when falling at the second last fence, the thought of the horses coming over the fence and landing on him had frightened the life out of him so that, though experiencing real pain for the first time, he managed to dive underneath the rails before the horses arrived. His brother, John, agreed that Fred 'was not a natural steeplechase jockey', finding it very hard: 'It was a job to him, a job he was determined to conquer because he had no wish to go into anything else.'

With that determination he learned quickly, developing a sense of pace, balance, tactical nous and the winning edge. Most notably, though, Winter was strong as an ox, especially in his arms, shoulders and back, and was able to drive his mounts forwards with legs and hands in preference to the whip. Writing in the *Daily Telegraph*, Lord John Oaksey, an astute judge of such things, simply labelled him 'the best jumping jockey I ever saw'.

In the 1952/3 season Winter became British jump-racing champion jockey for the first time, with 121 winners, a record-breaking figure that stood for 14 years. Beaten to the title by Dick Francis and then Tim Molony in the subsequent seasons, he went on to win the title for three more years and, in 1957, secured his first Grand National win on *Sundew*. However, all jump jockeys, literally, endure ups and downs; the hazards of the trade see to that. Jumping his very first fence at the start of the following campaign, Winter fell, fractured his leg, was out for the season and never won the title again.

Of all the many good horses Winter rode, Peggy Hennessy's *Mandarin* stood out. Twice, in 1962, he and *Mandarin* scored famous victories. The first was in the Gold Cup at Cheltenham, the second in the Grand Steeple-Chase de Paris. The latter is run at Auteuil, in the Bois de Boulogne, over 30 fences around a 4-mile figure-of-eight, and includes the 9-foot-high hedge called 'Le Bullfinch' and 'La Riviere', a huge water jump.

This heyday was one for the legends. Winter was already suffering from a severe stomach upset and then, at the fourth fence, the snaffle broke in *Mandarin's* mouth. The already indisposed Winter was now forced to try and steer the horse over the mammoth obstacles without the highly desirable facility to break or steer. Most would have given up. Not Fred. Somehow he manoeuvred and cajoled *Mandarin* round the course, keeping him in contention.

Only once, four fences from home, did *Mandarin* threaten to go the wrong side of a marker. Winter's Herculean strength hauled him back but *Mandarin* lost 4 lengths and his rhythm. No matter, turning for home they negotiated the Bullfinch and went on to win by a head. This was the stuff of a *Boy's Own* story. As the now-lame *Mandarin* hobbled back to the saddling enclosure, horse and rider were acclaimed by the French crowd for their sporting heroics. Winter himself could scarcely walk to the scales, and jockey Stan Mellor had to help him change.

That never-say-die attitude served Winter well, right to the end. At Newbury in his last season, he won four winners at a meeting, almost hauling two over the line with every last ounce of his now diminishing might. The jockeys rose spontaneously to clap and cheer upon his return to the weighing room. But the years of earnest effort took their toll and eventually he lost his edge; as he told jockey Tommy Smith, 'Courage is like a bank account: if you draw too many cheques, sooner or later one bounces.'

After his retirement Winter turned to training and excelled in this arena as well. He became champion trainer eight times and is the only person to have won the Cheltenham Gold Cup, Champion Hurdle and Grand National as both jockey and trainer.

13

RAISING THE BAR

If jump racing hooked you in, there was no rehabilitation. Once addicted, forever addicted. So the decisions made by the likes of Fulke Walwyn, Fred Rimell and Fred Winter to become trainers after their race-riding careers were over became a well-trodden path for those with the funds and inclination. Josh Gifford, a four-time British jump-racing champion jockey who rode 642 winners, was another who turned trainer, at the age of 28.

Others found different ways of keeping in the sport. Dick Francis – best known in the horse world for riding the Queen's *Devon Loch*, which spread-eagled so dramatically yards from the winning post at the Grand National in 1956 – turned to writing and enjoyed global fame and fortune as a novelist.

Another jockey–trainer was Stan Mellor. His achievements in the saddle dwarfed those of almost everyone else who had ever donned racing silks. Indeed, most observers felt that Stan Mellor's record would never be surpassed when this most stylish of master-craftsmen broke through the barrier of 1,000 career winners in 1971.

Yet from the mid-1970s through to the mid-1990s three men raised the bar and left their own personal stamp on the profession, not only in terms of the amount of times they visited the winner's enclosure, but also in the manner in which they did so.

Steve Smith-Eccles, no mean race-rider himself, inhabited the weighing room with all of them and became close personal friends, as is so often the case among National Hunt jockeys, and few are better qualified to provide insights into what made them tick.

JOHN FRANCOME, MBE

BIRTHDATE 1952–

BIRTHPLACE Swindon, Wiltshire, England

KEY FACTS
1,138 career winners, breaking the previous record
Awarded the MBE in 1986 for services to racing
British jump-racing champion jockey seven times between 1976 and 1985

Smith-Eccles's closest ally John Francome was the first and perhaps the finest horseman of the three. No surprise, then, that Smith-Eccles speaks so fondly of him. Yet the words come from professional recognition rather than kindness. He knows that few enjoyed Francome's horse-sense or developed a greater ability to coax a horse to jump fluently. Smith-Eccles said:

> '[Francome] came up through pony clubs and he reached the highs as a junior showjumper [he won junior international honours] so his forte was always going to be getting horses to jump and that's where Frank won most of his races, out there in the country. By the time it came to the business end of it, nine times out of ten he'd got the race in the bag. Tactically he was brilliant, in getting horses to jump he was second-to-none and that combined with his intelligence to bring him way, way above everyone else of that era.'

Francome's figures justify Smith-Eccles's approbation. He became Fred Winter's stable jockey in 1975/6 and remained in that role for 15 unbroken years. The two men linked up to remarkable effect, albeit with an absolute minimum of fuss and communication, as Francome himself once explained:

> 'We never had three cross words between us in all the years I rode for him. He never gave me a bollocking after a race. It wasn't his way. He knew what it was like to ride and how easily things could go wrong. He was no different when you rode a winner. You might get a "well done" off him. If he was really pleased, he might give you a pat on the back. He wasn't a great talker, just the odd grunt or nod. Driving to the races with him, you might get three sentences off him.'

Francome won the British Jump Jockeys Championship seven times between the 1975/6 and 1984/5 seasons, and chalked up 1,138 winners in Britain, surpassing Mellor's record for a jump jockey. This period includes the season of 1981/2, when Francome displayed a true sportsman's generosity of spirit. He had been neck and neck with Peter Scudamore for the title when Scudamore sustained a season-ending injury. Francome charitably decided to match Scudamore's total of 121 winners and then terminated his campaign so that the two riders could share the title.

Francome raised the bar both statistically and in terms of his mind-set and attitude to preparation. What is perceived as professionalism evolves through different decades. This was an era when jockeys such as Terry Biddlecombe were tough, courageous and talented but had a Captain Becher-like Corinthian spirit about them. They rode hard and played hard, drinking late into the night and sweating it out the next morning in Turkish baths. Francome, though, became a role model for others in the way that he dedicated and devoted himself to his profession.

Describing Francome as the 'ultimate professional', fellow jockey Smith-Eccles talks of how he was also 'a master at walking around the track, because even if you've ridden a thousand times the track will change from meeting to meeting – the positions of rails etc. – and with the changing weather there may be a boggy patch. And if you save half a length here and half a length there at the end of the race, that might be enough to win or lose. Francome was great at that, always looking for that edge.' Smith-Eccles also highlighted the fact that Francome didn't drink, so was never hung-over.

Despite this teetotal approach and the meticulous homework, Francome was very much one of the lads, often right at the heart of the banter in the weighing room before his retirement in 1985.

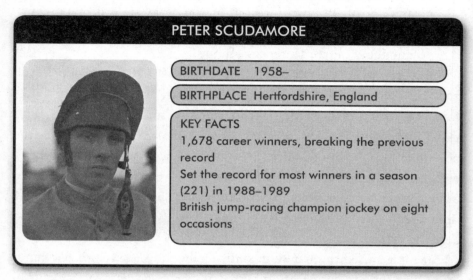

PETER SCUDAMORE

BIRTHDATE 1958–

BIRTHPLACE Hertfordshire, England

KEY FACTS
1,678 career winners, breaking the previous record
Set the record for most winners in a season (221) in 1988–1989
British jump-racing champion jockey on eight occasions

As Francome left stage right, so the spotlight fell upon Peter Scudamore, son of the outstanding jockey Michael Scudamore. Not that Peter particularly enjoyed the limelight – Scudamore was more of a grinder, a throwback to the days of Gerry Wilson and Fred Winter. Yes, he was a talented horseman, but he stood out because he was stoic and had a never-say-die outlook. Smith-Eccles speaks fondly of him:

> 'It's hard to describe Scu. He's one of the best mates, I love him to death. The thing about him was that he never gave up on a horse. He'd drive, push, kick – just didn't know when he was beaten. Even when he was out the back [at the back of the field with no chance to winning] and I'd be saying to him "go steady son" he'd pay no attention. He never knew when he was beaten. He's like a racehorse that never stops trying. Some of these good horses are scientifically proven to possess big hearts

– they get cut open after they die – and Scu's like that. He's all heart. Fearless.'

Smith-Eccles says that those traits can be traced back to his genes: 'He's the son of Michael Scudamore, who was a British jump-racing champion jockey, and he was born and bred to it. Even from a very early age I would imagine he lived and breathed jump racing. He had to succeed. There was no way he couldn't succeed and of course he was extremely successful. Now it's the same with his son, Tom [who is a current professional jump jockey].'

Scudamore became stable jockey for the stand-out trainer of the time, Martin Pipe. Pipe had a scientist's attention to detail and they formed a formidable pair. Despite this, some critics might compare Scudamore unfavourably with his predecessor, Francome, and his successor, Richard Dunwoody. He may have been less gifted, and never won either the Gold Cup or the Grand National, but eight championships and 1,678

Beautifully balanced and all heart. Peter Scudamore jumps a water fence during a race at Fontwell

winners (raising the bar again after Francome) speak for themselves. Scudamore invariably got the job done, fuss-free, until, like Francome, he retired with just a few hours' notice. At the age of 35 his hunger for the demanding lifestyle had waned and he admitted: 'I'd look down the list of runners in novice chases and I'd think that I didn't want to risk injury. I just wasn't in the right frame of mind for chasing titles anymore. I was coming towards the end of the season and, quite honestly, I didn't feel like putting in 100 per cent effort any more'.

Perhaps the most interesting personality of the three bar-raisers was the Belfast-born Richard Dunwoody. Like almost all top jockeys, Richard was born into the sport, being the son of jumps trainer George Dunwoody.

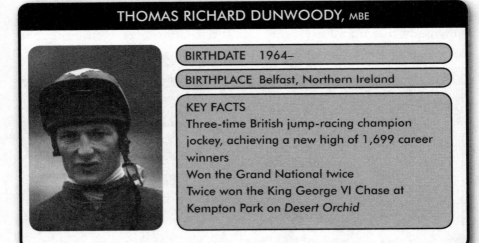

THOMAS RICHARD DUNWOODY, MBE

BIRTHDATE 1964–

BIRTHPLACE Belfast, Northern Ireland

KEY FACTS
Three-time British jump-racing champion jockey, achieving a new high of 1,699 career winners
Won the Grand National twice
Twice won the King George VI Chase at Kempton Park on *Desert Orchid*

Dunwoody turned professional at the start of the 1984/5 season and the next year he won the first of two Grand Nationals on *West Tip*. He took over from Peter Scudamore as David Nicholson's stable jockey and rode the legendary *Desert Orchid* to victory at the King George VI Chase in 1989 and 1990, as well as winning the 1990 Irish Grand National.

Dunwoody became British jump-racing champion jockey for the first time in the 1992/3 season, retaining the title for the following two campaigns. After a spell with Martin Pipe as stable jockey and as a freelance, Dunwoody passed Scudamore's record career total in April 1999, having ridden 100 winners per season for ten consecutive campaigns. Few had been more capable, and few more focused in the pursuit of excellence.

However, later that year Dunwoody was forced into retirement due to nerve damage that affected his neck and right arm. His career total of 1,699 winners in Britain was a record until Tony McCoy passed him in 2002. This astonishing achievement was, however, little consolation as he faced up to the challenge of life after race-riding and the unwanted question of how to spend his time thereafter. The careers of Francome and Scudamore came to a natural conclusion; they just knew the time was right to go and could move on with their lives. For Dunwoody, alas, this scenario was not to be, and being forced out of the game and to seek a new path was daunting for such an intense character.

Smith-Eccles reflects that Dunwoody's autobiography was accurately called *Obsessed: The Autobiography*. 'Again, one of my best mates. We rode together for many, many years, but he *was* obsessed, and he never really accepted being retired medically. He never accepted it. Even now he never got rid of being a jockey. It's still there.'

14

AP

Francome, Scudamore and Dunwoody raised the bar. They achieved that which many thought unachievable. But, just occasionally, a sportsman or woman comes along whose statistics are so much better than everyone else's that they render all 'who was the greatest' discussions redundant. Perhaps the most obvious example of this in another sport is Sir Donald Bradman, the Australian cricketer, who for 20 years collated a set of batting statistics that will surely never be beaten. By the time of his retirement, his test-match batting average was 99.94 per innings and in the 66 years since he retired no batsmen has come even close to

Another addition to a set of statistics that are without parallel. Newbury Racecourse, November 2014 – and AP wins, yet again

ANTHONY PETER (AP) McCOY

BIRTHDATE 1974–

BIRTHPLACE Moneyglass, County Antrim, Northern Ireland

KEY FACTS
Beat Sir Gordon Richards's record of 269 winners in a season in 2002, achieving a new high of 289 winners
The leading jump jockey of all time with more than 4,000 winners to his name, beating the previous record of 1,699 held by Richard Dunwoody
British jump-racing champion jockey every year since 1995/6

emulating him. The next-highest average is just less than 61 runs per innings, 39 per cent short of Bradman's tally. The gap is so cavernous that there is no need for debate: Bradman is the best. End of story.

The same phenomenon has occurred in National Hunt, and current observers are able to watch history being built every day. Yet the man who has achieved Bradman-esque statistics in the equine world is probably not even the most eye-catching or talented man within his peer group. Some people take a personal aura into each room they enter. The great American heavyweight boxer, Muhammad Ali, is probably the best sporting example of this. Even before he spoke, Ali turned heads, even those of people who somehow were not aware of his fame and unprecedented prowess in the ring. There was something about him that left people awestruck.

In horse racing, Frankie Dettori is a head-turner, a natural extrovert. You might hear his Italian accent before you see him and when he is on form he draws people towards him because of his fizzing energy and ebullience.

By contrast, there is nothing about AP McCoy from County Antrim in Northern Ireland that immediately demands attention. He is 5 feet 10 inches tall, with unremarkable brown hair and brown eyes. Unless you follow horse racing, you wouldn't guess that you were in the presence of greatness, yet greatness is what he represents. AP is the most prolific jump jockey ever, not so much a jockey as a freak of nature. Win by win, race by race, he has constructed a set of statistics that are without parallel.

There have been many more talented horsemen than McCoy but it's the 3 inches of grey matter between his ears that elevate him above the rest. Those 3 inches must be made of granite, because his mental fortitude may be without parallel in 21st-century sport.

In some ways, McCoy is just like the rest of us in that he possesses ordinary traits; his greatness lies with the fact that he has them to such an extraordinary degree. Many will make sacrifices for something they love to do – but not in the way that McCoy has, 365 days a year, for most of his adult life. Many possess reserves of courage and bravery, and can endure a degree of pain and discomfort – but McCoy has taken this to extremes. Many like to win and excel – but few pursue it with McCoy's insatiable persistence.

As a result of these extremes of behaviour, there is not a racecourse in Britain that McCoy would not visit to ride a winner. Usually, champions cherry-pick their venues, looking to reduce the tedious hours of travel on motorways if they can. Not McCoy. It's like the old joke about the Z-list celebrity who would turn up for the opening of an envelope. McCoy is the jockey equivalent. He'll go anywhere to ride a winner; it's a greed that can never be truly sated.

Three stories provide perspectives on the legend that is AP McCoy. The first is told from personal experience by Lisa Hancock, CEO of the Injured Jockeys Fund:

> 'He [McCoy] had a fall at Cheltenham in April [2013], and by sheer chance I happened to be there and jumped in the ambulance with him. He was in an extraordinary amount of pain and it

> wasn't particularly enjoyable for me. I've never seen somebody who I knew was very tough in so much pain – but because of the number of injuries he had sustained and because he's no fool he was very aware of which part of the body he had hurt. He was self-diagnosing that he had punctured his lung and that was why he couldn't breathe, and by the time he got to Gloucester hospital he told the A&E consultant what he had done. The consultant, slightly dismissively, said "Yes, we'll put you in the scanner first and then we'll assess it" but when AP came out of the scanner he was pretty much right on. He's a very astute guy who is very in tune with his body and knows how far he can push it – and that may or may not be a good thing.'

When asked about the same incident, McCoy corroborated the tale. 'Yes, I told them I'd punctured my lung and broken my sternum and some ribs,' he says. 'She'd never heard such a correct self-diagnosis before. But I'm so up on medical things now I nearly could be a doctor. I was so sore that I had an epidural in my back and was in intensive care for six days. You only worry about your head or spinal column. Everything else, some way or another, will repair in time.'

The second anecdote pertains to another fall, this time at Warwick in the middle of winter. Again, the injury was a bad one. The MRI scan revealed a fractured T12 and a shattered T9 and T10. In layman's terms, that's a broken back. He was operated on and the diagnosis was that he would be out for months: there was no chance he would make it back for the Cheltenham Festival.

But McCoy had heard about cryotherapy, which originated in Japan in the 1970s and involves medical therapy that uses extremely low temperatures to aid and accelerate the healing process. So McCoy went to a health farm for ten days to heal his back, undergoing one or two 3-minute sessions a day. He started off in a chamber at –65°C (–85°F), and then progressed to –100°C (–148°F). But here's the insight into McCoy's mindset: he got word that a professional footballer, Shefki Kuqi, held the unofficial record for enduring the lowest-ever temperature in the chamber at –145°C (–229°F). McCoy being McCoy set his mind to exceed that and withstood a session 5°C (9°F) colder than the previous low. He had been warned that the side effects would be disturbing, and indeed they were, but his pig-headed determination to beat all others and endure pain meant that he rode again just seven weeks after breaking his back and was able to participate at the Cheltenham Festival.

Even people in this abnormally tough profession are in awe of McCoy's competitive instincts and his remarkable pain threshold. His brain is no longer wired like those of normal people. 'The more [injuries that happen] to me the easier it has become to cope', McCoy once disclosed in an interview on Sky Sports. 'Your pain threshold becomes higher and you learn that it's part of your job, and the job is trying to get back from those injuries as soon as you can and not letting them have an effect on you. Just accept the fact that it's part of your job and it's going to happen.'

The third perspective is not so much a story as a reflection. People in sport often talk about the *will to win*, but many elite sportsmen and women who have hit the heights are in fact driven as much by fear – not physical fear, but the fear of failure, the fear of not winning and the fear of letting their Olympian standards drop. McCoy admits in his autobiography that this holds true for him too:

> 'There was pressure on me every day to win, self-imposed of course. I just wanted another number to add to the total, another winner, another tick. I obviously got a lot of satisfaction from winning, the same as I do now, but back then the satisfaction lay in the fact that that it was another winner, another one to add to the total. The fear of not being champion was my overriding feeling, not excitement at the prospect about being champion.'

These are just three insights into what makes McCoy tick, but they are pretty revealing and, regardless of his motivation, no one could doubt that he has been the dominant jockey of the modern era.

One of the downsides of this total dominance is that the outstanding contributions of his rivals in the weighing room have been somewhat devalued. In any other period, the likes of Richard Johnson and Ruby Walsh, for instance, would have been as garlanded and celebrated; they, too, are brilliant exponents of the craft.

Richard Johnson was born into a family with a rich horse-racing heritage and first rode at the age of four. Aside from McCoy, Johnson has ridden more National Hunt winners than any other rider in history, even though he has been a perennial runner-up in the Jockeys Championship. He is popular in the weighing room and respected by fellow jockeys and the public alike for his personality, professionalism and ability in the saddle.

Ruby Walsh, yet another Irishman, from Kill in County Kildare, also started riding early. He won the Irish amateur title twice before turning professional and secured the Grand National in 2000 at his first attempt, aged 20, on *Papillon.* Walsh has split his time between the Irish and British racing circuits and focused on quality as much as quantity, becoming leading jockey at the Cheltenham Festival in 2004, 2006, 2008, 2009, 2010, 2011, 2013 and 2014. Walsh is a stylist and possesses vast amounts of that intangible quality called horse-sense. Like Johnson, he is a jockey's jockey, one that others admire and want to copy.

So if the cards had fallen differently this chapter might have been about Johnson, Walsh and a few others. But they have plied their trade in the McCoy era, a rider who, at the time of writing (August 2014), has just broken his own record for the fastest 100 winners in a jumps season. The 40-year-old's powers do not seem to be diminishing. Many have suggested jump racing won't see his like again and it seems this is a fair bet. When he eventually chooses to retire then the bar of career winners will have been set at stratospheric heights and surely will never be raised again.

BRITISH JUMP RACING CHAMPION JOCKEYS					
Season	Jockey	Winners	Season	Jockey	Winners
1900	HS Sidney	53	1933/4	Gerry Wilson	56
1901	Frank Mason	58	1934/5	Gerry Wilson	73
1902	Frank Mason	67	1935/6	Gerry Wilson	57
1903	Percy Woodland	54	1936/7	Gerry Wilson	45
1904	Frank Mason	59	1937/8	Gerry Wilson	59
1905	Frank Mason	73	1938/9	Fred Rimell	61
1906	Frank Mason	58	1939/40	Fred Rimell	24
1907	Frank Mason	59	1940/1	Gerry Wilson	22
1908	P Cowley	65	1941/2	Ron Smyth	12
1909	R Gordon	45	1942/3	Racing suspended	
1910	Ernie Piggott	67	1943/4	Racing suspended	
1911	W Payne	76	1944/5	Frenchie Nicholson/ Fred Rimell	15
1912	Ivor Anthony	78			
1913	Ernie Piggott	60	1945/6	Fred Rimell	54
1914	Jack Anthony	60	1946/7	Jack Dowdeswell	58
1915	Ernie Piggott	44	1947/8	Bryan Marshall	66
1916	C Hawkins	17	1948/9	Tim Molony	60
1917	W Smith	15	1949/50	Tim Molony	95
1918	George Duller	17	1950/1	Tim Molony	83
1919	H Brown	48	1951/2	Tim Molony	99
1920	Fred Rees	64	1952/3	Fred Winter	121
1921	Fred Rees	65	1953/4	Dick Francis	76
1922	Jack Anthony	78	1954/5	Tim Molony	67
1923	Fred Rees	64	1955/6	Fred Winter	74
1924	Fred Rees	108	1956/7	Fred Winter	80
1925	E Foster	76	1957/8	Fred Winter	82
1925/6	Ted Leader	61	1958/9	Tim Brookshaw	83
1926/7	Fred Rees	59	1959/60	Stan Mellor	68
1927/8	Billy Stott	88	1960/1	Stan Mellor	118
1928/9	Billy Stott	76	1961/2	Stan Mellor	80
1929/30	Billy Stott	77	1962/3	Josh Gifford	70
1930/1	Billy Stott	81	1963/4	Josh Gifford	94
1931/2	Billy Stott	77	1964/5	Terry Biddlecombe	114
1932/3	Gerry Wilson	61	1965/6	Terry Biddlecombe	102

Season	Jockey	Winners	Season	Jockey	Winners
1966/7	Josh Gifford	122	1989/90	Peter Scudamore	170
1967/8	Josh Gifford	82	1990/1	Peter Scudamore	141
1968/9	Terry Biddlecombe/ Bob Davies	77	1991/2	Peter Scudamore	175
			1992/3	Richard Dunwoody	173
1969/70	Bob Davies	91	1993/4	Richard Dunwoody	197
1970/1	Graham Thorner	74	1994/5	Richard Dunwoody	160
1971/2	Bob Davies	89	1995/6	AP McCoy	175
1972/3	Ron Barry	125	1996/7	AP McCoy	190
1973/4	Ron Barry	94	1997/8	AP McCoy	253
1974/5	Tommy Stack	82	1998/9	AP McCoy	186
1975/6	John Francome	96	1999/ 2000	AP McCoy	245
1976/7	Tommy Stack	97			
1977/8	Jonjo O'Neill	149	2000/1	AP McCoy	191
1978/9	John Francome	95	2001/2	AP McCoy	289
1979/80	Jonjo O'Neill	115	2002/3	AP McCoy	258
1980/1	John Francome	105	2003/4	AP McCoy	209
1981/2	John Francome/ Peter Scudamore	120	2004/5	AP McCoy	200
			2005/6	AP McCoy	178
1982/3	John Francome	106	2006/7	AP McCoy	184
1983/4	John Francome	131	2007/8	AP McCoy	140
1984/5	John Francome	101	2008/9	AP McCoy	186
1985/6	Peter Scudamore	91	2009/10	AP McCoy	195
1986/7	Peter Scudamore	123	2010/11	AP McCoy	218
1987/8	Peter Scudamore	132	2011/12	AP McCoy	199
1988/9	Peter Scudamore	221	2012/13	AP McCoy	185

PART 4
OCCUPATIONAL HAZARDS

15

ONE PIECE

The esteemed sports journalist Ian Wooldridge wrote in the *Daily Mail* in 2005: ‘Like matadors they take their lives in their hands every time they ride. They smash collarbones, arms, legs and vertebrae round the clock and are back in the saddle when most of us would be taking tentative steps on a zimmer frame. Jump jockeys for me, remain the bravest of all our sportsmen.’

Another writer, Alan Lee, once half-joked that a jockey ‘grew up wanting to be a fighter pilot but decided to live dangerously and became a jump jockey instead’, while Sue Mott wrote in the *Daily Telegraph* in 2004 that she considered jump jockeys to be ‘a certifiable travelling band of madmen’.

All three sports writers had a point. Riding racehorses is not for the faint-hearted; it’s a survivor’s sport and there are few more perilous professions.

Jockeys’ careers are punctuated by stays in hospital beds while their battered and bruised bones recover from injuries, regardless of their capabilities. Despite being one of the greatest jump jockeys of all time, AP McCoy has suffered as much as most. He has fractured a leg, arm and ankle as well as both wrists, shoulder blades, collar bones, cheekbones and all of his ribs. He has also broken several vertebrae in his back, suffered punctured lungs and had to have all his teeth replaced due to racing injuries.

But McCoy, like the other riders, accepts these batterings as an occupational hazard and gets on with it, considering his body in a cold, detached manner. Most of us would view a broken leg, broken rib or dislocated collarbone as a major event in our life. Jockeys treat them with disdain and indifference. Yes, they are a nuisance because it stops them from working and earning, but they mentally divorce themselves from the emotion that could go with it. They take time off, they heal, and they get back on the horse as soon as they are physically able. They know they will be injured so pain, and the expectation of it, becomes an accepted part of their lives. Most develop a high pain threshold.

There used to be an informal ritual in the jump jockeys' weighing room at the end of each season during which the riders would congratulate each other on their survival with the simple utterance, 'one piece'. Nowadays, the gap between the end of one season and the beginning of the next is virtually non-existent but the sentiments remain valid – and the fact that the bodies of most of them are still intact thanks to the wonders of modern science is neither here nor there.

The dangers exist regardless of whether the jockey rides over jumps or on the flat, although jump jockeys fall more frequently. Point-to-point riders take a tumble, on average, once in every nine races; about twice as often as their professional counterparts within National Hunt. Because of their frequency those tumbles are anticipated and they develop skills to minimise the injuries, which can include being crushed by their mount.

On the flat, falls occur less frequently – on average once in every 240 rides – but, partly because of this and partly because they often happen within a fast-moving pack that has no opportunity to divert its course, the spills tend to be more dramatic and more likely to lead to serious injuries.

Overall, three-quarters of the injuries cause soft tissue damage; fractures and concussion make up the majority of the other quarter. Dislocations can also occur.

So, throughout the sport's history, every jockey has known that their fortunes in each race could change within an instant. One moment they could be in the heart of the action, absorbed in the contest, fuelled by adrenalin, their body taut and at one with their mount as they cover the ground at speeds of 25–40mph. The next they could be unceremoniously ejected from the saddle, hurtling towards an uncertain future.

If a rider is fortunate, he or she might gently plop onto the turf and manage to roll into a protective ball, untouched and unharmed by either the fall or the other horses thundering overhead. If so, the jockey will count their blessings, get up and try again next time with only their ego being bruised. If fate deals a different hand in this high-stakes game, however, the outcome can be altogether harsher. The rider might be speared down into the turf at speed and be kicked and trampled, not only by their own mount but the rest of the field. Worse still, the horse may land on them, and the damage brought about by half a tonne of racehorse – ten times the weight of the jockey – can be sickening.

The nature of race-riding means that broken collarbones are par for the course, but there is also the potential for damage to heads, necks and backs that, at worst, turns lives upside down; not just for the rider but also for their friends and family. Yes, there is a skill to falling, but ultimately it comes down to luck whether and where an injury is sustained. Either way, the jockey ends up alone and deserted on the turf as the field – the survivors – disappear into the distance to contest the prize.

Race-riding is similar to other high-octane sports such as rugby, boxing, martial arts, skiing, motor sport and mountaineering: if you take part, you'll get hurt – or worse – at some stage. Not that the participants of these activities dwell on such matters. In fact, for their own sanity they don't ponder them at all – and this has always been the case.

In the years leading up to and beyond the Second World War, most jockeys had a cavalier attitude towards risk. There was little in the way of protection, but most riders didn't give safety a moment's thought, and nor did the administrators who ran the sport. Former National Hunt jockey Ron Atkins is the ideal man to shine a light on an era before health and safety had been invented. The Londoner is probably best remembered for his long, trendy, rock 'n' roll brown hair, which protruded out from under a skullcap that very visibly carried his initials 'RA'. During a lengthy career in the saddle Atkins became a fans' favourite for his all-action riding style that produced over 400 winners for trainers such as Fred Winter, Ryan Price, Fred Rimell, Staff Ingham, Bill Marshall and Martin Pipe.

Despite these accolades, however, Atkins's most enduring service to the sport has been his work with the Professional Jockeys Association. As safety officer and vice president, he was one of the men responsible for conceiving the Jockeys Pension Fund and drove up the safety standards for the sport. So he took, and still takes, a keen interest in injuries and the related medical back-up that is required.

Certainly, Atkins experienced for himself the lack of safety precautions when he began his career in the 1960s, beginning on the flat before moving across to steeplechase as his weight increased. He remembers:

> 'When I first started and we were work riding at stables we didn't wear any protection at all. I've got photos in my office of me schooling over fences wearing just jodhpurs and a T-shirt. Nobody gave it a thought; and I think there was a more macho approach to safety.
>
> On the racecourse, when I first rode professionally on the flat we used to have a cork helmet – I've still got mine – that had no fasteners, no chin strap and it was pretty useless really. Nine times out of ten it came off when you fell.'

Atkins picks out concussion as the major issue for jockeys of his era, saying:

> 'In my time you could be concussed, be knocked out in the first race, but still ride in the third and fourth. I had an incident in my latter years in the 1980s, a bad fall in the first race at Hereford and missed the rest of my rides that day because I was out of it, but I was still allowed to come home in my car. I got as far as Oxford and booked myself into a motel overnight. I never rang my wife – who was wondering what had happened to me – because I wasn't thinking straight. I woke in the morning and wondered where I was.
>
> And there were a lot more incidents of concussion for the

> generation before me. Jockeys like Michael Scudamore, Peter Pickford and Dave Dicks rode in the 1940s and 1950s, and quite a lot of them became punch drunk. That was quite noticeable and they would slur their words. They were lovely fellas and some are still around today but there was quite a lot of damage being done which wasn't being picked up on.'

Atkins had been a schoolboy boxing champion and he says he looked towards that sport for guidance:

> 'I had a liaison with the British Boxing Board of Control. I spoke to their Chief Medical Officer in London and learned more about the protocols being put into place in boxing for when a fighter got knocked out. It was a major issue for them and that's no surprise. You can ride and not receive a blow to the head, but in the ring it's inevitable within the first couple of minutes. The things we learned from that liaison influenced our views on the dangers of concussion and the approach of the Jockey Club.
>
> As safety standards improved we also had a back pad that was made of foam rubber, a kind of polystyrene that went up your back. It was shaped like your back and strapped around your waist and looked bloody horrendous! Every jockey during the 1960s was going out like the hunchback of Notre Dame. It used to move, and wasn't very good but it was a step in the right direction. John Francome developed his own version, which was like a padded vest. In fact modern body protectors are based on Francome's self-designed version.
>
> When you fell, nine times out of ten it wasn't your horse that did the damage, it was the horses behind. You'd go down in a pack. If the horse behind is airborne and you're on the floor, they've got to land on top of you if you're in their path. The main thing I tried to do was keep rolling, get into a ball and keep rolling, If you get a kick don't resist it, because the horse is much heavier than you – half a tonne of horse coming at 35mph with a jockey on board.'

So there was a skill to falling? 'Yes,' Atkins replies, 'but unfortunately you have to survive a few to work out the best way. I was always told that the moment the horse goes down to get into a ball as quickly as possible, and I learned to do that. But I still broke the majority of the bones in my body once or twice. I've broken legs, ribs, collarbone, cheekbones and my nose.'

Atkins suggests that the jump jockeys, mainly through repetition, became more adept at riding with the blows:

> 'The flat jockeys didn't expect to fall, had no meat on them and the ground was firmer – so they broke up like eggshells. Normally on the flat the fall occurred because horses had clipped heels. When that happened, the jockey tended not to let go of the horse's head, which meant that they got pulled over the top. It was their own doing. Whereas, with greater experience of falling, the jump jockey would relax his grip on the reins. He knew that the horse has got to go down to come up again to balance itself. It's an instinct. The horse will extend itself to rectify the problem.'

Nor was falling the only danger, as Atkins explains:

> 'There were collisions with the wooden running rail, and the concrete uprights. Joe Mercer's brother, Manny, was killed cantering to the start at Ascot and I believe he got unshipped and went down and hit a concrete post and it killed him. Everyone suffered. Fortunately I'm still pretty sound. I don't limp, I don't ache. Recently I went to see Timmy Norman – 'Badger' as he was known in the weighing room – who won the National for Freddie Winter, his first runner in the National. He had arthritis. And Johnny Buck is also feeling the effects; his sight is a major problem. It gets you in the end.'

When asked about the sort of medical support provided by the St John's Ambulance Brigade and Red Cross at the racecourse, Atkins recalls how it was comparatively amateurish compared to the modern era:

> 'I can always remember that they were volunteers and they looked ancient to me. There's always been a doctor on a racecourse but it felt to the jockeys in those days as though he were there purely to have a gin and tonic and if a jockey fell off it was a bloody nuisance.'

Change was required, and the tipping point that finally brought this about was two shocking incidents at Aintree.

In December 1963, 34-year-old Tim Brookshaw, a previous British jump-racing champion jockey, rode *Lucky Dora* in a hurdle race. Having jumped the first four fences without alarm the inappropriately named horse suddenly jinked to the left, sending Brookshaw crashing through the wing of the fifth hurdle. Brookshaw was taken to Walton Hospital where he underwent an operation on his spine. He was temporarily paralysed in both legs, and although he regained enough movement to participate with distinction in the Paralympic Games in Tokyo in 1964 in the discus, javelin and weight-lifting events, the accident ended his riding career.

Four months later, Paddy Farrell, 33 years old, with a wife and four children, rode in the Grand National. His mount, *Border Flight*, ploughed through The Chair, and the injured Farrell was whisked to Walton Hospital and then on to Southport Hospital. Later that evening he was visited by his wife Mary, who, having spoken to the medical staff, had to tell him that he had broken his back and wouldn't walk again.

Tragic though those incidents were, they did act as a catalyst for change. A small group of leading lights within the horse-racing community, including the legendary jockey and trainer Fred Winter and the popular journalist and amateur rider John Lawrence (later Lord Oaksey), had the idea of setting up a fund to help Brookshaw and Farrell. That unstructured germ of an idea sowed seeds that eventually led to the formal creation of the Injured Jockeys Fund (IJF), a charity that in the 50 years since has been a safety net that has caught many jockeys and their families in troubled times.

The current Chief Executive of the IJF, Lisa Hancock, elaborates:

> 'Basically, we are a charity that provides support in a financial, medical and emotional way. We have supported over a thousand beneficiaries, using £18 million of charitable expenditure. We rely on generous supporters, donations, legacies and Christmas work. We are very fortunate that the racing community has taken the IJF to its heart.'

Over the years, as it has cemented its place in the horse-racing community, the charity has evolved and developed. Typically, it leaves the medical care to professional doctors and focuses on the logistics that can overwhelm friends and family. To that end they established a national team of almoners to work with the stricken jockey and their loved ones to assess what's required in the way of support, and then to supply it. Often the charity provides significant financial benefit, including the provision of mortgages.

Nowadays, it also enables rehabilitative work at Oaksey House in Lambourn. This is not only a home for retired jockeys but also a centre that provides physiotherapy, rehabilitation treatment, medical consultations and a fully equipped gym to aid recovery. In addition, the Injured Jockeys Fund is well on its way to building another rehabilitation centre, this time in Malton in North Yorkshire.

Of course, the IJF's main focus is on jockeys (although they do devote a quarter of their workload to stable lads and grooms) and the scope of that support is ever-widening, as Hancock explains:

> 'We help in different ways. Some old jockeys have suffered head-related injuries or require hip replacements. Others suffer from arthritis. They've spent a lot of time riding out on cold, wet, wintry mornings and they all ache when they get old, even though they are as tough as old boots.
>
> We do have a number of beneficiaries who fall into gambling, drinks and drug addictions. They may have struggled with life post-jockey and that may be because they've only ever dreamt of being a jockey, and it has finished or gone wrong. In those

cases the trustees usually offer support, but we say "you've got to come to the party; we won't keep bailing you out." We'll offer help in giving them a leg-up – for instance, retraining to become a carpenter or buying a van to become a plumber.'

When Ron Atkins was a jockey, buildings like Oaksey House hadn't been thought of, let alone built, but slowly, as the 1960s became the 1970s and beyond, there was an increasing awareness that the dangers could be reduced and that the brave sportsmen and, eventually, women who put themselves in harm's way needed some TLC.

As the IJF became increasingly established and respected within the racing community, people like Ron Atkins led the charge towards change. He became safety officer of the Jockey Association, and remained in the post for 21 years. In time, he brought in high-profile allies such as Lester Piggott, who became a vice president, and banged the drum for reform in an industry that, at least to Atkins's impatient mind, was criminally

Princess Anne, Princess Royal as Patron of the Injured Jockeys Fund presents a trophy at Ascot Racecourse

slow and resistant. 'We formed a small team of safety officers, one in the north, one in the south', Atkins recalls. 'It was purely jump racing that kicked that off, but while I was in the post we created the same for flat racing. Those officers looked at any incident to see if it could have been avoided and suggested improvements to stop it from happening again.'

One area that attracted Atkins's attention was the running rails, which used to be made of wood and attached to concrete posts, and were extremely dangerous. 'We were very determined to get other uprights and get plastic rails', he explains. 'With The Jockey Club we had quite a bit of resistance and I published many an article in *Sporting Life* when I was banging on about it. I was labelled a bloody nuisance because to change would involve cost and hassle for the authorities, but you've got to remember that I was the spokesman for the lads.'

He also focused on jockey's helmets:

> 'They were changed when I was a kid. By the time I got through my apprenticeship there was a newer version that had a chin strap. It was brought across to the United Kingdom by Laurie Morgan, a three-day event rider from Australia. It suddenly hit you that things could be better. Morgan's helmet was significantly safer than before. It could stand an impact on it before it crumpled, and was made mainly of fibreglass with an inner lining and a drawstring. It was an advance, but way behind what they have today, which has no drawstring but fits the head perfectly.'

Certainly, the composition of the modern-day version of the early helmet is an improvement on the type that Atkins used to ride in. The equipment meets the current European standard and is discarded after every head injury or concussion, but the current model has been around for a while now, and work is ongoing to find ways to upgrade materials and the kit's consistency. Helmet design remains at the top of the safety agenda.

Another catalyst for change – and it seems that horse racing needs a tragedy every so often to provide fresh impetus to health and safety – was the death of the 26-year-old National Hunt jockey Richard Davis.

He was the seventh jockey to be killed in action in the last 15 years, but the circumstances surrounding his loss stood out.

Davis was riding at Southwell in July 1996 when his mount struck the first fence and capsized, landing on Davis's abdomen. His liver was torn and there was considerable damage to the vena cava, one of the two large veins that convey blood to the heart. He lost 8 pints of blood before suffering heart failure and dying on the operating table. The inquest decided that his injury was so devastating as to be 'virtually untreatable', but a Jockey Club enquiry uncovered several causes for concern, in particular the facilities at the course and the quality of the ambulance cover: it took 39 minutes for David to be transferred between ambulances, and the medical support that he received also drew criticism.

Protocols needed to improve and Dr Michael Turner – chief medical adviser for the Jockey Club and British Horseracing Authority (BHA) since 1993 – fast-tracked those of horse racing into the 21st century. Largely thanks to Turner, racecourse facilities are now much better than they were at the time of Davis's tragic demise. National Hunt has at least three ambulances in attendance at every meeting – on the flat there are two – and those ambulances follow each race on inner ring roads with paramedics and doctors onboard. On every race day, trauma-trained doctors are on duty, and when a jockey falls a doctor or paramedic must attend to them within 1 minute. Before riding again the jockey must be examined and a decision made about their fitness. All injuries are centrally recorded and reported.

As horse racing has become more professional in its approach to risk, its advances and rules about concussion have put some contact sports to shame. By raising the bar in terms of safety, horse racing has set an example and cast a spotlight on how other sports handle issues such as concussion. Now the hottest of hot topics, this matter is causing governing bodies to grow twitchier as media focus sharpens and solicitors smell blood.

Concussion can be caused either by a direct blow to the head, face or neck, or by a blow, motion or impulsive force elsewhere on the body that causes the brain to move rapidly inside the skull. The vast majority of concussions don't lead to a loss of consciousness; more typically, they cause the onset of a short-lived impairment of neurological function that resolves spontaneously. Put simply, the brain re-boots itself.

Atkins's anecdotes about the 'punch drunk' jockeys who plied their trade just after the Second World War and his own befuddled attempt to make it home after a blow to the head send an icy chill down the back when they are considered in a modern context. We now know that playing on when concussed exposes the sportsperson to further injury and possibly even death.

Fortunately the Jockey Club implemented new rules about further participation based on whether or not a rider was knocked unconscious. If they weren't, the rider was suspended from riding for 2 days; if they were, but for less than a minute, the rider was suspended for 6 days; and if they were unconscious for more than a minute, the rider was suspended for 20 days.

This was progress way beyond that made by many other sports, but even this was superseded in October 2003 when, under Dr Turner's auspices, the BHA's Concussion Protocol was introduced. This remains in place to this day and has became acknowledged as a masterpiece; one of sport's most stringent and far-sighted protocols.

The benefits of these changes are not just anecdotal; they are supported by statistics. In the ten years before its introduction – taking into account point-to-point, National Hunt and flat-racing – if a jockey fell, there was a 2.54 per cent chance that they would sustain concussion. That's one concussion in every 39 falls. Since the protocol was introduced there is now only a 2.1 per cent chance of concussion, or one concussion in every 47 falls. (As an aside, it should be noted that concussion rates are much higher for professional female jockeys, who suffer concussion once every 16 falls.)

Paul Struthers, the current Chief Executive of the Professional Jockeys Association (PJA), is full of praise for horse racing's approach to this issue and is proud when he says:

> 'Concussion protocol was so far ahead of its time and is still better than other sports or on a par – and we are looking to enhance that. Racing is quite fortunate in that, unlike rugby for instance, it's 30 minutes before jockeys can ride again, so that gives time for them to be tested for concussion. We are looking to enhance that test because, anecdotally, some who pass it might be concussed. But they are few and far between. You saw in the winter Olympics skiers with cracked helmets, having fallen while performing, being allowed to ski a day or so later. That wouldn't happen in racing because of the protocol that's been introduced.'

The protocol recognised the importance of extracting anyone who had suffered concussion from the heat of the action. Failure to do so always places the competitor at great risk and this was highlighted, two years after the new protocol had been introduced into British horse racing, by a headline-making case in 2006 pertaining to American Football.

THE CONCUSSION PROTOCOL

The Concussion Protocol contains three main features:

1. Neuro-psychological testing: jockeys have an annual, 1-hour test at a designated centre located in a hospital or GP's surgery.
2. In the event of a fall a standardised concussion assessment is undertaken by the on-site doctor.
3. If the rider is diagnosed as having concussion, he or she will have to undergo a two-part evaluation before returning to racing, normally 6 clear days after the incident occurred. This includes a repeat of the assessment and an examination by a consultant neurologist (or neurosurgeon) at one of the regional centres.

Zackery Lystedt, a 13-year-old, suffered concussion during a match in Washington, but was allowed to play on. He subsequently suffered an intracranial bleed that resulted in a severe brain injury.

Zackery, his family and medical, business and community partners lobbied the state legislature for a law to protect young athletes in all sports from returning to play too soon.

THE LYSTEDT LAW

The Lystedt Law contains three elements:

- Athletes, parents and coaches must be educated about the dangers of concussions each year.
- If a young athlete is suspected of having concussion he/she must be removed from the game or practice and not be permitted to return to play.
- A licenced health-care professional must clear the athlete to return to play in the subsequent days or weeks.

In May 2009, Washington State passed the first Zackery Lystedt Law and almost all the American states have now followed suit. Yet concussion remains a white-hot topic in sport in the modern era, primarily because of the recent awareness of a syndrome called chronic traumatic encephalopathy (CTE). The emergence of this new condition has created what many observers warn is a ticking time bomb for many sports, including horse racing.

CTE is a disease of the brain found in those who have suffered repeated brain trauma. This trauma includes multiple concussions and triggers progressive degeneration of the brain tissue, including the build-up of an abnormal protein called *tau*. These changes in the brain can begin months, years or even decades after the last concussion or the end of active athletic involvement, and are associated with memory loss, confusion, impaired judgement, paranoia, impulse-control problems, aggression, depression and, eventually, progressive dementia.

Other sports with high concussion rates – such as boxing, ice hockey, football and, particularly, rugby union and American football – have already come under the microscope. Pioneering research on American footballers published last year by Boston University demonstrated links between successive concussions and degenerative brain diseases later in life. It revealed that CTE had been found in 30 former National Football League (NFL) players who, before they died, showed symptoms similar to boxers with punch-drunk syndrome. Around 4,500 former players consequently sued the NFL, who paid out US$765 million in compensation, as well as funding further research.

Many in the know think that all sports that involve repetitive head injury are at risk of cases of CTE and that what has been publicised so far is just the tip of the iceberg. They are more people focused on the supplementary questions: how many people will be affected? How many times does someone need to be hit on the head? Are there other factors that might increase the risk?

The recent response from Dr Turner took a cautious line regarding the link between repeated impacts and CTE: 'It's not 100 per cent', he

INCIDENCE OF CONCUSSION PER 1,000 PLAYER HOURS

Football	0.4
Ice hockey	1.5
Rugby union	3.9
Australia rules	4.2
Professional boxing	13.2
Horse racing (flat)	17.1
Horse racing (jump)	25.0
Horse racing (point-to-point)	95.2

said. 'You don't have thousands of football and ice-hockey players with CTE. Is it genetic? Are some people born with a predisposition to it? Can alcohol and drug use trigger it?'

So, there are more questions than answers at the moment, but horse racing will surely come under close scrutiny, not least because concussion rates for jockeys are higher than those of other sports.

At the moment, Paul Struthers is awaiting further data and information. He says that while the body is concerned and recognises the risks relating to CTE, there is little or no firm evidence as yet to suggest that it is a major long-term mental health issue for jockeys. He explains:

> 'CTE is becoming such a big issue in contact sports such as American football and rugby. Boxers used to get it, causing dementia. It's the result of multiple concussions and jockeys suffer concussion at a rate higher than that of any other sport. Yet we don't seem to have an incidence of CTE and dementia in retired jockeys and we don't know why that is. There's no historical data and the Injured Jockeys Fund don't have a list of ex-jockeys who have to be looked after because of dementia.
>
> We know that if you've got concussion and have a second impact then that can cause major problems – and there would certainly have been many jockeys who suffered from that. Yet we are not seeing issues with CTE, depression or dementia. The only way of progressing research in this area is for ex-jockeys to donate their brains once they have died. This concept is being supported by Bob Champion and the Injured Jockeys Fund, so we'll see where the research takes us.'

This is the area in which Dr Turner, who has now left his position at the BHA, is now devoting his energies. CTE appears likely to remain in the news for a while yet; certainly it highlights that even in the enlightened modern world there is no room for complacency when it comes to safety.

Meanwhile, as CTE bubbles just beneath the surface, other issues are being addressed. For instance, Paul Struthers is particularly keen to improve the medical support given to jockeys at NHS hospitals by providing staff with footage of the fall in order to aid accurate and swift diagnosis. This measure was brought into practice as a result of the injuries sustained by Hayley Turner at the 2013 St Leger meeting, when she suffered a gasp-inducing fall. Taken by ambulance to the A&E department at the Royal Doncaster Infirmary, she had a distinctly discomforting dialogue with the medic, as she remembers: 'I was asked "what hurts?" I said "I hit the ground at 40mph, everything hurts". I needed someone from the PJA to explain that this was a proper high-speed trauma.'

X-rays failed to help the NHS consultant to diagnose Turner's broken back and fractured hips. Nor was this a one-off. Jockey Mickey Fenton was discharged from hospital after a fall and drove from Chepstow to his home in York with what was later revealed to be a broken neck. Struthers believes the NHS can occasionally let itself down and so the PJA are trialling sending footage of falls to hospital with the injured jockeys. Since introducing the trial, the PJA have reported that there have been 'six jockeys diagnosed via vertebral fractures and only one missed. One didn't get sent off with a DVD and [they] still don't know whether he's got vertebral fractures because he went to the hospital at Newcastle and he's still never had his X-rays. He's going private for scans.' Overall, the trial has been encouraging and Struthers reports that the PJA will look to formalise the procedure.

Another area of concern is the use and design of body protectors. It is compulsory for jockeys to wear current versions, which meet the European standard and are mainly designed to mitigate against rib fractures. However, work is in progress to upgrade the standard. Lisa Hancock of the Injured Jockeys Fund explains that they are currently looking at the inflatable body protectors used by eventers, which are attached with a lanyard, 'so when they fall off the saddle they are projected forwards and the body protector bursts open in Incredible Hulk style!'

Paul Struthers endorses this work while pointing out the challenges:

> 'Making them [body protectors] mandatory has undoubtedly saved jockeys' lives. It won't stop you breaking your arm or

leg but they stop a lot of bruising. The BHA and IJF have been trying to trial an inflatable vest like the ones they have in other equestrian disciplines, but the practicalities are tricky. There are several problems: they can get dislodged on the way to the start, the canister makes a noise when it goes off, plus there's the weight. So it's still work in progress.'

Aside from body protectors and other safety equipment, the Injured Jockeys Fund is helping riders to become more prepared by improving their physical conditioning and their fall technique, as Lisa Hancock clarifies:

> 'We are now much more involved with currently licensed jockeys than we were pre-Oaksey House, and are involved in their fitness and well-being. We have strength and conditioning coaches, nutritionists and a doctor all resident there, looking after jockeys past and present. So if you were to go there now you'd see the gym full of currently licensed jockeys all trying to get fitter. That's fantastic. It doesn't stop them falling but it does mean that if they do fall their bodies are in a better shape to get fitter quicker. That's our reasoning.
>
> Of course you can't eliminate the risk; obviously the more skilful you are the less likelihood there will be that you will fall, but that also applies to the horse. There are so many differing factors and influences that we wouldn't be bold enough to say that making a jockey fitter and more skilful is going to eliminate the risk.'

Hancock is right. Danger and risk are inherent within horse racing and the day-to-day life of a jockey – and the potential for a tragedy can't be extinguished.

On Monday 5 August 2013 in Darwin, Australia, Simone Montgomerie rode a horse called *Riahgrand* in the sixth race of the day. Aged 26 and a mother of two, Simone came from a noted racing family: her father, Peter Montgomerie, trained the runner-up in the 2005 Melbourne Cup. Along the home straight, without warning, her mount buckled and

Nicholas Hall wins aboard About Square *in the Simone Montgomerie Tribute during Melbourne racing at Flemington Racecourse in 2013*

she was thrown from the horse and trampled by the rest of the pack, suffering traumatic injuries. Two doctors treated her at the scene but she passed away shortly after arriving at Royal Darwin Hospital. The young mother was the 503rd jockey to die on an Australian racetrack. The remainder of the meeting was cancelled and the Darwin Turf Club donated the $200,000 prize money to a trust fund for her daughter.

The loss of Simone Montgomerie highlighted that even with all the best intentions and innovations, horse racing remains a highly dangerous sport. Although there have been improvements in safety it is not possible to bubble-wrap a rider or strap them inside a strengthened cockpit like the one that cocoons a motor-racing driver. Somewhere, soon, there will be another tragedy. It may occur in the UK, a thought that sends shudders down the spine of Paul Struthers, who says: 'we've not had a recent major, catastrophic injury on course that leads to loss of life. It's not happened in racing since young Tom Halliday died at Market Rasen in 2005, but it's the thing that I dread. Because I know it will happen, and I'm not looking forward to when it does. And it will be *when*. It won't be *if*.'

Lisa Hancock admits that the serious injuries came as a shock to her when she moved into the role and had greater exposure to this darker side of the sport:

> 'Particularly in the first two years – and we did have a run of very bad head injuries – it did make me think "Oh God, this sport is so dangerous." I'd seen the devastation for individuals and families and there was a period where I thought "Is it really worth it?" I've enjoyed racing all my life but hadn't really thought about the devastation that can come as a side effect.
>
> And then I came around in a circle because Robert Allner was injured in a car crash and he had ridden all of his life – but the injury that made a career-ending difference to him occurred in a car. So that brought reality into it.
>
> Is being a jockey worth the risk? I guess it's down to the individual. It really is. Every time you get on a horse, or even go near a horse it's a dangerous game but the enjoyment it brings is enormous and individuals have to weigh that up and make their own decisions.'

16

WASTED

On the day of the QIPCO 2000 Guinea Stakes, the 14 jockeys line up, mainly for the benefit of the cameras, just before they enter the parade ring. They do so self-consciously and impatiently, like footballers lining up to meet dignitaries before a cup final. It does, though, provide a rare opportunity to observe the race-riding elite together. The group reflects the global nature of horse racing nowadays. From France: Christophe Lemaire, Olivier Peslier, Christophe Soumillon and Mickael Barzalona. Andrea Atzeni from Sardinia. Frankie Dettori, almost a naturalised Englishman, but born in Italy. Kieren Fallon, Joseph O'Brien and Richard Hughes from Ireland.

The majority stand at around 5 feet 4–5 inches in height, so the eye is naturally drawn to the Gullivers in the land of Lilliput. These include 21-year-old Joseph O'Brien, who is 6 feet tall. It will be a challenge for him to sustain a long-term career as a jockey on the flat, although the 41-year-old Dubliner Richard Hughes is only 2 inches shorter, and he has conquered long odds to do just that, racing since 1996 and, over the past two seasons, becoming British flat-racing champion jockey.

The sight of Hughes's pencil-slim frame this day in Newmarket brings to mind a caricature of Fred Archer, more than a hundred years ago, who was also 5 feet 10 inches tall and went through agonies to restrict his weight before he eventually committed suicide.

Fred Archer's regime was, out of what he saw as professional necessity, brutal. When he won his first race at the age of 12 he weighed just 4st 11lb; in his first championship season his weight had risen to 6st and by the time he finished growing he struggled to make 8st 7lb.

He became very tall for a jockey, particularly in the Victorian era, and during the winter filled out to 11st. As a result, his career became an ongoing, irreconcilable conflict between his talent and the length of his frame.

In order for Archer to shed weight, a Newmarket doctor prepared him a special concoction that became known as 'Archer's mixture'. One teaspoonful was enough to consign anyone else to a lengthy stay in the nearest lavatory; Archer drank it by the sherry glassful. His diet during the season consisted of castor oil, a biscuit and a small glass of champagne at midday. If he ate a good dinner, his weight ballooned by 3–4lb, but he could lose 6lb in two days when it was most needed. Certainly he had to fast even more than his peers.

Back in the present, by the normal rules of nature Hughes should be too tall and too heavy to meet the weights required to be a jockey but, like Archer, his talent and his desire to race-ride has encouraged him to fight the unequal fight.

Like Archer, this ongoing battle against his weight has taken him to some dark places and, without doubt, there has been a personal cost – though not, thankfully, such a terminal price as the one Archer paid. In his revelatory autobiography, Hughes explains that he mistakenly used alcohol to manage his weight and, in time, became an alcoholic. It wasn't the only way that he wasted his emaciated body. By his own admission he has also supplemented a day-to-day diet of nicotine, caffeine and chocolate with so many 'pee pills' (diuretics that flush liquid out of the body) that he became almost immune to them. The task cannot be getting any easier, and few can fully appreciate the daily deprivation that Hughes endures so that he can ride horses of the quality of *Toormore* in the 2000 Guineas.

Of course, it's no mean feat to ride a highly trained, highly strung racehorse in competition. In a few minutes *Toormore* will stretch out down the Rowley Mile at a speed that will peak at 40mph. On top of the horse, Hughes will perch precariously on short stirrups, with just the insides of his feet and ankles in contact with the animal. The minimum requirements just to complete the course will be a combination of tactical nous, technique, strength, balance, concentration and cardio-vascular fitness, but to give the horse the best chance to win Hughes needs to be full of vim, vitality and vigour; fit, focused and at the top of his game.

It doesn't require much imagination to appreciate the debilitating impact that dizziness, weakness, tiredness, slow reactions, anxiety, fatigue or visual distortion could have on a jockey's ability to ride at all, let alone well. Yet the day-to-day dietary habits of many riders make these sensations an all-too-familiar reality. Most feel they have no choice but to almost starve themselves.

The most obvious explanation of why this happens can be found in black and white within the rules of horse racing – and, in particular, the handicapping system that has been in place as long as the sport has existed. The aim of these regulations has always been to handicap the better horses by requiring them to carry more weight. That way, all should have an equal chance of winning, evening out the field – making the races more competitive, difficult to predict, and encouraging that essential part of the sport's prosperity: gambling.

To achieve this equality, in many races each runner is allocated a weight or *handicap* to carry on their back based on their ability and past performances. When the weight of the jockey – and their equipment – falls under the required amount then the balance is made up with extra mass; if, however, jockeys weigh in above the required value then they have committed the cardinal sin. There is not one owner or trainer who would voluntarily want their horse to carry more than the handicapper dictates.

And, of course, from race to race the target weight changes. A jockey may ride, say, five times in a day and all the events could require different weights. So every time he or she steps on the scales (and they may do that up to 28 times a day) the pressure is on.

If a jockey fails to make the weight, word soon gets round and trainers and owners will ditch him or her in favour of another who can achieve the target. It's the slipperiest of slopes and, once a rider starts to find it hard to stick to the correct weight, it may be a good time to consider a different profession. Fewer rides means less income and a career heading south. Jockeys' financial security depends on their ability to take light rides at minimum notice.

So the lighter riders are the better. It's been this way since the days of Samuel Chifney Senior in the 18th century, placing a physical and psychological burden on race-riders. The jockey's lifestyle is one of sacrifice that few would entertain. Even if they are naturally diminutive in stature, almost everyone is required to deny their body the nutrients and hydration it demands and maintain it a level that is significantly leaner and lighter than nature intended. Some look skeletal to the point of anorexic, their waxwork faces pale, gaunt and sallow.

Of course, jockeys are not the only athletes who battle against the scales. Boxers, wrestlers and rowers – to name but three other groups – have targets to hit, but it's an unfair comparison because jockeys – more akin to willowy, pencil-thin supermodels – have no respite. They weigh out 30 minutes prior to each race and weigh in immediately after. Minutes later the cycle begins again with the next race. There's no opportunity to refuel or rehydrate. This gruelling process is not one that is experienced by boxers, for instance, who weigh in just once, 24 hours before a fight.

Nor do many jockeys have an off-season during which they can feed up. Both on the flat and over fences the seasons are lengthy and many jockeys work all year round. Yes, flat racing is at its height in summer, but in winter all-weather racing takes place and several jockeys compete abroad in Dubai, Hong Kong, the USA and the like. The requirement to go hungry is present 24/7 and pretty much 365 days a year. No wonder it nags away at the mind as well as the body.

This relentless battle has, to a degree, been rewarded and glamourised by owners, trainers and the media within the racing industry. And the quirky, extreme methods of weight management have long been a cause of amused curiosity by horse-racing followers.

Back in the 19th century, Jem Robinson liked a party, and his winter extravagances invariably saw his weight balloon up to nearly 10st, but he could fall 2st in a month by swallowing 'physics' and undertaking marathon walks in heavy clothing. The weight dripped off, but Robinson was often discovered feeling faint and had to be taken home in a cart.

In more recent times, Lester Piggott – nicknamed 'The Long Fellow' – also found height a curse, like Archer. Although Piggott started small – the 12-year-old tipped the scales at 6st 9lb when he won his first race in 1948 – six years later, when he won his first classic, he was a lofty 5 feet 7½ inches and weighed 8st 5lb. So Piggott had to watch the pounds more than most. Early in his career he went for the short-term fix. He admitted: 'My solution was to wear a plastic running suit, which covered me from foot to neck, and turn the heater in the car on full blast. I got my weight down but my passengers didn't always enjoy their lifts.'

In time, however, Piggott came to rely on a regime of a thin slice of toast with black coffee for breakfast, a sandwich for lunch and an evening meal of tongue and salad. Occasionally he indulged in a dollop of ice cream, a block of chocolate or half a glass of champagne. He drank no more than a pint of liquid each day and smoked three or four appetite-suppressing cigars. He once said: 'I never let myself get heavy, even in winter because I'm afraid I'll never get it off ... I don't eat potatoes, rice or bread. You can take dehydration pills and lose 2–3lb in a few hours but they are bound to affect the kidney and liver.'

With hindsight, Piggott's long-term attitude towards weight loss seems considered. More recently Frankie Dettori admitted in his autobiography, *Frankie*, that he was not averse to taking shorter-cuts to drop weight:

> 'Over the years I've tried various dire methods to lose unwanted pounds, including laxatives and pee pills. They all work for a time but the horrible side-effects make you pay and can seriously damage your health. Most mornings I needed to lose 3lb before going racing. I did it with a mixture of running, walking, sweating in the sauna and working out in the gym. When I had

> to lose weight in a hurry as a youngster the first thing I tried was laxatives. They work fine by clearing you out quickly. But you end up feeling a bit weak and light-headed, and if you use them regularly you start to suffer from the most agonizing stomach cramps.'

In the educated, enlightened 21st century you might expect the sport's governing body to have pinpointed the potential threat this kind of dieting poses to riders' well-being and to have adjusted the rules of the sport accordingly. You might also reasonably believe that the prehistoric approach to weight loss adopted by the likes of Fred Archer would have long ago been consigned to ancient history, replaced instead by the appliance of sports science and a holistic approach. The truth is, these assumptions are both right and wrong.

The modern-day, recently refined regulations state that the minimum weight carried in flat racing is 8st, and for National Hunt it is 10st. This minimum requirement for the flat leaves Britain trailing behind Ireland, Australia and the USA – where the minimum weight is either 8st 4lb or 8st 7lb – but in line with France. More typically, a jockey is usually required to ride at between 8st and just over 9st. Prior to a race, a rider must weigh out fully clothed at the target amount. In addition to the jockey's mass the weigh-out (and weigh-in) includes the mass of the riding boots, saddle, jockey's skull cap, whip, horse's bridle, plates, blinkers, hood, visor, eye shield or eye cover and anything worn on the horse's legs. A 2lb allowance is given for the jockey's body protector.

To sustain a living in either code, most jockeys want to be available to ride on or around these minimum weights. If they can't do this then they are denying themselves rides and income. It doesn't help that the human species has evolved to become taller and bigger, with the mean weight of a member of the British population rising at a rate of 1lb every three years. Currently, the average adult British male weighs 13½st. Of course, some of that figure reflects the trend towards a more sedentary lifestyle and over-indulgence, and riders are generally more diminutive in height than the norm – but the difference between the nation's average weight and the ideal for a professional flat-racing jockey is still at least 5st; by modern standards, a jockey needs to match the average weight of a 14-year-old boy.

In this context, it is understandable that the regulations that set the minimum weights were described – albeit before the 2lb increase in minimum weight in 2013 – by informed judges as being 'archaic, arbitrary and potentially dangerous'. Minimum weights, the argument goes, are not keeping pace with the evolution of the human body.

It is perhaps no surprise, then, that research suggests that only one in ten flat-racing jockeys can comfortably ride at the minimum weight (it's one reason why more females, who tend to be naturally lighter, are entering the profession), while most jump-racing jockeys make their required weight only after wasting and hours in the sauna.

Two-thirds of jockeys reported that they struggled with weight and the majority identified it as the most challenging aspect of their professional life. So most riders follow a dull, unrelenting routine that messes with their minds and bodies.

WEIGHT MANAGEMENT STRATEGIES EMPLOYED BY RIDERS

This data is taken from a survey of modern riders on which methods they use to manage their weight.

Additional exercise	98%
Riding exercise	96%
Sauna use	78%
Food restriction	74%
Fluid restriction	64%
Exercising in a sweat suit	59%
Exercising in a hot environment	41%

Many jockeys also said that they smoked and some drank alcohol to excess. Alcohol has little nutritional value, may impair rehydration and glycogen storage after exercise, and, when heavy drinking is combined with smoking, it can lead to poor bone health and fragility that increases the risk of fractures. The same is true of restrictive diets.

Despite these data, a recent assessment of over 40 Irish apprentice jockeys highlighted a chasm between what they should be eating and drinking and the reality.

TWO EXAMPLES OF DAILY DIETS OF APPRENTICE JOCKEYS

Apprentice one, who aims to weigh 8st 6lb, reported s/he followed a typical diet of:

Breakfast – tea with whole milk and two sugars; sausage roll
Main meal – take-away chicken curry and rice; apple; glass of whole milk
Evening meal – chicken roll and coleslaw; three chocolate biscuits; tea with two sugars.

Apprentice two, who aims to weigh 8st 4lb, listed:

Breakfast – ham; Capri-Sun
Mid-morning – energy drink; bar of chocolate
Main meal – chicken, stuffing and mayonnaise sandwich on white bread; one can of energy drink
Afternoon – small chocolate bar
Evening meal – chicken stir fry with noodles; water
Before bed – cup of tea; plain biscuit

On race days both jockeys had a breakfast consisting of orange juice and chocolate bar, then nothing until they ate a take-away on the way home at the end of the day.

With help, both apprentices have since reduced the amount of calories and fat in their intake; but there will be others who won't. Of the three out of four British jockeys who restrict their food intake, several adopt diets that wouldn't be approved by a nutritionist. They fail to meet the recommended daily allowance for nutrients, with not enough fruit and vegetables included and too much fast-food being consumed. Nearly half of those surveyed regularly consumed chocolate, sweets or biscuits at least once per day.

Richard Perham, jockey coach at the British Racing School, is not surprised: 'I know that the mentality of some jockeys would be to say "I've worked my socks off today. I've taken 4lb off in the bath, I've taken another 2lb off in the sauna at the races and I've had a bad day – so I'm going to have a beer and a packet of crisps on the way home."'

Of course a lack of nutrients deprives their body of what it needs and can lead to fatigue, physical weakness and poor reactions, which are all detrimental to a rider's performance in the saddle and downright dangerous for those who frequently drive hundreds of miles to race meetings. The consequence is that when faced with the boring and unpleasant demands of constant wasting some have turned to short-term, hard-core options: 'flipping' and the use of laxatives.

Flipping involves self-induced vomiting. This was once so prevalent in the USA that some racetracks (the iconic Churchill Downs included) had specific 'heaving bowls' installed to accommodate jockeys before a race. At such a course, there might have been a row of toilet cubicles with, at the end, one designated for flipping that contained a bowl rather than a toilet seat. Most riders would 'flip' by sticking a finger down their throats, while the bodies of others become so used to the process that just standing at the bowl was enough to induce vomiting.

Frankie Dettori confirmed his experience of it:

> 'A lot of jockeys in the States are in the habit of throwing up, or "flipping" as we call it, after a meal. It's a drastic method of eating well and not putting on weight afterwards. Steve Cauthen used to do it from time to time when he was here and I throw up

> occasionally too. When you are wasting hard all the time you get to the point where you will go nuts if you don't eat a proper meal. So you dive into a big plate of food aware that you will then have to lose 4lb in a hurry. Flipping is the easiest way to do it.'

Walter Swinburn, another top jockey, admitted: 'Eating for me was not very pretty. I had it down to a fine art. The whole idea is that you drank fizzy drinks when you bolted [your food] and I knew how to get it back up within minutes. The more dehydrated you were the easier it was to get it up.'

If the whole flipping concept sounds absurd, then imagine you are a typical journeyman jockey trying to maintain a weight that is well below what nature intended for you. Maybe, like most of us, you enjoy your food. Maybe, given a free choice, you prefer chocolate to fruit, crisps to salad, and beer to water. Maybe, at times, you get hungry and lack the willpower to resist the healthy option of meeting your body's needs. So, when your career rests on you making a light weight – ironically putting food on the table for your family – perhaps you too might opt for the short-term option that you know is bad for you. Perhaps you too would pay a visit to the toilet and flip?

How many jockeys take this route? This is difficult to judge. Research may be misleading because jockeys are concerned that this practice would be viewed unfavourably and don't own up to doing it. Most informed judges will tell you that there was a period when it was rife and that it still occasionally happens now.

Paul Struthers, Chief Executive of the Professional Jockeys Association, feels however that the trend in Britain is towards a more enlightened approach:

> 'I don't doubt that there are some people out there using old-fashioned methods to manage weight but they are in the massive minority. With regards to flat jockeys – are some of them still flipping? Well, we know they are. There are some. It worries me. We gets things reported back to us informally and through that informal reporting the numbers are small – whether that's

jockeys who are flipping or jockeys who might use drink to manage weight. It's less than one or two per cent. Several, less than a handful, probably some we don't know about. But we're told in confidence so we can't go up to them and we try to educate indirectly.'

No doubt Struthers is right about the fact that the new breed of rider is more professional, but the minority that he mentions remains a concern because flipping is a step along the pathway to bulimia and anorexia, and has severe potential side effects: decayed teeth, caused by frequent exposure to stomach acids; water retention, swelling and abdominal bloating; acute stomach distress; swallowing difficulties and rupture of the oesophagus.

In addition, it is thought that some jockeys have used laxatives or diuretics, though it is difficult to know exactly how many as these substances are currently banned under the rules of racing in the UK, and their use is veiled in secrecy. Dettori has admitted in the past that he once dabbled in this area. In his autobiography, he admitted:

'I tried Lasix, which is the same as a pee pill. You take a tablet – the same type used to stop horses breaking blood vessels. It's easy, too easy, that way because you can lose 4lb of body fluid in an hour. Compare that to the four or five hours you'd need to spend in the sauna to have the same effect. But Lasix also has nasty side effects, including sudden cramps, particularly in your feet and calves.'

Dettori was right about the side effects. Lasix is a diuretic generally used to treat cognitive heart failure, but it can cause damage to the colon and the liver as well as that eternal enemy of the jockey: dehydration.

Most jockeys suffer from a lack of the most abundant and crucial component of the human body: water. Water should comprise 50 per cent of body-fat weight, 60 per cent of body weight and 65–75 per cent of muscle mass; it is essential for health and performance. When there isn't sufficient fluid present in the body to maintain these levels, dehydration can occur.

Certain levels of dehydration are tolerable, but it is unlikely that jockeys can ever physically adjust to high degrees of dehydration. They may get used to the tiredness and persistent thirst but there are other, more serious, side-effects relating to their mental and physical state and, as a result, their ability to perform at their best. These include the part of the brain that controls attention, wakefulness, thought, memory and perception.

Much of the dehydration is self-induced in the equine world. Sunken-eyed jockeys deliberately and systematically remove fluid from their bodies. This is often because of a short-term need to make a weight, rather like last-minute revision before an exam. They run in a sweat suit, drip in the sauna, soak in a burning-hot bath, drive in a car with the heater at full blast, take a pee pill or a laxative, or simply resist the temptation to quench a raging thirst. All of this wrings out juices from the body; not just water, but important salts such as sodium, potassium, magnesium, calcium, zinc and iron.

These short-term fixes might solve their immediate problem that day, but what about tomorrow? Research in 2001 suggested that most jockeys were habitually dehydrated and nine out of ten had 'high to severe' levels of dehydration on race days. In addition, because of the need to maintain their weight throughout the race day, there was no opportunity for them to rehydrate prior to or during the event.

No wonder, then, that there have been numerous reports of jockeys who are unable to see straight after a race and stumble into the weighing room, notably in the USA, where the race weights have hardly changed in the last 50 years. This has given rise to tragic stories, such as the one of 22-year-old apprentice jockey Emmanuel Jose Sanchez, who fell into a coma on the floor of the shower after a ride and died later in hospital. A month earlier, after a win that was the high point of his career, it was observed that he was so unsteady after crossing the finishing line that he needed help guiding the horse into the winner's circle.

Severe dehydration was Emmanuel's killer, and was also a factor in the death of 31-year-old James Herrell. According to his bereaved fiancée, he spent an excessive amount of time in the sauna – or 'hot box' as it is known in the States – overused pee pills and was in the habit of flipping his food up to 15 times a day. Sanchez and Herrell deprived their bodies of nutrients and fluid to such a degree that they could no longer function – and the consequences were tragic.

Of course the challenge for jockeys is two-fold. Not only do they need to make the weight while maintaining athletes' physiques, but at one and the same time they need to be, to use the modern parlance, 'in a good place' in their heads. The two requirements are not always compatible.

Any sports' performer will tell you that being 'in a good place' helps an athlete achieve peak performance and results, yet the torment and tyranny of constantly weight-watching is more likely to create the opposite emotional states, including: anxiety; anger; irritability; fatigue; confusion; tension; mood swings; short-term memory loss; and difficulty in concentrating and maintaining mental alertness. Exhaustion and lethargy, irritability and difficulty sleeping are all identified as being part of general anxiety disorder.

Research suggests these symptoms can have an impact upon performance, relationships and overall well-being, particularly when exacerbated by the other challenges that are part of the job of being a jockey: endless travelling; concerns about where the next rides are coming from; the never-ending pressure to win; the threat of future injuries and the challenge of recovering from past ones; the preservation of links with trainers and owners; and, of course, the need to keep beating the scales.

Is it any wonder that jockeys – particularly flat-racing jockeys – are not always seen as being the 'life and soul' of a party? If their race-day demeanour in the paddock is more akin to that of an undertaker than a clown, then they can point to a host of extenuating circumstances. They are probably undernourished, on edge and living off adrenalin. On average, pretty much all of the jockeys who go into the paddock to receive last-minute instructions from owners and trainers will be hungry; some will feel moody and on edge and a couple may be fighting a day-today struggle with some form of depression. Yes, they are about to receive an injection of the addictive drug of high-speed sporting competition and, for one lucky rider, the ultimate thrill of success – but it's just a short-term fix.

Frankie Dettori explains in *Frankie*: 'When you are sitting in a sauna for hours on end, boiling away unwanted pounds, your craving for these things [food and drink] dominates your thinking. Of course when you give in to temptation all your hard work is undone. That's why some jockeys who live in the sauna eventually become so miserable.'

This has been the case down the decades. As Peter O'Sullevan said of Lester Piggott, 'the austere regime further isolated him his fellow men, promoted irritability, and fostered the gunfighter's delusion of being above the law'.

Little wonder that prolonged wasting can encourage addictions and depression. It preys on the mind. If you constantly deny yourself something that you know you need, then it can end up becoming a craving that drives you to distraction. Paul Struthers recognises that the sport need to acknowledge this hazard:

> 'We're aware of some issues in relation to drink, drugs and depression within the sport. I'm aware of one or two drink- or drug-related issues with younger jockeys and we try to help when we get wind of someone with a problem. We have outstanding counsellors available to the industry and usually close friends and family are aware and help. But the British Horseracing Authority's testing regime on course – with 500 breath and urine samples taken a year – would pick up misuse and we haven't had a positive sample for a while.'

Perhaps the potential for depression is of greater concern. High depression, tension and confusion scores have been found in elite rowers during periods of rapid weight loss. What of horse racing? Paul Struthers certainly has this on the Professional Jockeys Association's radar, not least because he admits he has suffered personally:

> 'With regard to depression, we know that one in four people every

year will suffer from some form of mental illness (that's not just feeling down for a few days) and if you think about the lifestyle of an average jockey – restricted diet; restricted hydration; tricky finances; risk of injury; often carrying an injury; long days; lots of travelling; constant uncertainty about your future; going from high-adrenalin moments of riding to long drives home on the motorway; public scrutiny and criticism, particularly in this day and age of social media and with two dedicated broadcasters

Sweating it out. Jockey Richard Winant sits in the sauna at Boston's Suffolk Downs trying to make weight

> devoted to horse racing – all the evidence suggests they should suffer from mental-health and well-being issues more than is normal. But as yet there's no evidence of it. I suspect people who are suffering keep it to themselves, so I don't think we currently know.'

You suppose it is an area that Struthers and his team will continue to research and investigate, but for now, if jockeys face this very real danger to their health and emotional state, why don't more adopt a more forward-looking, scientific approach to weight management?

Few are better placed to judge the reasons for this than Daloni Lucas. Lucas has a background working in the NHS and is grounded in professional rugby, and she recently graduated from the University of Bath with a MSc in sports physiotherapy, for which she researched the human physiological demands of horse racing. She is now hoping to continue the research and work towards a PhD by further investigating the physiological demands, epidemiology and injury-prevention aspects of the profession.

Lucas has also become one of the sport's foremost physiotherapists and currently works extensively for the Injured Jockeys Fund. Although she had an equestrian background, Lucas is comparatively new to the culture within horse racing and admits it was a shock: 'Coming from a rugby background with an emphasis on creating a lifestyle that supports performance and fitness, I've found in racing that although these jockeys work hard, their lifestyles, in many cases, completely contradict what they are trying to achieve.'

She cites the fact that so many jockeys smoke and drink as being contributing factors in this unhealthy lifestyle, but is most vocal about their eating habits:

> 'To some extent the day-to-day lifestyle of jockeys results in them making poor food choices. They are often too tired to cook and eating what is readily available affected what they ate most frequently. Racing takes place in the afternoons and also in the evenings in summer months. Jockeys are therefore likely

> to eat very little in the morning prior to racing and then choose the most convenient and quickest meal in the evenings following racing as they are likely to be very hungry having eaten very little during the day. Ninety-two per cent of jockeys missed lunch on race days, which is likely to be due to the timing of races and their need to maintain a low body weight to make their racing weight.'

Lucas adds that the food available at the racecourse is the most convenient option for jockeys, but suggests that what's on offer to them at most racecourses is out of kilter with what they need:

> 'Racing will say it is sensitive to the needs and well-being of jockeys but more research needs to be done. I think we've missed a trick. Often the food on the racecourses is not desirable. We can tell a racecourse that we want fresh produce, fresh chicken and the like and they provide turkey twisters because they're cheap. Racing is a business as well and racecourses have budgets to adhere to.
>
> Jockeys need convenience because of their lifestyle, because they are up early and on the road. So they might stop at motorway services for a pasty. It would be so much better if they could prepare something more nutritious the night before, but that might seem like too much effort when you got up at five in the morning and you're tired. That's why racecourse food is important – because it's their opportunity to refuel on good nutrition rather than crap.'

But Lucas does not apportion all of the blame to racecourses. Ultimately, the jockeys need to take responsibility for their eating habits and she thinks there is work to be done:

> 'We're all working towards changing the culture in racing. We are trying to move forward the weight-control measures that are currently in place so that jockeys are more educated about their weight-management and become healthier.
>
> But there is a certain type of person in racing. They have been

brought up in a certain way and are not aware of other lifestyle practices. They follow their role models. There is a historical culture and people conform when they see someone they've always aspired to have healthy eating and drinking habits. They aspire to these people, so they follow their ways.

I know firsthand from dealing with current jockeys that they almost become conditioned to that feeling of dehydration and when they have wasted for a ride and dehydrated and they've been successful that reinforces that practice. It felt good. So they do it again and again. It's that feel-good factor. They get into a cycle of binge–purge–dehydration.

At 5 per cent dehydration your reaction times are affected along with your ability to concentrate. It's the way that a lot of these jockeys manipulate their weight and this is what we are trying to change. It's the easy option. We've discussed the possibility of getting fitness equipment at a racecourse so they could do something proactive rather than sit in a sauna and sweat.'

Jockey coach Richard Perham supports Lucas's views and shares some of her frustrations:

'There is a culture to get through and a stigma if you are seen to be eating the right foods. When I was riding – and it still happens particularly with the senior boys – many jockeys would opt for diuretics, laxatives, vomiting, saunas, driving to the races for 2 hours with the heater on full blast at 32°C (89.6°F), with a sauna suit on, with a ski suit on, wearing a bobble hat and gloves to sweat the weight off. That was after having spent a couple of hours in the sauna and an hour in the bath and maybe done some running.

We try to promote good practice, but the reality of course is that 95 per cent of jockeys would be at least a stone beneath their natural body weight. When I was a jockey, every single day I would go to the sauna and sweat off 2–3lb in the sauna, I'd have something to drink and eat but I'd be back to square one the next day. It's not quite so prevalent nowadays, I'd guess there would be a more mature attitude. Weights have gone up so that's making life easier. The alternative that we are advocating is to be on a consistently good diet. We want jockeys to think "I've got my cool box in the boot with some prawns and some chicken, salad and vegetables to pick up with a bottle of hydrating liquid." It's not rocket science to figure out which approach will work best, but that isn't always the chosen option.'

Lucas and Perham know that these strategies are driven by a herd instinct and cultural trends. In the past, the norm has been to adopt disordered eating and unhealthy weight-loss practices. Jockeys tended to follow their peers and learnt to tolerate persistent thirst and hunger, accepting them as a part of their lifestyles. All racecourses have saunas installed and there was a camaraderie and ritual surrounding jockeys and sauna use. So, damaging ways of losing weight became an entrenched and accepted aspect of the sport.

Slowly that appears to be changing. With virtually no downtime or off-seasons for jockeys, Lucas sees convalescence periods following injury as her opportunity to get in the jockey's ear and broaden their thinking:

'When you are looking to rehabilitate someone from a fracture, for example, that's when I see the opportunity to start from scratch. If they've had a poor diet and they smoke then the chances are that their bone density is going to be reduced, so this is your opportunity say "right, now is the time to change. Let's get you involved with a nutritionist, let's get you down the right pathway."

Lads that have been injured have adopted more positive self-management and seen the benefits. We want jockeys to be healthier, fitter and have longevity – and we want to see a decrease in injury rates. Of course, when jockeys eat better and tire less they are far more likely to make the correct decisions in the saddle and less likely to fall or experience some other

> negative consequence.
>
> Jim Crowley is an ex-jump jockey who went on to the flat. He's addressed how he manages himself. He exercises, he diets, he supplements his intake with protein and he will tell you that this is the best he's felt. His self-management is more in keeping with other sports. Noel Fehily is another who is very proactive.'

In the past few years there appears to have been a shift in thinking. The likes of Crowley and Fehily – established pros with a desire to learn and improve – have reaped the rewards. They are being watched and copied by others. Apprentice jockeys, making their way in the sport, are receiving informed and helpful advice from coaches, mentors and the racing authorities. And the sport's elite role models – AP McCoy, Ryan Moore and Richard Johnson, among others – are setting a positive example.

Yet for all Daloni Lucas's optimism – and the admirable efforts of the Injured Jockeys Fund, the British Racing School, the British Horseracing Authority and the Professional Jockeys Association – she knows the culture within horse racing is centuries-old and reform will happen more slowly than she or the authorities would like:

> 'While in recent years research has enabled a greater understanding of the pressures and demands placed upon jockeys, it appears that this knowledge has not fully filtered down to the jockeys themselves, particularly young jockeys at the start of their career.
>
> More support and information should be provided to young jockeys at the start of their careers to prevent them damaging themselves. This is a controversial thing to say, but although people will tell you that this "waste and flip" culture doesn't exist in modern-day racing, when you are there on the ground you know that it does. It is the easy option, and until we change attitudes and educate more people that won't change significantly. Old habits die hard, don't they?'

PART 5
ANATOMY OF A JOCKEY

There can be few more demanding professions than being a professional jockey. Does any other athlete require such a broad range of skills, knowledge and mental attributes? Few need to be so brave, so fit, to work so hard and to sacrifice so much. Then there's the ability to coax a half-tonne racehorse to run or jump to its best.

Despite these challenges, thousands of young hopefuls aspire to be the next AP McCoy or Ryan Moore. Of course, almost all fall by the wayside. Only the crème de la crème, the best of the best, make it. Without a deep-rooted desire there is no point in even setting out on the expedition – and even with a bellyful of ambition there are innumerable pitfalls and challenges to negotiate.

In truth, most aspiring jockeys will just have a passing, vague interest in getting to the top that they never act upon with any conviction. Some will ride in their youth but take it no further; others will progress to become stable lads and lasses but ultimately decide it's not for them, or fall short of the mark.

By this stage, the vast majority of wannabe champions have been weeded out. Some, though, do earn a licence to become an apprentice or conditional jockey and ride against the pros. And some even get beyond claiming an allowance and become a bona fide professional. By then, only the elite remain, yet there are still three more rungs of the ladder to climb before a rider can become the new McCoy or Moore.

The first of these tiers is the one inhabited by those who turn pro and, for a couple of years, are regulars on the circuit, but can't quite make it work. The level above that is inhabited by sound, steady, solid pros who make a long-term living out of racing without hitting the headlines. Then, as we approach the summit, we find the stars, those elite jockeys who regularly compete at events such as the Derby, the Grand National, the Cheltenham Gold Cup, the Kentucky Derby and the Melbourne Cup. And, at last, comes nose-bleed territory, the stratospheric final pinnacle that is home of the icons whose names are writ large in the legend of the sport.

What characteristics define how far each aspirant reaches on this journey – and how long he or she can stay at that level? Of course, it's not an exact science but this part explores some of the key factors, primarily in the company of five specialists who are well placed to appreciate what it takes.

Martin Lane – Born in Kilworth, County Cork, Ireland, 25-year-old Lane moved to England in 2009, whereupon he experienced immediate success, becoming champion apprentice on the flat in 2010. Lane is one of the new breed of jockey – a smart thinker, professional and keen to learn – and has established himself on the professional circuit.

Michael Caulfield – Universally known in the horse-racing community as 'Corky', Caulfield is the former Chief Executive of the Professional Jockeys Association and now a successful sports psychologist, based in Lambourn, Berkshire, England. More than most he understands how jockeys think.

Steve Smith-Eccles – A former National Hunt jockey, Smith-Eccles now coaches and mentors jockeys. He had 900 winners, riding for the likes of Harry Thomson-Jones and Nicky Henderson in a career that stretched from 1970 to 1994. He was known as a livewire in the weighing room.

Dale Gibson – Former jockey over the flat, primarily in the North, Gibson had 9,700 rides and 528 winners across a 24-year career. He is highly respected within the racing community for his dedication and professionalism, and now works for the Professional Jockeys Association.

Richard Perham – Former jockey, now Senior Jockey Coach at the British Racing School, Perham trains and assesses the majority of aspiring jockeys, both amateur and pro, for National Hunt and the flat.

17

HORSE-SENSE

The first characteristic required by a rider, horse-sense, is both fundamental and intangible. All professional jockeys can ride a horse competently. They can coax it to start, stop, turn left, turn right, go quicker and slow down – and ride in the textbook shape of a cocktail glass with their head, elbows and heels in a vertical line. But that's not enough. They also require the ability to 'read' the horse and be sensitive to its quirks and foibles. They need to be able to encourage it to race at approaching 40mph or jump National Hunt fences. In racing parlance, they need to be able to 'get a tune out of it', regardless of its character and personality.

American journalist Jim Murray outlined the requirement in prosaic terms in Bert Sugar and Cornell Richardson's book *Horse Sense*: 'You have to be half-man, half-animal to be a jockey. You have to, in a sense, be able to think like a horse. You have to sense his mood, gauge his courage, cajole him into giving his best.'

Former jockey Dale Gibson cites Ryan Moore (flat) and AP McCoy (jumps) as master craftsmen of this art:

> 'Ryan Moore is probably the best jockey in the world at the moment – that's not to undermine what Richard Hughes has done – and he's got the whole package. He's absolutely world-class. He can transmit that feeling to the horse and makes riding look effortless. AP McCoy has a sixth sense, knowing what he wants the horse to do during the race and nine times out of ten the horse responds, often making an average jumper better and generally ending up in the winners' enclosure. He is a remarkable jockey.'

Of course the critical question that an aspiring jockey might ask is whether this ability to 'transmit' is something riders such as Moore and McCoy have to be born with. When people talk of a jockey being 'natural' or 'gifted' was it always in their blood, in their DNA? If you haven't got *it* – whatever *it* is – then can you ever get it?

Certainly it's not just the thoroughbreds in horse racing that have good genes. Many jockeys, too, follow in family footsteps. Take Lester Piggott, for instance. The achievements of his ancestors, such as John Barham Day, Tom Cannon and Ernie Piggott, illuminate a family tree that outlines a dynasty of eight generations of trainers and jockeys across both codes. In racing terms, he is more blue-blooded than the racehorses that he rode. Did this bloodline contribute to Lester's recognised genius as a rider?

Two-time British flat-racing champion jockey Charlie Elliott once said that he thought it 'true to a large extent that great jockeys are born, not made, that the ability to communicate with a horse so that he'll run for you, give you his maximum, is some kind of natural gift'. However, he also acknowledged that jockeys had:

> 'to work to develop it and ... have a lot of self-confidence to make the most of it on the big occasion. What it is that makes one jockey so much better than another at getting a racehorse to do its best, I defy anyone to define ... at the end of the day there's a lot of mystery. There's something strange and marvellous that happens between the horse and certain men who get on his back and you can't explain it, you can only demonstrate it by getting up on the animal.'

Former National Hunt jockey Steve Smith-Eccles believes that some aspects of becoming a jockey are intuitive and can't be taught, but he says it's not all about bloodlines:

> 'I see lots of jockeys, trainers and owners who have sons and daughters who can have any amount of practice and still can't ride for toffee. They might be able to get from A to B but they haven't got that natural talent.

> Now if that natural talent isn't there, it doesn't matter how much coaching you give them, you can't bring it out. There are jockeys with natural talent, natural flair because they are born with it. It's like musicians. If you've got an inner ability, it can be brought out and finely tuned, but if it's not there to begin with, you can forget it. The ones with natural flair do things so easily; they do it without thinking about it; it's second nature. You don't have to tell them or coach them.'

He reflects on his own experience to elaborate the point. Born in a mining village in Derbyshire, the only horse he'd sat on before starting his racing career was 'a donkey on Skegness beach and a pit pony when it came out of the mines.' From the age of 15 he'd served a six-year apprenticeship and it was on his first day of the apprenticeship that he was to see a racehorse. However, it wouldn't be long before he was to ride a horse: 'Within seven days they put me on one to round the sand ring and within three months I was on the gallops alongside a guy called Lester Piggott', he recalls. 'Now that's what I call progress. I think I was lucky that I was put into a sport that I was ideal for. That little bit of flair was there for me, thank God.'

The aforementioned 'genius' Lester Piggott agrees somewhat with Smith-Eccles's view that you need a 'little bit of flair' to begin with and a suitable horse racing environment to release it. Piggott was tutored by his father and started riding for him, aged 14. The boy had flair but he also had to graft. He muses: 'I think that for anyone to be good at anything they need some help and they've got to be pushed a bit. Nobody's a natural really. They've got it there but they've got to be put right at the beginning.'

Richard Perham thinks that for those with natural flair and aptitude it's never too late to start riding, although an early familiarity with and ease around horses is obviously an asset:

> 'People who have never been around horses can become very good jockeys. There are many jockeys – Daryl Holland for example, who at 16 hadn't been near a horse before – who

only go into horse racing because they aren't very big. There is nothing else there for them. Their career adviser may have said something like "You're a small person, why don't you become a jockey?"

But if you've get someone who's a horseman but also a very good jockey they end up being like Tony McCoy, Ruby Walsh or Kieren Fallon. They have an affinity with horses. My belief is that you mostly get that horse-sense through growing up and spending time around and riding horses rather than having a natural ability, but others would argue it's just in them.

Someone like Pat Eddery had talent oozing out, he just fitted on a horse, Frankie Dettori is another one. Is it nature? Is it nurture? A bit of both I'd say. You can teach people to be more relaxed on a horse but I think that born-in instinct is difficult to teach.'

Dale Gibson adds his views to the debate, supporting the notion that growing up surrounded by all things equine is a contributing factor in a rider's success:

'I think it comes from an early age, from riding ponies, being around horses. I think it's easier if you have it engrained into you and are brought up in and around horses. I was brought up in Newmarket and had a pony when I was younger. My grandfather was head lad to multiple-champion trainer Sir Noel Murless for 20 years and my mum was a riding instructor. I was naturally very light and I had an interest and that's why I did it.

By 14 or 15 I knew that that was what I was going to do. I remember standing up, 30 years ago now, at a technical drawing class at school and saying that's what I'm going to do, and the teacher laughing. I was the only one to do that. I thought "I'll give it a bash."

And yet Daryl Holland didn't sit on a horse until he was 16, Willie Carson didn't until he was 16, Chris Catlin didn't sit on a

> horse until he was 16 – and, believe it or not, Johnny Murtagh didn't sit on a horse until he was 15. I can't believe that – but it's true, so one of the world's greatest jockeys in the past 20 years didn't sit on a horse until he was 15.
>
> Ultimately, one way or another, you have to become a good horseman to be a good jockey. You can't get away without it. You have to get inside the heads of some horses. Every horse is different and you've got to work 'em out pretty damn quick.
>
> If you've not ridden them before you can get an idea from the form, from what the trainer says and by watching videos – but you haven't got very long to work them out. So, you pick it up by watching how they act around the paddock, how they are in themselves, how they are behind the stalls – but sometimes it's split-second stuff. You can be off the bridle, pumping along, and the horse will suddenly pick up; or conversely you can be travelling very well on a horse and they let you down. You need to take note of all that.'

So, the specialists agree that when an aspiring jockey has natural flair, athletic coordination and good hand–eye coordination it will help them. They will learn quickly and make a difficult craft look easy and stylish. Yet anyone who has worked with youngsters knows that talent alone is not enough. Many blessed with talent achieve nothing of note. So, it's more complicated, more subtle than that.

All the experts also concur that to develop horse-sense you also need to graft, a philosophy that has recently been underlined by Matthew Syed's compelling book *Bounce: The Myth of Talent and the Power of Practice*. The book promotes the view that winners are *made* rather than *born*. That, in turn, suggests that when the likes of Piggott are viewed as possessing 'horse-sense', this understanding has actually come about as a result of a person growing up in a environment that fosters such skills – a setting in which riding a horse is as normal as learning to walk or ride a bike – so they accumulate innumerable hours on horseback and gain racecourse experience that helps them to learn their trade.

Gibson tends to agree with Syed: 'You gain experience and refine your craft with rides, and I had 9,700 professional rides. It's all about repetition', he says. 'After a while it becomes second nature and you develop a sixth sense about how each individual horse will behave and how to deal with each of the fantastic, idiosyncratic tracks – the likes of Goodwood, Chester, York, Aintree, Epsom – that we have in Britain.'

One example of horse-sense that is acquired through nature, nurture and practice is that of balance; an indefinable but critical part of a jockey's skills since the Georgian days of Samuel Chifney. Look back in history and most of the iconic jockeys have been widely praised for their sense of balance. The Derby specialist Steve Donoghue was one such rider. In *Derby 200*, Michael Seth-Smith and Roger Mortimer said of him:

> 'There is a physical as well as a spiritual side to Steve's success. It is called balance. Watch him coming down the hill at Epsom. You never see him holding on to the reins as many of his colleagues are compelled to. His touch is as light downhill as it is on the flat, and that I believe is why he is so successful on the Downs course. His mounts have never any shifting dead weight to carry.'

In more recent times the American Bill Shoemaker was described by Tanner and Cranham (in *Great Jockeys of the Flat*) as having:

> '... balance, intelligence, the ability to switch the whip from one hand to the other and back again, making the right moves most of the time, and a rapport with horses. Most of the outstanding riders have these qualities. The uncanny ability to achieve and maintain the perfect balance so that weight appears to be taken off the horse's back; the uncanny ability to transmit confidence down the reins and through the bit so that the horse realises his tender mouth will not be abused whatever exertion is asked of him. Revelling in this freedom the horse can use himself to the full, responding to every request from the saddle; horse and man are as one.'

The critical role that balance plays was further confirmed by Australian-born jockey 'Brownie' Carslake, who wrote of Sir Gordon Richards in the *Sunday Express* in 1929:

> 'I attribute his success to one word: balance ... Richards, because of his perfect balance, is carrying less weight than would another jockey of a similar weight. His perfect balance helps him to stick close to the rails on a round course and when he throws his reins at a horse in a driving finish his balance keeps the horse straight. Make no mistake about it. No other jockey could copy Gordon Richards. He is a law unto himself. If any of us tried throwing the reins at a horse the way Gordon does, the horse would swerve all over the place.'

Nothing has changed in the 21st century. Indeed the appliance of sports science is leading to an even greater focus in this area. The senior jockey coach at the British Racing School, Richard Perham, explains:

> 'In the 1980s, everybody used to ride with their full foot wedged into the stirrup, and we rode incredibly short with our knees well above the pommel of the saddle on the horseback. After 20 years people are now riding deeper and the majority of jockeys are riding with their tiptoes in the stirrups. To an untrained rider that's incredibly difficult but to a trained rider it does give them a greater sense of balance, presuming they are fit enough and strong enough to secure their weigh evenly across the horse. That's the main difference. Before there was a lot of body movement; there's less movement now. It boils down to the fact that less is more. In a finish if you flail about the horse might become unbalanced.'

Perham and the British Racing School are using a scientific approach to understand more about the subject, as Perham clarifies:

> 'We've done studies, working with the Royal Veterinary College, looking at the interaction between a rider and a horse. Are the jockeys making it more effective or being a hindrance? We are looking at weight ratios, how a jockey moves laterally and

> how much weight they put into a stirrup. And we're working on getting an audible, real-time feedback to the jockey on what weight ratio they have on each foot in the stirrup. We are trying to create a jockey that can feel more balanced and feel the horse move at speed. It's ground-breaking in horse racing but we are so far behind because if you spoke to someone in dressage, or in eventing, they would be able to tell you at gallop or at canter how a horse is moving, the leg it's moving and leaning on and so on.'

Former English flat-racing jockey Dale Gibson says that judgement of pace is another example of a skill that is mainly gained through experience and trial and error:

> 'Yes, you can teach it, but it's part of the race-riding skill that is gained through experience and through riding work in the morning with experienced jockeys and lads. It took me a bit of time in the mornings before I got my licence, but in the last three or four years of riding I had a pretty good reputation that once I got to the front I could stack 'em up behind and play with them. You had to have the horse of course; there were days when I got it wrong, tracked the wrong horse, when I gave one too much to do – but I became a pretty good judge of pace. For most jockeys it comes with experience and rides.'

The Australian Scobie Breasley was a skilled exponent in judging pace but, again, it was down to the way he grew up rather a genetic gift. Like most Australian apprentices, Breasley was weaned on riding against the clock and taught to hug the rails. He certainly became a superb judge of pace, sticking to the rails like glue and always looking to win by the smallest margin, something that Irish trainer Vincent O'Brien confirmed: 'The best Australian jockey could win a race by a neck or half a length for you with 7lb or more in hand and, of course, they were very good judges of pace. He would wait and wait. Your horse had the easiest possible race. He'd just put him in front on the post. He was so gentle with horses.'

Scobie Breasley hits the front with his usual impeccable timing. On Malberry, *Windsor Races, 1964*

That clock-watching was clearly a good way of racing. Ten-times British flat-racing champion jockey Steve Donoghue learned how to judge pace during his grounding at Chantilly, which, in his autobiography, he once reflected 'taught us to be keenly on the alert to get away the instant the flag fell: then, knowing that our times would be clocked, each rider learnt to pay great attention to the speed of every other animal on the gallops as well as his own'.

According to Steve Smith-Eccles, 'jumping is a lot, lot different to [riding on] the flat. But [he] could ride [his] horse without giving it any thought which then allowed [his] brain to be aware of what was happening around [him]'. The former jockey believed that skill largely comes from experience:

> 'If you ride in thousands of races, you know if you're going too fast or too slow. If they were going too quickly, I wouldn't get

involved with those who were setting the pace, I'd wait for them to hit the brick wall, which invariably they did, and they'd come back to me. If the race was run at a slow pace, I'd be ready and waiting for when someone pushed the button to go with them.

Yes, it's a lot to do with pace, but the more you ride the easier pace becomes to judge and you get a sense of what's normal. But you've got to be prepared for the unexpected. Some horses might make a break for it and not come back, and you can look a bit of a fool – but that's racing. Riding a horse in a race is like building a jigsaw. You build up your jigsaw and the final piece is when you jump the last, but that jigsaw is formed by the horse you ride.'

This conveys a key point about riding without thought. When a jockey can ride unconsciously they can devote all their attention to the race – the jigsaw – as it unfolds around them. It's like an onboard computer. When the brain spends so little time on the act of riding it is freed up to compute the mass of incoming data received through the senses. It can focus on the other horses and jockeys, seeing what's going to happen before it happens; gauge where the gaps exist; assess how much each horse has left in the tank; be aware of the jockey getting ready to make a move.

That information helps those jockeys make the right tactical decisions as the race develops. After years and years of experience this race management, like riding the horse, can also become a largely unconscious act. It just happens. The trick is to get to this advanced level as quickly as possible by tapping into the experienced wise heads in the weighing room for hints and tips.

18

LOOK, LISTEN, LEARN

If much of horse-sense and race management is learned from experience, then there is a requirement that a jockey has the aptitude and desire to learn. Great jockeys tend to be students of their craft, humble enough to know that there is always more knowledge to be gained; they are eager to improve, no matter how accomplished and acclaimed they become.

Some lesser mortals walk with a self-satisfied strut. They think they've made it and know it all when they become an apprentice or turn pro. They are resistant to guidance, blind to the ways in which they could get better. Jockey coach Richard Perham says he knows the warning signs when a group of jockeys enters his classroom at the British Racing School: 'Many walk in the door of the training room and sit down with their arms folded and their legs wide apart', he says. 'Their body language states "there is nothing you can tell me that will make a difference to my job". You know their minds are not open to learning anything.'

Historically, the culture in horse racing has been so strong and deep-rooted that many have been blinkered to innovation. So they stick in the mud; doing what they've always done and what others have done before them. Perham adds:

> 'How easy or difficult is it to change the culture and the way jockeys think? It's like banging your head against a brick wall!
>
> For many, the whole concept of jockey training has a stigma. They think "I don't need training, I'm doing just fine and I'm wasting four days going up there [to the British Racing School] to be trained when I could be riding in races."'

But, more and more, stagnant jockeys who carry the burden of an old-fashioned mindset are trailing behind. The sport and their competition are moving on without them. In contrast, Perham says it's just as easy to spot the one (or ones) who will make it when a group of wannabe jockeys settles in his classroom:

> 'It'll be the person who comes in looking really smart, shakes your hand, sits down, makes eye contact, listens, makes notes on what you are talking about and absorbs the feedback they get. They'll do well.
>
> I can see the psychology changing but it has taken five years to see jockeys come back to me from the licence stage. Luke Morris, William Carson, William Buick and Andrea Atzeni are four pro jockeys that have been through this classroom as rookies, looking for their first licence, and they bought into the ethos of training and how much good it can do.
>
> It's been gratifying to see them do incredibly well. Take William Carson. He didn't get it easy from granddad [top jockey, Willie Carson] and William Jnr has had to work for everything that he's got. He came on a course when he was 16 and he was keen about what he wanted to do, he asked questions and he already had a basic knowledge. You'd be astounded by the lack of basic knowledge of some of the youngsters who come through here. I knew he [William Carson] would do well.
>
> Tactical acumen comes with time. If you study the formbook and prepare properly, you will learn. The new, young breed of jockeys – such as the four I mentioned – are students of everything about racing. They ask questions. They will seek out a mentor to give them advice.
>
> Fortunately, nowadays there are strong, positive role models. Tony McCoy doesn't smoke, take drugs or drink. He's probably a really boring person – and he'd agree with that – but that's because his whole life is devoted to preparing for racing every single day of the week.'

Smart operator. William Carson, with a famous name and an impressive attitude, wins at Windsor in July 2014

Irish jockey Martin Lane was one of those who fell under the tutelage of Richard Perham and the fact that he became champion apprentice in 2010 and, four years on, is building an impressive professional career points towards a worthy mindset. Lane believes attitude is massively important and cites examples of apprentices who didn't have the right outlook:

> 'You see so many jockeys who look the part as an apprentice, look like the next big thing, but don't improve. You get your chippy, arrogant young lads who have been told all their life that they can ride – and they can ride – but they're the ones who kick off when they get jocked off [lose a ride to another jockey] and they have the shortest careers. They are probably better than nine-tenths of us but they don't have the attitude.
>
> There's so much distraction around, for apprentices. They get a lot of publicity and money. They might be 17, 18 years old and driving a Mercedes. They're the next big thing, probably living

on the yard, no kids, no partner, the money is theirs, life is good, there's nothing to worry about, no accommodation or fees. And temptation is all around them – girls coming their way, their friends going to night clubs. A lot don't deal with it and end up on the drink or have weight problems.

Personally, I always want to keep improving. I've been lucky to be around Ryan Moore more than normal recently and I asked him questions – about his fitness regime and about various horses. Often it's little things. The other day he was sweating [using the sauna], which is unusual for him, and I asked him why. He doesn't speak a lot but when he does he's worth listening to. His mind is full. If you can get it out of him, he's very interesting to listen to. If you ask Ryan or Frankie Dettori or Richard Hughes a genuine question, they'll speak to you all day long. After all we've all got to work together, 300 days a year and it works both ways; Ryan had to ask me the other day about a horse that I'd just ridden first time out.'

These days, apprentice and conditional jockeys have the opportunity to be assigned a mentor and, at the time of writing, 125 individuals out of 230 have taken up the option. Former English flat-racing jockey Dale Gibson says that they would be well advised to pick the brains of those with greater experience: 'When it came to race management, the likes of Ray Cochrane, Bruce Raymond and Michael Hills helped me. They were real, good solid pros who had been around the block. They knew the little, tiny details that I didn't. I'll always remember the help I got.'

But he adds that this acquisition of knowledge can only be constructed slowly, brick by brick. You can't become an instant master craftsman any more than you can become an overnight sensation: 'Patience is so important', he states. 'My best season was when I was 38 and I'd been going 20 years. Most teenagers want to do it tomorrow. We live in that age. George Duffield had his best times in his late 30s, early 40s; Willie Carson was phenomenal in his 40s; and then there's Piggott. To become the whole package takes time.'

Although the new breed of jockey appears to be more open to new ideas, older dogs can learn new tricks as well. Perham cites as an example Graham Lee, who won the Grand National when he was a jump jockey but got his weight down and transferred to riding on the flat:

> 'He's brought a different persona into the flat weighing room, partly because he's been brought up and nurtured by Michael Caulfield. Graham wasn't always the way he is now. He didn't always have a professional, well-prepared approach, but that has been instilled into him. And when it worked for him he probably decided he really liked it.
>
> And there's a jockey who retired two years ago, Philip Robinson, who was British flat-racing champion jockey in Hong Kong. He's ridden classic winners in the UK and had over 2,000 winners worldwide and was the oldest jockey riding until he retired. He said to me "the last five years I was riding I would always go on the simulator in the morning and give 600 pushes on that, then I would go on the cross-trainer for 40 minutes before I went racing. How could I compete with the younger riders if I knew that my body wasn't warmed up properly?" And he was still riding at the top level when he was 50.'

The moral of this story is crystal clear. The smart young jockeys look, listen and learn, and they never stop trying to improve throughout their career.

19

PILLARS OF PROFESSIONALISM

Given horse-sense and an appetite to improve, the smart jockeys – and it's no coincidence that they tend to be the most successful ones – will gravitate towards an all-round professional approach. Particularly in the past ten years, the culture in the weighing room has changed, and there are three key areas in which the canny ones have become more painstaking: preparation, physical conditioning and the management of personal relationships.

First, preparation. Despite long working days and busy schedules, more jockeys are finding time to do their homework. Dale Gibson became more diligent as his career progressed, as he explains:

> 'The modern-day jockey has to have the whole package of skills and mindset, and one aspect of that is pre-race preparation, doing your homework. That really begins in earnest once the horse has been declared – 48 hours before the race on the flat, 24 hours for jumps. The research involves knowing where the likely pace is going to be and the likely dangers when the tape goes up or the stalls open.
>
> Graham Lee says that there is far more homework and preparation time required on the flat than over the jumps. A lot more [time] is spent studying the *Racing Post*'s website and replays and just getting to know the opposition.
>
> You also get mentally prepared and do your weight preparation. At declarations you know what your weight will be – whether you will ride at your minimum, whether you can have your tea the night before.

I was keen on walking the course, finding the best ground, making sure that there were no deviations in where we were going up the straight, no rail movement. The course might have been watered so the paper might have said it will be slow going at Nottingham today, but in fact it might have been slightly quicker on the stand side. I found out those little variables by walking the course.

I started that in 2003 – and was conscientious in doing it for the last six years that I rode. I'd say that when I started the course walking, somewhere around a quarter of jockeys were doing the same. There would be those that pretended they hadn't done homework, but they had done more than they told you.

Some jockeys got away without doing it and were still successful because they had natural ability. I only had slightly above-average ability so I had to make up for that by doing my homework. I would like to think I was a good communicator. I'd always ring my trainer to get instructions before the race in case they weren't going. Your owner and trainer won't always be there – they'll be there at the big days, but not necessarily at Warwick or Fakenham on a wet Monday. I'd also speak to the clerk of the course to make sure they hadn't done anything to the track that might affect the result. I tried to get an edge where I could, because of a lot of the horses I rode were pretty average and exposed. They were Monday to Friday horses, for which I needed to find a bit to make them run a bit quicker.

I prided myself in squeezing every ounce out of them. If it meant finishing third – because I'd done my homework – instead of finishing fifth I got a kick out of that – and the winners came as well.'

Gibson wasn't alone in his diligence. At the British Racing School there is a small black book that was owned and written by Kevin Darley in 2004 (Kevin went on to become the 2009–2012 Chief Executive of the Professional Jockeys Association). This book is a diary of Darley's every ride during 2004, with extensive and meticulously written notes, building up a picture of the performance and character of each horse.

Jockey coach Richard Perham says Darley is a role model to others: 'He was a good jockey. He had ability and would have been a lot of people's role model. He rode well, he prepared well, he presented himself well, he was a brilliant communicator and he was incredibly driven – so he had all of the attributes that are needed.'

Perham adds that these days pre-race preparations are ratcheting up to another level. In addition to reading the *Racing Post*, walking the course and linking up with the trainer and owner, the enlightened jockeys now appreciate the need for their bodies to be warmed up when they ride.

> 'Any jockey will tell you that they work incredibly hard when they ride a horse. It's an intense physical activity and we confirmed this with a study in conjunction with Exeter University, which provided data that proved that their bodies work as hard as an Olympic athlete's when they are riding in a race.
>
> We had three ways of measuring what the body was doing: a metabolic analyser measured the oxygen input and output; heart-rate monitors picked up how hard the heart was working; and the lactic acid in the blood was assessed through finger-prick blood samples after the warm up, just before the start of the race and then at the finish.
>
> We found that that the bodies of all ten jockeys who did this study were more effective and economical in race two and race three than race one. All jockeys have always said that the second ride of the day always feels much better than the first. The reason is that they've warmed up. But now we've got some evidence from this study that confirms it.
>
> So, clearly the message from the study was to warm up before the first race. Younger jockeys all got it, but some senior jockeys are very, very blinkered and said "I'm fine, I've always been fine, I just get the first ride out of the way." What they are

failing to understand is what about if you've only got one ride on the day or it's a really important ride. It's all about preparing professionally and being the best you can.'

One of those younger jockeys who 'gets it' is Martin Lane, who also undertakes his own post-race post-mortem, win or lose:

'I'll watch the video after the race at the racecourse and if there's something I question I'll go home and watch it, maybe once, maybe 20 times. I'm mainly looking at the tactics. Sometimes you get beat and you're angry with yourself and you have a look at the video and think "that's won well; there wasn't anything I could have done". But there's other times when you have messed up and that's when you go home to watch how you can improve and win the next time. It's normally because you haven't known enough about the animal. By then watching the video, 90 per cent of the time you learn something about the horse that you can use to win next time – assuming you get the chance.'

Lane is also a strong advocate of the second pillar of modern-day professionalism: physical conditioning. He outlines his own regime:

'I work out for an hour, twice a week, with a personal trainer doing weights in riding positions. I don't have much time so using the trainer makes sure that I make the most of the time I have and work the right muscles. I'm lucky; I'm one of the lighter ones so I can do quite a lot of weight work. They've made a big difference. I also try and get out on a racing bike, doing 100km, 120km a week. I can do 25km in 40 minutes and that helps with the cardio. But nothing gets you race-fit like riding. It's unique.

We diet a lot and the more you sweat the slower your reaction times become. We all sweat, but if you're unfit and you're sweating, you're going to hit a massive wall. But if you are as fit as you can be, then you'll always give a good consistent ride, no matter how many rides you have that day.'

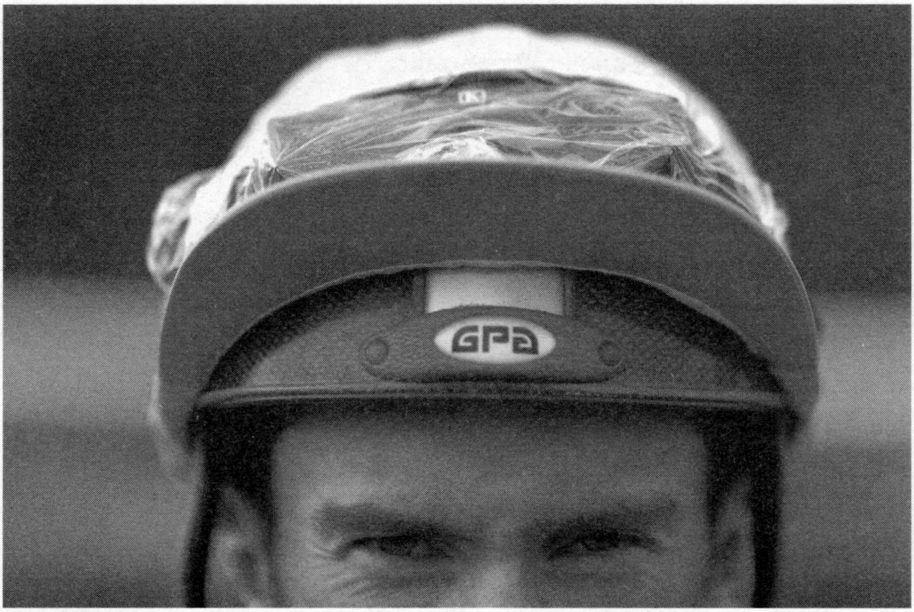

Eyes of the tiger. Martin Lane, focused on a long-lasting and successful career

Jockey coach and former jockey Steve Smith-Eccles says fitness can be the difference between winning and losing. 'First and foremost, the fitter you are the better you ride. Fitness is paramount', Smith-Eccles states. 'The technical stuff you can teach, but holding the normal body position on the bridle expends energy and a tired body affects the mind, which in a race situation is dangerous.'

Richard Perham agrees, emphasising that muscle tone is as important as aerobic vigour:

> 'Getting race-fit starts with building the key muscles. The legs, lower body and core are the three areas that the jockeys focus on in training. Upper-body strength is also important. Nowadays most jockeys don't have an ounce of fat; they are literally muscle and bone. Balance and fitness are equally important for jockeys but balance must come first. In the same way that in yoga you need to hold these positions for a period of time, a jockey also needs core stability to maintain his balance.'

After preparation and physique, the third pillar of professionalism in the 21st century is the management of a network of connections. This is just as important for a jockey as a senior manager working in the office-based corporate world. The whole horse racing industry is built upon an ever-shifting foundation of alliances. For jockeys, the ability to connect and 'get a tune' out of each racehorse is undeniably pivotal, but perhaps of more importance is the triad of relationships between the owner, the trainer and the jockey. The saying 'it's not what you know, it's who you know' might have been invented for horse racing.

The elite jockeys earn the right to make some choices about who they ride for and, to some extent, don't have to try quite so hard to gain rides. Their track record keeps them trendy. Most, though, come at the bottom of that owner–trainer–jockey triad, so they need to build relationships using a set of interpersonal skills that bear no relation to those required to ride a horse. Can they make a positive first impression? Can they build rapport? Can they communicate effectively, saying the right things at the right time in the right way? All are required to induce people to employ their services and give them repeat business. Many jockeys don't find these aspects of the job easy.

Take Kieren Fallon, for example. In an interview in *The Telegraph*, he once said, 'Outside riding, I find life a little more difficult. When I'm on a horse, it's completely different. Nothing bothers me. Whereas, I feel uncomfortable around different people.'

Martin Lane says that the culture in modern-day racing is putting extra emphasis on these interpersonal skills:

> 'Relationships with trainers are massive. Horses get beat, owners aren't happy and you get a lot of strain on the relationships. You have to keep your head. There are so many jockeys readily available and, because of the economic times, it's easier for a trainer to blame the jockey than say the horse is no good to the owner.
>
> There's not a lot of loyalty around. Some days you'll get jocked off horses, some days you'll jock off other jockeys. There are a

lot of jockeys around of equal ability and if I give a horse a bad ride then, if they fancy it, Ryan Moore or Richard Hughes will be ringing up the trainer the next day. You can't deny an owner who pays the bills the opportunity to have the best jockey. Of course it sucks, massively, but you just have to keep your head down and hopefully he's [the person who jocked you off] riding for his own boss the next time and you can get back on it. You get your knocks on the way. You can't let people walk all over you but you also need to know when to shut up and say as little as possible. The fiery jockeys will go through trainers pretty quick.'

In the jockeys' changing room, too, it's vital to be able to communicate, hold your own and become accepted as one of the gang. There will always be banter and it's no place for the sensitive. It's almost an initiation that novice jockeys have to go through. Particularly if they are innocent or gullible, young riders can expect to be tested out by teasing and practical jokes. In a way it is part of their development, because being a pro jockey is not for the weak, soft or easily distressed. You need to be gutsy to survive and you need to understand and adhere to the unwritten code of conduct that exists within the weighing room. Sports psychologist Michael Caulfield explains:

'You have to earn their respect. Sam Waley-Cohen is an example. He's a lucky young man, he's got wealth and a family fortune behind him but he's had to earn the respect of the weighing room by his riding and by his manners, not by being wealthy and owning a good horse.

Within the weighing rooms the jockeys operate with manners, courtesy and standards. Take the Cheltenham Festival for example. For the jockeys that week is all about performing well yet under the pressure they remain courteous. There's no cheating, no conning. It's just raw competition. Their manners are impeccable under pressure. It's competitive, it's feisty, but it's based on manners and standards that have been handed down

> over the years. The code of conduct that jockeys operate by will never be written or published. It doesn't need to be.'

Caulfield adds that it helps jockeys to develop skills that hold them in good stead outside of the inner sanctum:

> 'Pat Eddery once said that being a jockey is 50 per cent what you do on the course and 50 per cent off it. If you don't manage those relationships well, particularly in times of disappointment, you'll be finished. Trainers, owners, media – you've got to manage them. You look at AP. He was a very shy boy from Northern Ireland and now he's this blossomed, trained communicator. Richard Johnson is a shy boy from Herefordshire, but if you put him with people in the paddock he knows how to behave. That's what the weighing room teaches you.'

Each jockey creates a team around him or herself that also need to be managed: the valet, the agent, the accountant and the support network of friends and family. Those that make it through the levels will also benefit from becoming media-savvy and able to give interviews. So while many might overlook the importance of communication and interpersonal skills, they do so at their peril.

20

LABOUR OF LOVE

Every jockey needs a resilient mind and steely resolve to handle the hard work, the sacrifices and the relentlessness of the job. This is no easy task. Yes, it might appear glamorous when the elite jockeys arrive in a helicopter at Epsom Downs, Churchill Downs or Flemington Racecourse to compete with the eyes of the masses upon them and a baking sun on their back. But that's misleading, and Richard Perham paints a rather more downbeat picture:

> 'When you go into racing, wanting to be a jockey, at 16 years old you start at the lowest level. It's shovelling shit into a wheelbarrow. You work in the cold, you get up at six every morning in the peeing rain, get wet four times a day in the same clothes and get cold. And when you've finished you've got to sweep the yards, working your socks off. You don't go into racing and immediately become a professional sportsman.
>
> Why do people want to be a jockey? Often because there is nothing else. Because I grew up around horses, I went point-to-point racing, and when I was 14 I was still 5st. You either grow up watching racing and going "wow, that looks fantastic and I'd love to do it" or you're a small person that hasn't got that many options. You don't need academic qualifications but you have to be a bit tough, prepared to work your socks off and bounce back from someone giving you a thump – because that's what happens.'

Dale Gibson agrees that these harsh realities soon sort out those who are genuinely committed from those who are toying with the idea of being a jockey:

'Those that haven't had the upbringing have to have a real desire to do it. I see some people who start off in racing and lack a bit of desire. You've got to enjoy doing it and you've got to make a lot of sacrifices. Sacrifice is a word that is underused in the industry. People don't realise the mental and physical sacrifices that a professional jockey makes. The hours that a professional jockey puts in must be very high up the scales of professional athletes: driving yourself to the races; the preparation the morning beforehand; the dietary needs, surviving on one and a half meals a day; the falls; the let-downs. It's a tough game, a really tough game.

I didn't go to a wedding or many social events for 20 or more years. It's pretty sad really. I turned a lot down on a Saturday night because I was riding the next day. Particularly now, with

Life in the fast lane. Jockey Tom Scudamore gets into a helicopter at Doncaster Racecourse for a dash to Cheltenham. But much of a jockey's life is less glamorous

breathalysers, you have to act like a true professional. There were lots of things I missed out on to pursue my career. I'm convinced my son – who's a bit sharper than me – doesn't want to follow in my footsteps because when he was seven or eight years old I got busy and quite successful and he equated Dad riding horses with me not being here. I was driving constantly, thousands and thousands of miles per month, and sometimes I'd say to him on a Sunday night, "I'll see you on Wednesday," and his face would drop a mile.

You need to want to do it from a very young age and once you are on the treadmill you've got to stay on it. I have seen jockeys try to get off the treadmill, having come back from riding a lot of horses, thinking that they can just ease off. But it doesn't work. You can't ease off in this job. You think you can, but you can't. You've got to keep going.

When a jockey gets off the treadmill he or she loses the momentum they had. It's a fickle game and out of sight is out of mind for connections. Nothing advertises a jockey more than riding a winner of any race at any time of year. Jockeys quite often only take a week off in a year as they don't want to give up rides to their opponents. I did the same when I was on a roll.'

Most sports' performers enjoy a cycle of play–rest–train–prepare. There is light and shade. The spells of high-intensity activity are balanced by downtime. Footballers play once, maybe twice a week. A golf tournament lasts a maximum of four days. County cricketers play regularly during the summer but have a long off-season. Yet the life of a jockey is utterly relentless. They ride six, possibly seven days a week and there is virtually no off-season during which they can recharge their batteries. It requires more perspiration and dedication than inspiration.

So, a jockey in regular employment – and the more successful they become the more rides they get offered – will follow a day-to-day routine of an early rise to ride work before they travel to an afternoon meeting and have several rides. In the summer they may also head off for an evening meeting. Depending on the location of the meetings they may not get home until late at night – and are up early the following morning to do it all again. Coping with the travelling alone is a test, as Dale Gibson testifies:

> 'Jockeys spend a large proportion of their life in a car. I worked out that over 23 years of driving and riding as a professional I was in the car for 2½ to 3 of those years, which is an amazing statistic. I was doing 60,000–70,000 miles a year in my own car for six or seven years and 80,000–90,000 miles in total. There is a jockey called Joe Fanning who sold his car last year, having had it for 19 months, and he'd done 160,000 miles in it. He's at Hamilton one day, Brighton the next, Musselburgh the next. The car salesman could not believe it. That's 2,000 miles a week. Only the top half dozen in both codes might be able to afford to have a driver.'

For the elite jockeys, that travelling doesn't just involve cars; it's in helicopters and aeroplanes. These days it's a global sport and Martin Lane is just one jockey who prefers to escape for 2½ months each English winter to the racing in Dubai. He says he looks forward to the trip, not least as a respite from Britain's motorways:

> 'It's still work but you're not driving every day. Whereas in Britain it's never-ending. You do 70,000–80,000 miles a year in your own car, 100,000–110,000 miles in total – and it's pretty much wasted time. You can't look at the form. Our physios complain to us about our bad posture and the travelling puts fatigue in your body. By comparison, riding horses is the easy bit!'

Moreover, Richard Perham pinpoints an additional element: many do all of this while starving. He says:

> 'Richard Hughes is our current British flat-racing champion jockey, he's 39, 40 years old, he has struggled with his weight all his working life because he's a beanpole. I know the pain he goes through to draw the weights on a daily basis. Second to that, in the first week of November he was in California in the USA for

> the Breeders Cup, he flew from there to Melbourne to ride in the Melbourne Cup, he then went to a worldwide challenge in South Africa; and from there to Japan to ride in the Japan Cup; and he will ride in Hong Kong next weekend. He's a jockey that lives off fresh air, and that travel after a full season of riding is a heavy workload.
>
> The exhaustion is the thing that gets to you, the constant wasting, the pain, the hours and hours of eating nothing but a bit of lettuce and a piece of white fish. It all takes its toll. Constant miles driving from home to a trainer to test the skills of a particular horse, then on to a race meeting, and then another race meeting, and then home and bed, and the same thing starts all over again the following morning.'

Lane agrees, but makes an interesting observation about Hughes:

> 'At least Hughesie gets the rewards. He's riding 150 winners a year, Group One winners. He knows if he has to miss a meal then he's maybe riding five favourites that day, so he's gaining from it. Mentally that makes such a difference. Whereas other tall jockeys, who weigh 3st less than they naturally would, like George Baker and Adam Kirby, don't get the same rewards. For them it's tough. Yes, they're still doing well but it must be so much easier when you get out of bed knowing you're going to ride Group One winners.'

Michael Caulfield confirms that when this relentlessness is accompanied with deprivation it becomes a mind-blowing endurance test:

> 'Wasting is torture, it's head-wrecking. If I told you now that you need to lose a stone by Saturday night, you wouldn't think about a lot else between now and then. You'd think about what you couldn't eat, what you couldn't drink, what you couldn't do. Living life permanently hungry and thirsty is testing to say the least.
>
> There are obvious challenges because you are living your life on the edge of pain and without food, but the other thing about

horse racing is that of all the sports I've worked in it's the one where you get beat the most. Even the good ones get beaten an awful lot. So it needs perseverance, knowing that most of the time you're going to get beat. And that takes a different mindset. You need the sheer perseverance to go through hell. A lot of the jump jockeys talk about how they have to get past the "f*** it factor". Which is when you want to say "f*** it, I can't do this anymore – it's just too brutal and too painful", but most get through it and just keep going.'

So within the sport, much kudos and respect is given to the jockey's jockeys – the solid, reliable pros (it would be demeaning to call them journeymen) who stay on the treadmill year after year, seldom in the headlines, by no means rich, and grind out a living. Caulfield identifies a few such riders:

'Brian Harding, up north, would have my complete and utter respect. He's 42, he's riding better than ever, he's ridden for the same yard all his life and he's incredibly loyal. He's as straight as a gun barrel, he commands the respect of everyone in the changing room, he has come back from a horrific, career-threatening injury, yet at 42 he loves it as much as ever.

Then there's Joe Fanning up north and Paul Hanagan – he's done it in the north, he's now doing it for Sheikh Hamdan, he's come through from nowhere at the beginning and I think it's a remarkable achievement.

They love every part of race-riding. Riding a proper racehorse at speed is exciting, but it's also the network in the changing room, the friendships they form, the thrill of winning and making people happy in their work. It's a complete package – all the good ones love what they do.'

21

JUST CHAMPION

All of the characteristics detailed in this section will help a jockey sustain a career, but there are two specific traits that are held in abundance by the superstars and elevate them into the higher echelons of sporting achievement. The first is self-belief. It exudes from them. Their confidence is rock-solid and bomb-proof. They *know* they are better than the competition. That encourages them to keep going year after year, helps them to get back to their best after injury and allows them to just 'let it happen' in the frantic last few furlongs of a big race. They don't try too hard.

Richard Perham agrees that self-belief is invaluable, not least because he looks back on his own career and recognises that he would have liked more of it:

> 'I had no confidence or arrogance when I rode. I lacked self-belief, just like the majority of young riders, whereas the top riders have self-belief in abundance. Look at someone like Pat Eddery, an idol of mine. He was the top dog, a jockey's jockey. He had an amazing self-belief. Just like Richard Hughes. He will go out, unflustered, to ride in a big race and if his horse is favourite, he will say, "Brilliant, the job's easy, I'm on the best horse, all I need to do is perform and I know I can perform well." So he does it. Others would go: "I'm on the favourite, which means pressure. I hope I don't mess up." But he just deals with it.
>
> Hughes says "Listen, if it's good enough it will win. Don't get wound up about it just because it's a Group One race. Treat

it like a seller. You can't go wrong. If it gets beat, there'll be another day." What a great attitude.'

Confirming its importance, previous studies of sports performers have identified that self-belief is the most crucial trait when it comes to separating the truly elite from the merely outstanding – and sports psychologist Michael Caulfield certainly recognises its value:

'Self-belief is important in any walk of life, whether you are writing, broadcasting or working in the medical profession. You need an element of belief throughout your career. Belief also comes from loving what you do, because you know you'll crack it in the end. The majority of those who survive as a jump jockey for 20 years have strong self-belief. They've got lots of evidence to back it up, but they wouldn't keep doing it [riding] without

Role Model. The highly regarded, totally professional Richard Johnson in action. 2007 at Wincanton

> that absolute cast-iron belief in their own ability. The ones who don't have it don't last.
>
> I think that almost the perfect athlete in sport is the jockey Richard Johnson. He's got everything. AP has almost gone on to a different level to beat him for 20 years running but AP will tell you that Richard Johnson is the man most respected in professional sport, because he's done it for 20 years, day in, day out. It's his ability not to get too high, his ability not to get too despondent, he's remarkably consistent, he doesn't leave a single piece of effort behind him so he knows that he's given everything to his profession. I think if anyone can look at himself or herself in the mirror at the end of his or her career and say, "there's nothing else I could have done", then it'll be Richard Johnson. He's the perfect role model for me. He does what he does; he does it for the sheer joy of it. Of course he gets rewarded for it, which he should do, but he has such a desire and joy in doing what he does. He's as hungry to win as he's ever been, but that's underpinned by a belief in his own ability and a love for doing it. He doesn't need to do it, he just loves it.'

Martin Lane believes that confidence is just as important to a jockey as any other sports' performer. They all dip in and out of that intangible called 'form', as he explains:

> 'Confidence is massive for a jockey. When you feel confident you let things happen rather than forcing things. You feel calm with no fear and nothing else in your mind. If you wait a split second, then the gap comes whereas when you're panicking, you end up rushing and doing stupid manoeuvres. The top boys will just let it happen. And besides, Ryan Moore has the confidence of knowing that he can go into a race and not worry about getting beat. He'll still ride the next time.'

In addition, like high achievers in many professions, the most successful jockeys have an edge. They seize opportunities to win with the icy, killer instinct of an assassin. Their behaviour might be more obsessive,

McCoy. Simply the best

driven, blinkered and competitive than other, perhaps more rounded human beings: they are not like most of us. Fred Archer was not normal, Piggott was not normal, Dunwoody was not normal, McCoy is not normal. Willie Snaith summed it up nicely when he described his great friend Piggott as being 'always greedy for winners, like he'd never had one before.'

What drives them on in this way is unique to each individual. AP McCoy has said that the fear of losing is his motivation. For others it might be the adrenalin buzz of the competition and the lure of the winner's enclosure. Some will crave the money or the pampering of their ego. Ruby Walsh was once asked in an interview on Channel 4 about his success at the Cheltenham Festival. Wasn't riding more than 30 winners there over his career a bit greedy? He pondered for a moment, then replied:

> 'There is a bit of greed in most sportspeople who have any bit of success. AP's as greedy as hell. Somewhere in there, there has to be that little bit of selfishness that makes you want more, makes you push yourself that little bit it harder. Yeah, I'm a bit greedy.'

22

BRAVERY, BOTTLE AND GOODBYES

Finally, we need to focus on another much-needed characteristic: a vast quota of daring and bravery. It's particularly true of jump jockeys, but it applies to all riders. In Chapter 4 Martin Dwyer said that he actually enjoys the fact that there is a risk to what he does. It sharpens his senses and heightens his enjoyment.

People like Dwyer are illogically fearless and courageous, though, of course, they would never describe themselves in that manner. It's just us observers who think that way. They do not consider that they are in any way heroic and there is good reason for this: jockeys can't afford to be self-congratulatory about their bravery or even ponder the inevitability of injury because, rather like a golfer considering the concept of the yips when putting, they run the risk of allowing the subject to seep into their subconscious and affect their performance.

During the course of interviewing jockeys, there was a remarkable degree of consistency in the way in which they answered questions about falls and injuries. All said it is essential to acknowledge that accidents will happen but just as important to blank out this fact in your mind. And all offered the same health warning at the end: once you start thinking too much about getting injured while you are involved in a race then it's time to hang up your boots. 'It can get tough when things go wrong', Dale Gibson agrees. 'I had a bad fall in 1996. I was off for 20 weeks. It took an inordinate amount of mental strength to get back. Only my family and close friends know that I needed every ounce of my mental strength – and I think I've got plenty – to want to do it again.'

In *My Autobiography*, the made-of-steel, multi-champion jump jockey AP McCoy outlined his approach to injuries:

> 'If you go on a horse afraid of falling, afraid of pain, then it's time for you As long as you are happy to ride the bad jumper once it has a chance of winning, as long as you are happy to get up on the horse that has fallen in its previous three races knowing that if you get it around it will probably win, then kick on. Psychologically I always think that as long as I am happy to crash, I can keep riding.'

To adopt the McCoy mindset, to simply kick on, is in itself an admirable mindset, but it is one that needs to be retained over the length of what can be a 20-year career. If jockeys – and other sportsmen – were able to regulate their thinking patterns then they might be able to maintain that equilibrium. But they can't.

Professional excellence is no protection against the inevitability of a jockey's ups and downs. Few have a higher pain threshold than AP McCoy

For some, over time, a sense of fear, of being afraid, does begin to seep into the subconscious and nags away in the recesses of their grey matter. It is the most unwelcome of visitors. It can happen to boxers, test-match batsmen, rugby players, Formula One drivers, skiers – but jockeys are particularly at risk, simply because their chosen occupation is so dangerous to life and limb.

Being afraid is certainly not a conscious choice, far from it, and often jockeys won't admit they feel it – either to themselves or others – or even be aware of it (in fact their friends in the weighing room will probably notice it first) but the dark shadow of anxiety can creep up on them, like a sporting Grim Reaper. And, by common consent, that's the beginning of the end. It begins to affect the way they go about their job. Their decision-making is influenced and word begins to get around. There's virtually no way back. 'If you think about the dangers of riding, then you pack up', jockey coach Richard Perham says. 'The moment you start thinking that it's scary there is no point in going out there because people will see it a mile off. It's called losing your bottle. It happens all the time, to everyone in the end, sooner or later.'

Steve Smith-Eccles agrees with Perham: 'It's a dangerous job. We do it without even thinking about it because you have all the falls and the injuries; you accept it mentally so when it happens physically it's no big deal. I don't wish to sound blasé but you know you're going to get injured. If you thought about the danger, you couldn't do it. I've seen jockeys lose their bottle.'

But what's the catalyst for the beginning of the end? Perham is brave enough to admit that it happened to him and points to an accumulation of injuries as being at the root cause of his loss of nerve:

> 'In the latter stages of your career after you've fallen off and had a good hammering, had concussion a few times, broken ribs, punctured lungs, broken arms and legs, then when you are in the thick of it the desire to say "I've seen the gap and I'm going for it so get out of my way" lessens completely. You begin to ease back and slow up. I felt that happening. The trigger for the loss of bottle could be lack of motivation, outside influences such as family commitments and age. But the more accidents you've had the more cautious you become because you experience fear.'

Lisa Hancock, CEO of the Injured Jockeys Fund, concurs that age alters the way we think:

> 'As we grow older and more mature, our thoughts change. I'm sure that jockeys' take on things change. If you compare a

> 19-year-old jockey with a 39-year-old jockey, their outlook on life generally would be enormously different. The 39-year-old has probably got a family at home and is aware of what's in their bank account and is a bit wiser in their mental reasoning of how to ride a race. In comparison the 19-year-old won't have a clue about their bank account and it would all be a bit of fun. Their take on the world would be different. They may just be desperate to achieve. So, as it is in the general cycle of life actually, attitudes to risk may also change.'

And when it does happen, the implications are significant. Steve Smith-Eccles says the first person that knows that a jockey has lost his daring is the guy who's riding against him every day. He explains:

> 'Francome used to know what I was going to do before I did it, and vice versa. You'd be riding against them the whole time, you'd see them on TV, and so you'd know what they were going to do before they did it. And if somebody does something out of the ordinary it makes you think. Maybe instead of giving it [the horse] a kick they hold back. Once or twice you might overlook this but if it keeps happening on a regular basis you know their bottle has gone. If that happens you can't help them, in truth you'd probably look to take advantage of it. The thing about our sport is that it's man to man; it's not a team game. We're on our own. The camaraderie is great but when you're out there on the racetrack it's every man for himself.'

Perham agrees that to the trained eye it's not difficult to spot when someone has lost their nerve and that others in this competitive industry will smell the fear and seize the opportunity it presents:

> 'I would know it when I saw it happening – and so would every other jockey. They'll intimidate them knowing that they will go "no thank you". They'd squeeze them and make life scary for them. Believe me, when you are doing 40mph and in the middle of 20 other horses and someone starts squeezing you so that you are slapping against a white railing, you've either got the option

> of saying "get out, get off and leave me alone" or you start slowing up and they take your position. But then you are in a compromised position because you are boxed in and you end up at the back of the field.'

This brutal truth leads on to the last and perhaps the most challenging characteristic required of jockeys: the ability to hang up the boots and the silks and move on. Ideally this happens once a jockey has enjoyed a long and successful career and they instinctively know the time is right to stop. John Francome and Peter Scudamore are two examples of riders who acknowledged that their time had come and quit while they were at the top of their game. In such cases, if they feel that they've lost their edge then it's almost a welcome signal from the body and the mind that enough is enough. However, when the end occurs prematurely through injury – as happened to Richard Dunwoody – then that can be tortuous.

The average retirement age for a jockey is 33½ on the flat and 30 in National Hunt, but the career span is increasing and the ages are going up. Michael Caulfield, who set up the highly successful Jockeys Employment and Training Scheme (JETS) that helps jockeys with career advice and training to help them gain employment after race-riding, thinks that's a welcome trend:

> 'The 2014 Grand National summed that [the increase in jockeys' age] up for me. The winning jockey was 37, Richard Johnson was 37, AP is coming up to 40, there's Paul Moloney, there's Paul Carberry. Because they are now getting better support and treatment the whole year round they are lasting longer than before, and that is of particular interest to me. They are now riding longer and better than ever. It's down to improved support and knowledge, their mindset is so much stronger because they know they've got proper support around them. Successful jockeys can go on longer than 25 years. They don't regard 35 as old any more.
>
> Nevertheless, retirement is the biggest challenge they face – and that's true across all sports. If you love what you do and

you have to stop doing it in your junior years – and 35 and 40 years of age *is* junior – it's the hardest time they'll ever face. They've coped with change in the past and they've coped with disappointment but not being able to ride again takes time to come to terms with. If it's through injury, it's even worse, it's galling.

Some of them just know that the time is right to stop putting themselves and their family under that amount of pressure. It's risk and reward: at 23 you're fearless, at 33 you might think "do I need to do this anymore?" and it's time to move on. And they are now better prepared for the future. They reach that day of stopping with much less fear than they did in the past.'

Dale Gibson says that the secret to coping with retirement is to think ahead and make plans:

'You have to mentally prepare for retirement. I tell that to some of the guys I ride out with on a Saturday morning – who are still successful in their early 30s. I was lucky. In March, April 2009 I gave myself time to retire. The wheels started to fall off, the rides started to dry up, I was maybe a fraction off my game, the quality of the horses had dipped. My wife knew that I wasn't particularly happy through 2009. I'd still go racing, but some days it was for one ride at 33–1 and then another ride, two or three days later, at 33–1. I knew I could still do the job but if my body was a car, the fuel was on red.

I was offered a couple of jobs and I knew I was going to retire six months before I did. One of the best things I've ever done was to give myself some free time because it made me a better person, in that I could accept not being a professional sportsman.

I still play cricket and table tennis, and help, organise and ride in a successful charity race under rules for a bit of competition, but I was ready to shake hands with riding racehorses for a living. I had a lot of miles on the clock. I've remained doing a lot of what I did when I was riding: I've still got media work, I'm still involved. I didn't need to reinvent myself. But for many others it's bloody hard when they stop being a professional sportsman, particularly a jockey, because you have sacrificed so much over the course of your life.

A lot of jockeys don't have a full education and it's a unique sport that's in your blood. Part of you dies when you stop riding. So if you're in your late 30s, early 40s, I'd suggest you do it gradually because it's when you stop quickly that the problems can kick in. Fortunately, thanks to JETS, jockeys are getting better support than they have in the past for what lies ahead of them and how to cope with it.'

Maybe the challenge of retirement highlights an inherent irony within the profession. Yes, you need to be a remarkable sports' performer, with a remarkable array of skills, to sustain a career as a jockey. But, chances are, the really difficult bit comes when you stop.

PART 6
LAST HURRAH

23

NATIONAL TREASURE

When most jockeys get knocked down they get back up again. Most love what they do and refuse to be beaten by adversity – and it would be a literary crime to complete a book that celebrates the profession without an affectionate touch of the cap to one the greatest stories of them of all, not just in horse racing but in British sport as a whole: Bob Champion, cancer, *Aldaniti*, the Grand National.

For many people of a certain age the legend is easily recalled. They can cast their mind's eye to Champion, in white racing colours with the royal blue sash, under a cloudless Liverpool sky – and they can recall the commentary of the BBC's Peter O'Sullevan, scarcely audible above the noise of the crowd, in the run in from the last fence:

> 'It's *Aldaniti*, as they reach the elbow. They've got a furlong to run. It's *Aldaniti* in the lead, but now being pressed by *Spartan Missile*. It's *Aldaniti* from *Spartan Missile*. And here comes John Thorne, 54-year-old John Thorne putting in a storming finish. It's *Aldaniti* from *Spartan Missile*. *Aldaniti* is going to win it! *Aldaniti* wins the National!'

The first sight of Bob Champion, MBE, in the flesh triggers those memories before he has even introduced himself. It's immediately uplifting to see that two weeks short of his 66th birthday he is a picture of prosperity and health, even though he has suffered from cancer and, more recently, two heart attacks. Yes, he's carrying a few more pounds than he was in his heyday and the still-dark hair has thinned, but that familiar open face is tanned, making his teeth – treated after the battering they took when he was a race-rider – appear all the whiter. He's well dressed in a charcoal suit and a checked shirt, which hides a tell-tale long diagonal surgeon's scar across his chest that must provide him with a regular reminder of what he endured and what he has achieved.

Champion is a kindly, genial character, which is just as well when he's asked to re-tell the same story he has already told a million times. He still gets lost in the tale, reliving it again. Indeed when the subject strays away from Aintree and *Aldaniti* he unconsciously brings it back, keen to unload. It's certainly comfortable territory and even now, 33 years on, you sense that it still gives him a buzz to talk about the day that changed his life, and, in turn, allowed him to change the lives of many others.

For Champion is an excellent ambassador for jockeys, but not because of the fabled deeds of bravery that celebrated Saturday in Liverpool. It's because, despite these heroics, he is, at least by the extraordinary standards of this tribe of 'warriors on horseback', unremarkable.

Bob Champion. Aldaniti. *Aintree, 1981. The Chair is negotiated and a place in the sporting legends beckons*

He is a Yorkshire boy who grew up with horses and hunting and dreamed of winning the National; a youth who learned his craft and turned pro; an adult who loved what he did, rode nearly 500 winners across 11 seasons and became one of the most respected jockeys of his generation, with an intuitive feel for horses, a will to win and the fortitude to cope with the constant weight-watching and broken bones.

So, in many ways, Champion was just like John Francome, Jonjo O'Neill, Ron Barry, Bob Davies and others who frequented the changing rooms of Sandown, Kempton Park and Huntingdon. Yet in July 1979 Champion, then 31 years old, faced a challenge that dwarfed the challenges of food deprivation and broken collarbones. He was persuaded to have a suspicious lump investigated, and the medical diagnosis was chilling. He was urgently operated upon, surgeons removing malignant growths, one testicle and half a rib. He was told that, in all probability, he was about eight months from the grave and had the disease been found 18 months earlier there could have been no recovery because there would have been no treatment available.

Champion confirms this verdict, saying: 'Yes, I'd have been dead. A goner. End of story. And they only gave me a 30–35 per cent chance of living, so still the odds weren't great.'

Indeed, following the initial operation and diagnosis, it took a while for the stereotypical jockey's mindset towards misfortune – resolute, pig-headed, keep-calm-and-carry-on – to kick in. For a while Champion was going to just give up, as he can recollect only too well:

> 'I wasn't going to have the treatment at first because I didn't feel too bad, and I'd had a couple of ops to remove the tumour and I kept thinking I'll just go back and ride and hope for the best. Because the stable jockey at Josh Gifford's, Dougie Barrett, had got killed in the Whitbread at Newcastle and I took over dead man's shoes, I thought well, with a bit of luck, I'll get killed on the racecourse. I said that to Professor Peckham and he looked at me like I was bloody stupid and I'll always remember he said, "Bob, you're not a bad novice chase jockey, if you were offered a

> 6–4 shot, you'd give it a ride", and it made me think "I suppose I would, this is worth a try." I suppose he just said the right thing at the right moment.'

So Champion took up the challenge, now a willing guinea pig for a pioneering if barbaric treatment. Six times he was admitted to a Surrey hospital for an agonising five-day stay during which time he intravenously received a cocktail of drugs that included platinum. Of his treatment, Champion says:

> 'The side effects of the chemo were horrendous. There were some bloody bad days with the treatment – fortunately there are better drugs now – and it was tough. I suppose being a jockey could have helped to make me more determined. To be honest my number one aim was that I didn't want to die.'

He became sick, emaciated and bald. Septicaemia nearly pushed him over the edge. Yet through the darkest days of the treatment Champion tried to look ahead and keep upbeat: 'Although I was a bit out of it I kept giving myself goals, thinking certain horses like *Aldaniti* will be back next spring', he says. 'Those goals kept going through my brain.'

In truth, they were forlorn hopes. In all probability the odds suggested that he would die, and even if he did survive, never get back to the fitness required for negotiating the likes of Becher's Brook. Besides, if he were to ride at Aintree it looked unlikely that *Aldaniti* would be there: the horse had suffered two serious tendon injuries and a fractured hock, and Champion remembers that things looked bleak: 'The old horse broke down so many times. The last time it happened, at Sandown, it was bad and the vets wanted to put him down. But he was such a great patient. He stood in a box for six months in plaster. That's hard for a horse.'

Fortunately, Champion and *Aldaniti* had good people in their corner; principled, loyal people, in a sport in which owner-horse-trainer-jockey alliances are formed then broken from week to week without a second thought.

Champion says that the trainer, the now late Josh Gifford, was a key ally, and *Aldaniti*'s owner, Nick Embiricos, was equally steadfast:

> 'I was good friends with Josh and he was amazing. I know now that Josh never thought I would be back riding. He never gave it a second thought. He just kept saying your job's there when you come back. But in his heart he never thought I would. He was a man of his word, loyal to all his jockeys.
>
> Nick was also amazing. I think it helped that I had won on *Aldaniti* at Leicester and I said then that he would win a National one day. So that gave Nick hope.'

By January 1980 Champion's ravaged frame had endured the chemotherapy and he had been given the all-clear. Yet there were many more fences to be cleared before a Champion-*Aldaniti* reunion at Aintree could be considered. For a start, the jockey needed to regain his vitality and vigour. He was thin, weak and had little feeling in his hands and feet. Fortunately he had the bright idea of escaping to the sun, a decision that he recalls with satisfaction:

> 'Once I started to recover the best thing I did was to go to America. I just couldn't cope with the British weather, it was cold and frosty, and I couldn't breathe because my lungs had lost 35 per cent of their capacity. I tried riding here but I wasn't getting anywhere so I went to South Carolina for eight months where I knew the weather would be good. It did help but I had to work really hard to get fit. I don't think anybody realises, to this day, just how hard I worked. I had lost all my muscles so I had to start again, like a baby. If I had stayed in England, it would have delayed my comeback for another three or four months.'

Fast forward to April 1981 and a glorious springtime in Liverpool. A sense of renewal. Fresh hopes and optimism. Certainly psychologists could write case studies about Bob Champion's mental state around then, in the lead-up to and throughout the Grand National. It is one aspect of this much-told tale that has often been overlooked. Given how much the event meant to him, Champion's confidence and Zen-like serenity were astonishing. Those who believe in fate would argue that not only was it written in the stars that the Champion–*Aldaniti* story should end in glory, but that the jockey subconsciously knew that would be the case.

For whatever reason Champion didn't hope or expect to win. He knew:

> 'I was very confident. I just couldn't see myself getting beat. It was a funny feeling. I travelled to Aintree with Jonathan Powell, who was writing my book with me at the time, and he was amazed how confident I was. In fact I felt very confident for six weeks before. The way he'd won at Ascot. Every time I went to the National I felt confident I suppose – and I didn't always win – but this felt a formality in a way. I remember Jonathan saying to me when we were having breakfast – a tiny bit of breakfast, like a mouthful, at the hotel – "at least we've got here", and I said "we've got here and we've won".'

Warming to a familiar story like putting on comfortable slippers, Champion adds:

> 'I remember down at the start Josh Gifford came down to check the girths. He used to smoke like a train, and I said "if I win today, you'll give up smoking will you?" and he said "yes". And he did actually. The plan was to hold *Aldaniti* up like we always did. He wasn't too great over the first two fences but he had a brain and he adapted very quickly. I jumped Becher's about 29th but I must have had a better run around the Canal Turn than anyone else and three fences later, still 3½ miles from home, I was at the front.'

That was contrary to the plan. Was Champion worried?

> 'Yes and no. I'm thinking "jeez, I'm getting some bollocking in the stands now; I better start thinking of excuses." Once you've hit the front you can't just pull back and go last again. You have to keep him in rhythm. And he was eating the fences really. But deep down I was happy because I was always good in that situation. If I hit the front in a race, I rarely got beaten. I was a good judge of pace and I was happy because

I was getting a lot of breathers into him and he was jumping really well.'

So while *Aldaniti* pinged over the toughest fences in steeplechasing, Champion's mind wandered. A natural horseman he had no need to consciously consider how to ride – that was all happening subconsciously on auto-pilot – and he had enough confidence and faith to just let it happen. Those in the know will tell you that this is the ideal mental state for an athlete. Most experience a fleeting but blissful period of time when they trust their skills, when mind and body (and in this case horse) work in harmony and they can do no wrong, when their thinking is clear and alert, serene and absorbed, and they perform extraordinary feats with ease. In modern parlance this is labelled 'flow-state' and it's annoyingly difficult to create. Sometimes it just happens. Fortunately for Bob Champion it occurred during the race of his life. Perhaps it was fate. He takes up the story:

> 'Yes, I kept thinking back to previous Nationals and how they were won. I seemed to have a lot of time out there, I don't know why! I went through *Red Rum*'s Nationals in my mind. I looked on one side and saw *Sebastian V*, who was second in 1978. On the other side I spotted *Rubstic* who had won in 1979. I just kept jumping, trying to keep him sound. I'd had a look at the third last and Philip Blacker on *Royal Mail* looked to be going the best of the others and I thought "I've got you beat", and he made a mistake at the second last because he was getting tired, so that made me happy. I got to the last fence still in front, in the right place at the right time. I knew I wasn't going to get caught.'

But what about the challenge of veteran John Thorne on *Spartan Missile* as they passed the elbow? Did that threaten Champion's confidence for a moment?

> 'I never saw him to be honest. I tracked him to Becher's on the first circuit and I thought he'd gone, but he did come to me at the elbow. He got within about three-quarters of a length of me, but I kept thinking if I get to the running rail ahead my horse

> will keep galloping. And I knew that something would have to have some acceleration to come by me and after 4½ miles horses don't quicken. I actually started going away again and I won by 3 lengths in the end.'

Did Champion realise at that moment quite what he had achieved? That people would still be talking and writing about it 30 years later? 'No, not at all. Not a clue,' Champion responds. 'I never thought what a story it was. As I went past the post the staff nurse and the other nurses came up to congratulate me and my first thoughts were for the patients because I'd had so many telegrams. I had hundreds wishing me luck.'

Strangely, moments after one of the greatest feats in sport, Champion made the error that he says he most regrets:

> 'If I look back on my life, I made one big mistake. When I pulled up I thought this is the time to retire. I knew I was getting to the end of my career anyway, at 33 years old, and I thought "what a way to go out". But two seconds later I thought I'd like to do this again next year, so I decided to carry on. In hindsight I'd have been best to go out on a high and at the top. I do regret it.'

Either way, Champion's life could never be the same again, because the tale kept on being told long after he passed the finishing post. A book was released and, in 1983, the book was turned into the movie *Champions*. John Hurt played the lead and Champion worked with the scriptwriter, went to the press days and acted as a technical adviser during the filming. He was delighted with the end product.

More significantly, the publicity from his win encouraged so many charitable donations that Champion set up his own trust. This is still going strong more than 30 years later, and has raised more than £14 million. Once he had retired as a jockey, Champion's devotion to fund-raising was so great that he cut short a career as a trainer.

To the delight of the public, he often brought along *Aldanti* to fund-raisers – at least until the 'old horse' passed away at the ripe old age of 27. Champion recalls that he was 'wonderful with the public – a nice kind horse who loved the attention'. Partly through Champion's efforts, the odds of survival for those who suffer from testicular cancer (if diagnosed early) have risen from 30 per cent to 95 per cent, and he is clearly proud the charity's achievements:

> 'The first laboratory we build in the Royal Marsden means a lot to me. It's doing a really good job. And now we've started building one in Norwich at the new science park focusing on prostrate cancer. That will be phenomenal, one of the biggest places in Europe. We'll fund the scientists and the research.'

Maybe those who believe in fate and a higher being may consider that Champion's victory in 1981 was pre-destined so he could help others. Now, given 30 years of hindsight, does he look at his illness as a positive or negative? He considers. It's a question he's not been asked much before, if at all. On one side there's the unfair infirmity and suffering he endured and the residual impact of the treatment on his body, which may have been a factor in the two heart attacks that he has suffered in more recent years. On the flip side, the illness was the vehicle that allowed him to meet so many and do so much good. After a moment's consideration, Champion replies:

> 'Certainly, what means the most to me is the letters I've had from people. Through the years I've had thousands of letters. I've always written back to them, and it's nice when you get another letter back from them a few years later saying "thanks, I'm still alive. Your letter gave me confidence." That's what means the most to me.'

INTERVIEWS

The following were face-to-face interviews unless stated otherwise.

Ron Atkins (by phone)
Michael Caulfield (by phone)
Bob Champion
Frankie Dettori
Hollie Doyle
Martin Dwyer
Dale Gibson
Lisa Hancock
Martin Lane
Daloni Lucas (by phone)
Richard Perham
Steve Smith-Eccles
John Snaith
Willie Snaith
Paul Struthers
Phil Taylor
Hayley Turner

BIBLIOGRAPHY AND FURTHER READING

The following titles were used while researching this book:

221: Peter Scudamore's Record Season by Dudley Doust (Hodder and Stoughton, 1989)

A Sportswriter's Year by Simon Barnes (Heinemann, 1989)

A Trainer to Two Kings by Richard Marsh (Cassell, 1925)

Born Lucky, An Autobiography by John Francome (Corgi Books, 1985)

Bounce: The Myth of Talent and the Power of Practice by Matthew Syed (Fourth Estate, 2010)

Channel 4 Racing: Complete A–Z of Horse Racing by Sean Magee (Channel 4 Books, 2001)

Classic Horse-racing Quotes: Horse-racing History In The Words Of Those Who Made It by Graham Sharpe (Robson Books, 2005)

Derby 200: The Official Story of the Blue Riband of the Turf by Michael Seth-Smith and Roger Mortimer (Guinness World Records Limited, 1979)

Eclipse: The Horse That Changed Racing History Forever by Nicholas Clee (Bantam Press, 2009)

Foinavon: The Story of the Grand National's Biggest Upset by David Owen (Wisden Sports Writing, 2013)

Frankie: The Autobiography Of Frankie Dettori by Frankie Dettori (Collins Willow, 2004)

Front Runners: More of the Best of Brough Scott by Brough Scott, (Gollancz, 1991)

Genius Genuine by Samuel Chifney (1804)

Great Jockeys of the Flat by Michael Tanner and Gerry Cranham (Guinness World Records Limited, 1992)

The History of Horse Racing: First Past The Post by John Carter (Abbeydale Press, 2010)

Horse Racing's Top 100 Moments by 'Blood Horse' Publications (Eclipse Press, 2006)

Horse Sense: An Inside Look at the Sport of Kings by Bert Sugar and Cornell Richardson (John Wiley & Sons, 2003)

The Injured Jockeys Fund: Celebrating Fifty Years 1964–2014 by Sean Magee (Injured Jockeys Fund, 2013)

Jumbo to Jockey: One Midlife Crisis, a Horse and the Diet of a Lifetime by Dominic Prince (Fourth Estate, 2011)

Just My Story by Steve Donoghue (Hutchinson, 1923)

My Autobiography by AP McCoy (Orion, 2011)

The National Horseracing Museum: A Concise History of British Horse Racing by Hilary Bracegirdle (Heritage House Group, 1999)

Newmarket: A Year at the Home of Horseracing by John Carter (SportsBooks, 2008)

Obsessed: The Autobiography by Richard Dunwoody (Headline Book Publishing, 2000)

On and Off the Rails: The Best of Brough Scott by Brough Scott (Gollancz, 1984)

Post Haste by Edgar Britt (Macmillan Australia, 1967; 2000)

Racing Post's 1000 Racing Quotations by Graham Sharpe (Highdown, 2007)

Racing's Greatest Characters: Fabulous Stories of Winners and Losers, Runners and Riders by Graham Sharpe (JR Books, 2009)

The Racing Tribe: Watching the Horsewatchers by Kate Fox (Metro Books, 2005)

Sporting Excellence, a study of sport's highest achievers by David Hemery (Willow Books, 1986)

Steeplechasing: A Celebration of 250 Years by Anne Holland (Little, Brown, 2001)

The World of Horse Racing by Brough Scott and Gerry Cranham (Bounty Books, 1987)

ADDITIONAL MATERIAL:

'Jockeys and their practices in South Africa' by D Labadarious, J Kotze, D Momberg & TJ Kotze (1992)

'An investigation into appropriate weight standards in top level Irish flat and National Hunt jockeys' by G Warrington, A McGoldrick & M Griffin (2005)

'Psychological effects of rapid weight loss and attitudes towards eating among professional jockeys' by MJ Caulfield & CI Karageorghis (2007)

'Eating habits and body weight control methods of national hunt and flat race jockeys in the UK' by A Higham (2012) (unpublished Master's thesis: University of Chester, UK)

Presentations and research (courtesy of the Professional Jockeys Association) from the International Conference for the Health, Safety and Welfare of Jockeys, 2013 including 'Importance of nutrition' (by Gillian O'Loughlin) and 'Concussion systems' (by Dr Michael Turner)

WEBSITES

www.bbc.co.uk/sport/0/horse-racing

https://sites.google.com/site/jockeypedia/www.nhrm.co.uk

www.racingpost.com

www.telegraph.co.uk/sport/horseracing/6017626/Kieran-Fallon-I-know-this-is-my-last-chance.html

www.theguardian.com/sport/2005/nov/06/horseracing.theobserver

www.wikipedia.org

INDEX

abroad, riding 36, 44–5, 49, 91, 160, 207–8
agents 38, 44
Aldaniti xiii, 223, 226, 227, 228, 229–31
Ali, Muhammad 127
Apprentice Jockeys' Licence 56
Archer, Fred 74–5, 76, 77, 78, 101, 157–8, 212
Arkle 112, 113
Aspell, Leighton 18, 20, 29
Atkins, Ron 139–43, 145–6, 148
attitude, apprentices' 193–4

Baker, George 40, 52, 57, 208
balance 186–8
Balding, Andrew 49
Batchelor, Matthew 22
Becher, Captain Martin 107–11
Becher's Brook 10, 111
Biddlecombe, Terry 121, 133
body protectors 114, 140, 141, 153–4
Boss, Glen 113
Bradman, Sir Donald 126
Breasley, Arthur 'Scobie' 5, 91–2, 188
Brew, Charlotte 59
British Racing School 56, 179, 187–8, 191–2, 197
Britt, Edgar 88–9
Brookshaw, Tim 143
Buckle, Frank 69–71

camaraderie xiii, 13, 19, 21–3, 24, 46–7, 202
Carberry, Paul 18, 218
Carson, William 192
Carson, Willie 100, 184, 192, 194
Caulfield, Michael 178, 195, 202–3, 208–9, 211–12, 218–19
Cauthen, Steve 93, 95, 165
Cecil, Sir Henry 6, 95
'The Chair' 8–9
Champion, Bob xiii–xiv, 21, 152, 223–31
changing room culture 16–29, 202
characteristics of a professional jockey 177–220
Chifney, Sam 67–9
Chronic Traumatic Encephalopathy (CTE) 150–2
Clerk of the Course 32
communication and interpersonal skills 100, 201–2
concussion 47–8, 140–1, 147–52
conflicts 25–6
Cooper, Brian 23
corruption 66–7, 68–9
courage 20, 214–15

Darley, Kevin 198–9
Davis, Richard 146–7
dehydration 167–9, 173–4
depression 13, 169–71
Derby 49–50, 51, 59
Dettori, Frankie 51, 52, 98–100, 103, 127, 157, 161–2, 165–6, 167, 170, 184, 194
Donoghue, Steve 81, 82–3, 102, 186, 189
Doyle, Hollie 56–9, 62
Doyle, James 52–3
drink- and drug-related issues 144, 158, 164, 170
Dunwoody, Richard 25–6, 27, 123, 124–5, 212, 218
Dwyer, Martin 34–55, 214

earnings and expenses 28–9, 44, 50
Eddery, Pat 40, 89, 95–6, 103, 184, 203, 210

Elizabeth II, Queen 5, 6, 85
Elliott, Charlie 182

Fallon, Kieren 25, 47, 52, 96, 103, 157, 184, 201
Farrell, Paddy 143
fear, and loss of nerve 215–18
female jockeys 31, 56–62, 96–8, 153, 154–5, 163
flat racing 22, 63–103, 162, 196, 218
Flatman, Nat 72–3, 100–1
flipping (vomiting) 165–6, 167, 169
food and eating habits 31, 52, 161, 164, 165, 172–3, 174
Fordham, George 74–5, 76–8, 101
Francis, Dick 117, 119
Francome, John 21–2, 24, 120–2, 123, 133, 141, 217, 218
Frankel 6, 113

Geraghty, Barry 18, 20
Gibson, Dale 179, 181, 184–5, 186, 188, 194, 196–7, 205–7, 214, 219–20
Gifford, Josh 119, 133, 226–7, 228
Golden Miller 112, 113
Grand National 8–9, 10, 16, 17–18, 33, 59, 225, 227–30
Greaves, Alex 59, 61

Hamer, Josh 23
Hancock, Lisa 128–9, 143–5, 153, 154, 156, 217
handicapping system 159
Hannon, Richard 39–40, 56
Harding, Brian 209
helmets 114, 140, 146
Herrell, James 169
Hills, Richard 40
Holland, Daryl 50, 183–4
horse-sense 76, 91, 114, 131, 181–90
Hughes, Richard 39–40, 52, 57, 157, 158–9, 194, 202, 207–8, 210–11

Injured Jockeys Fund 4, 6, 13, 143–5, 152, 154
injuries and fatalities 6, 11–12, 19, 23, 32, 33, 47–8, 58, 61, 97, 114, 128–30, 137–56, 175, 214–15, 216

Jacob, Daryl 23
Jockey Club 59, 65, 66, 69, 88, 146, 148
jockey-trainers 119
Jockeys Employment and Training Scheme (JETS) 218, 220
a jockey's life 34–53, 204–9
Johnson, Richard 130–1, 176, 203, 211–12, 218

Krone, Julie 96–8

Lane, Martin 178, 193–4, 199, 201–2, 207, 208, 212
laxatives and diuretics 161, 167, 174
learning and development 191–5
Lee, Graham 195, 196
Lucas, Daloni 171–4, 175–6

McCoy, AP xiv, 22, 23, 30, 107, 125, 127–30, 131, 133, 137, 176, 181, 184, 192, 203, 211–12, 213, 215, 218
McNamara, John Thomas 23
Maguire, Adrian 25–6, 27
Maguire, Jason 20, 23, 28
Makybe Diva 113
Mason, Frank 112, 132
medical care 32, 33, 142–3, 144, 147, 153
Mellor, Stan 118, 119
mentors 194
Molony, Tim 114–15, 117
Montgomerie, Simone 154–5
Moore, George 92
Moore, Ryan 96, 176, 181, 194, 202, 212
Mould, David 10
Murless, Sir Noel 6, 7, 87, 184
Murphy, Isaac 78–9
Murphy, Timmy 24–5
Murtagh, Johnny 185

National Horseracing Museum 3, 12, 14–15
National Hunt 8–9, 10–12, 22, 59, 107–33, 162, 196, 218

O'Brien, Joseph xvii, 157
O'Sullevan, Peter 8, 9, 170, 223

pace, judgement of 7, 24–5, 188–90
Perham, Richard 165, 174, 179, 183–4, 187–8, 191–2, 193, 194–5, 198–9, 200, 204–5, 207–8, 210–11, 216, 217–18
physical conditioning 28, 154, 199–200
physiotherapy 32
Piggott, Lester 7, 25, 87–91, 92, 93–4, 145, 161, 170, 182, 183, 212, 213
Pipe, Martin 123, 124, 140
Pollard, John 'Red' 85–6, 113
pre-race preparations 41, 121–2, 196–8
Professional Jockeys Association 44, 49, 61, 152, 153
professionalism 28, 121, 196–203

Queally, Tom 113

race management 24–5, 188–90, 194
race-riding bug xvi, 9, 13, 15, 29, 125, 205
Rees, Fred 112, 132
retirement 52, 124, 216, 218–20
Richards, Sir Gordon 4, 6–7, 83–5, 87, 88, 89, 92, 102, 187
riding work 10, 35, 36
Rimell, Fred 114, 119, 140
Robinson, James 'Jem' 71–2, 161
Robinson, Philip 195

safety issues 140–3, 145–54
Sanchez, Emmanuel Jose 168–9
saunas 32, 60, 174, 175
Scudamore, Peter 24, 121, 122–4, 133, 218
Seabiscuit 85, 86, 113
Secretariat 113
self-belief 210–12
Shoemaker, Bill 93–4, 186
silks 31, 65–6
Sloan, James 'Tod' 80–2
Smith-Eccles, Steve 21–2, 24, 26, 27–8, 119–20, 121–3, 125, 178–9, 182–3, 189–90, 200, 216, 217
Snaith, John 7–8, 9–15
Snaith, Willie 3–8, 9–10, 15, 212–13
Stevens, George 111
Stewards Enquiry 33
Stott, Billy 112, 132
Struthers, Paul 61–2, 148–9, 152, 153, 154, 155–6, 166–7, 170–1
Swinburn, Walter 166

Taaffe, Pat 113
Taylor, Phil 17–21, 22–7, 28–9
Thornton, Robert 18, 19, 20, 24
trainer–jockey relationships 39–40, 197, 201–2, 226–7
training, attitude to 191–2
travelling 28, 42–3, 206–8
Tufnell, Meriel 59
Turcotte, Ron 113
Turner, Hayley 59–61, 62, 153
Turner, Dr Michael 147, 148, 151–2

valets 17–29, 30, 31, 46

Waley-Cohen, Sam 202
Walsh, Ruby 23, 24–5, 130–1, 184, 213
Walwyn, Fulke 114, 119
wasting 22, 157–9, 161–2, 165–7, 168–9, 173, 176, 208
Webster, Stuart 25
weighing in/out 30, 32
weighing room xvii, 30–1, 32
weight allowances, apprentice 60–1
weight management 32, 52, 58, 157–8, 160–76, 196
weight requirements, minimum 162, 163
welfare support 44, 144–5, 170
see also Injured Jockeys Fund
Wilson, Gerry 112–13, 114, 132
win-at-all-costs mentality 7, 25–6, 130, 212–13
Winter, Fred 115–18, 119, 120–1, 140, 142, 143
working jockeys, number of 36